UNRULY SOULS

UNRULY SOULS

The Digital Activism of Muslim and Christian Feminists

KRISTIN M. PETERSON

RUTGERS UNIVERSITY PRESS

New Brunswick, Camden, and Newark, New Jersey, and London

Library of Congress Cataloging-in-Publication Data
Names: Peterson, Kristin M., author.
Title: Unruly souls: the digital activism of Muslim and Christian feminists /
   Kristin M. Peterson.
Description: New Brunswick: Rutgers University Press, 2022. |
   Includes bibliographical references and index.
Identifiers: LCCN 2021045844 | ISBN 9781978822665 (paperback) |
   ISBN 9781978822672 (hardback) | ISBN 9781978822689 (epub) |
   ISBN 9781978822696 (mobi) | ISBN 9781978822702 (pdf)
Subjects: LCSH: Digital media—Social aspects. | Digital media—
   Political aspects. | Feminists—Political activity. | Feminism—Political aspects. |
   Women conservatives—Political activity. | Religious fundamentalism—
   Political aspects. | Fundamentalism—Political aspects. | Islamic
   fundamentalism—Political aspects. | Digital communications—
   Social aspects. | Digital communications—Political aspects.
Classification: LCC HM851 .P479 2022 | DDC 305.42—dc23
LC record available at https://lccn.loc.gov/2021045844

A British Cataloging-in-Publication record for this book is available from the British
Library.

References to internet websites (URLs) were accurate at the time of writing. Neither
the author nor Rutgers University Press is responsible for URLs that may have expired
or changed since the manuscript was prepared.

♾ The paper used in this publication meets the requirements of the American
National Standard for Information Sciences—Permanence of Paper for Printed
Library Materials, ANSI Z39.48-1992.

www.rutgersuniversitypress.org

Manufactured in the United States of America

For all the unruly souls

CONTENTS

UNRULY SOULS

INTRODUCTION

In a catchy music video titled "Dog," the Muslim hip-hop star Mona Haydar calls out the misogyny embedded in a lot of Islamic communities when male leaders criticize Muslim women for not dressing modestly enough and then harass or even assault women. The whole song is a powerful takedown of the hypocritical men who objectify women both by placing them on a pedestal as the perfect, modest icons of Islam and by using women as objects of sexual desire. As Haydar repeats throughout the song, "Say you can save my spirit / But you're a dog at night / We can see right through him; he's a dog."[1] Since even the few Muslim women who can achieve the ideals of modesty and perfection are not safe from harassment and abuse from men, Haydar's music video flips the script and places the blame on the men who can't control their sexual desires.

Meanwhile on Twitter, members of the growing ex-Evangelical Christianity movement address similar critiques of misogyny and sexual harassment, but in this case, within purity culture—that is, the abstinence-based teachings that spread throughout American Christian communities in the 1990s and 2000s. In Twitter discussions about recovering from the trauma of purity culture, individuals discuss ideas related to Haydar's song, such as how women are blamed and shamed for sexual indiscretions. Purity culture promotes an ideal version of what it means to be a pure Christian woman. In a Twitter conversation from July 2016, one of the participants explains that these purity teachings "normalized the idea that girls who won @ the courtship game had to be white, petite, & dress like middle-aged housewives."[2] Furthermore, Keisha McKenzie, one of the facilitators of this Twitter discussion, writes that purity culture promotes "theologically justified racism" and "cis/heterosexist culture."[3] Again, women are objectified and become the bearers of sexual purity for the whole community. Those who don't meet these high standards because of their sexuality, gender identity, or race are deemed as inherently flawed.

These two examples reflect activist movements around feminist and queer causes in wider U.S. society (#MeToo, Black Lives Matter, and the movements for equal pay and transgender rights), but they also demonstrate the ways that feminist concerns within American religions are interweaving and intersecting.

Activists raise awareness of the ways that discourses around purity and modesty reinforce misogynistic and racist ideals, but this narrow view of piety also inflicts spiritual harm. The interconnections between Muslim and Christian feminists are more noticeable in digital media. Podcasts have become alternative communities for those who feel like misfits in religious spaces. Black Christian women pull up a seat with the hosts of *Truth's Table*, queer youth explore deeper questions of faith on *Queerology*, and young people join gatherings through *The Liturgists*. Instagram pages expand beyond photo spreads of fashion styles to challenge the narrow expectations of modest dress, share infographics about gender-based violence in religious communities, and circulate resources on racial justice. Twitter threads create a powerful network to call out religious leaders who are sexual predators and abuse power. Digital videos and hip-hop music provide flexible and layered spaces to celebrate the hybrid experiences of Muslim Americans and the messiness of spirituality. While much of the wider social and academic discussions around media and gender have dismissed religion as backward practices and irrational beliefs that restrict women's agency, there are growing movements (consisting mostly of women, but also containing some men and transgender and genderqueer individuals)[4] seeking to root out patriarchy, white supremacy, colonialism, and homophobia within more traditional religions and in larger society.

Public discussions and academic work explore intersectional feminist activism and also the visibility of "popular feminism."[5] This project seeks to address the activism that is growing among young people, particularly within Islam and Evangelical Christianity, and the unique role that digital media play in enabling these projects. Some of these activists leave their religions, others join or start more progressive religious communities, and some remain to reform religions from the inside. While valid arguments have focused on the ineffectiveness of what has been called slacktivism in the digital moment,[6] the individuals profiled in this book are well aware of the limitations of online activism. At the same time, they come from religious communities that rarely offer ways for marginalized perspectives to be heard. Digital media may be one of the few spaces for activists to address these injustices, provide support for victims of harassment and abuse, and collectively work for reform.

Having studied the self-representation of Muslim Americans in digital media for the past several years, I became interested in this comparative project when I started to notice overlaps in the discussions around Islamic modesty and Christian purity. These discussions centered on how only certain women—white, straight, and thin virgins—were able to maintain this purity. Individuals shared stories from religious education around abstinence that compared women who were too sexual or immodest to uncovered lollipops, chewed-up gum, used pieces of Scotch tape, and roses without petals. The women who fall outside of these unachievable norms express their exhaustion, anger, and deep hurt after years of being told that they are inherently sinful, impure, immodest, and hyper-sexual. The host of the podcast *Truth's Table*, Michelle Higgins, clearly explains these spiritual wounds that come from her identity as a Black Christian woman being misconstrued as a hypersexual temptress. "Along with believing that men have all the answers, is the idea that women are the source of the problems," she says in an episode on April 14, 2017. "I don't even remember the beauty that God has blessed me with, and I tend to think that my body is more of a curse than it is a holy vessel."[7]

These Christian and Muslim figures express similar frustrations with being criticized for not meeting these unachievable standards within religious com-munities while still having to deal with sexual abuse, harassment, racism, homophobia, transphobia, and classism. These young people reject the modest and demure icons of their religious communities and turn to digital media to connect with those who have similar experiences, rearticulate their values, play with categories, and create new meanings within their religions. This book seeks to explore how the creativity and flexibility of digital media facilitate this growing intersectional feminist activism within religions, specifically how this work develops a new space of acceptance and healing for the unruly souls who have been dismissed from religious institutions. By comparing the activism of Muslim and Christian misfits, we can observe interconnected projects to develop nonbinary interpretations of faith that bring marginalized voices to the center.

DIGITAL ACTIVISM DEMONSTRATES
THE EQUALITY OF UNRULY SOULS

Through a variety of examples in this book, I examine how young Americans raised in religions that reinforce traditional norms of gender and sexuality use digital media to celebrate their inherent value and dismantle intersecting forms of oppression. This book lays out a theorization of the current digital media moment by arguing that the hybrid, flexible, playful, and sensory nature of digi-tal spaces facilitates intersectional feminist activism within and beyond religious communities. This activism often grows out of a desire to dismantle powerful forces of oppression within religions, but these cases illustrate how online media can help foster empathetic communities for those recovering from religious trauma. The distinctions between the cases allow for a specific theorization of the affordances of media, such as Twitter hashtags, photos, podcasts, and music videos. By examining different forms of religious expression, this book takes a wide-angle look at the deep trauma inflicted when religious teachings are fueled by patriarchy, colonialism, and white supremacy. Discussing these different cases together enables broader and deeper theorization of political activism in the cur-rent digital moment while addressing the specificities of religious expression.

While previous scholarship has examined how digital media spaces encourage social action, this book specifically examines the religious dimensions of digital activism. The individuals in all of the cases presented here face intersecting forms of oppression within society based on their race, ethnicity, class, gender, sexuality, or ability, in addition to experiencing a deeper pain from being dismissed within their religious communities as inherently flawed. Rather than attempt to fit into the narrow symbolic role of the demure and pious virgin, the women embrace their status as religious misfits. The creative projects discussed in this book demonstrate how digital media provide hybrid styles and flexible spaces to insert critiques of religion from marginalized perspectives. My analysis of these creative projects draws on work from queer theory, decolonial theory, and Black feminist theory that examines how those who have been marginalized find innovative opportunities for resistance through various tactics. Building on these theories, I assert that the women are able to effectively deploy their disregarded status as unruly souls along with digital media tactics to construct a new religious understanding built on the equality of all people in the eyes of God.

Although digital media spaces are highly structured by corporate forces; government oversight; and cultural discourses around gender, sexuality, and race, the women in these cases deploy creative tactics to contest dominant labels and binaries. While the playful and spreadable features of digital culture are also responsible for an increase in trolling and the harassment of marginalized voices, the women in this study enter this messy space fully aware that their words, values, and bodies will be scrutinized. Because they face physical threats and intersecting forms of oppression within religious communities and wider society, these women are unable and unwilling to remain silent. My analysis of these cases addresses this tension, as the women are deeply wounded and harassed within online spaces but still find digital media to be productive platforms to creatively resist patriarchal religious institutions and support each other.

DIGITAL MEDIA AND ACTIVISM

From the chat rooms and message forums of the early days to current concerns over misinformation, trolling, and extremist propaganda, online media have been theorized as spaces that enable or inhibit political action. Some media scholars have questioned the potential of digital spaces to facilitate significant change. With the explosion of social media sites and the availability of cheap consumer products, there appears to be endless opportunities for individuals to express themselves—often through consumer choice. At the same time, it remains unclear how much of an impact individual voices can have in the larger cacophony. Rather than promote progressive actions or political participation, Alice Marwick finds that "social media applications encourage people to compete for social benefits by gaining visibility and attention."[8] It's all about the number of likes and views. Furthermore, we see how these spaces of expression are co-opted by capitalist forces to market to certain desirable audiences.[9]

Additionally, new media technologies often offer the promise of political change while simply creating a space for the endless circulation of information. Jodi Dean formulates the concept of "communicative capitalism" to describe this "deadlocked democracy," which promotes circulation and consumer choice as political action instead of revolutionary change.[10] Communicative capitalism takes hold through the new media technologies that emphasize networks, participation, circulation, and exchange. As individuals are endlessly producing and circulating information, Dean argues that the "messages get lost."[11] People contribute information to the circulation stream, but the stream dampens the political power. It often feels good to participate online, Dean acknowledges, but "this feeling is unconnected from any larger collective practice that might actually affect change."[12]

Furthermore, spaces like online fandom communities are often theorized as sites of resistance and subversion in the same way that early cultural studies scholars looked to comics, punk music, and romance novels as cultural spaces of meaning making.[13] However, it remains unclear whether an interest in fandom relates to political action or just the shallow pleasure of cultural consumption. In addition, participatory online culture does not necessarily encourage progressive political actions. As Christian Fuchs asserts, participatory culture "idealizes community and fan culture as progressive and ignores the fact that the collective intelligence and activity of cultural communities and fandom can easily turn into a fascist mob."[14] Fuchs's assertion predicts the rise of the Alt-Right in the United States and the organized rallies and instances of violence (which stemmed from participation in online communities) centered around white nationalism.

These concerns about the emancipatory potential of digital media reflect the common critique of overemphasizing popular culture while neglecting to account for political and economic forces. However, I want to complicate the assumption that the corporate-owned digital media spaces can never allow for political action. In the current media context, there are few spaces that are not owned by large media conglomerates, and almost all digital spaces are influenced in some ways by the neoliberal market logic that infuses most aspects of Western society. In addition, the few alternative media spaces that exist outside of corporate control are often not easily accessible to a mainstream, less technically savvy audience, and the materials produced in these spaces rarely circulate to larger audiences. Because of this context, I incorporate Sarah Banet-Weiser's approach to studying the "ambivalences" of contemporary branded culture as a way to take seriously the cultural work that is produced within these neoliberal, branded spaces. Banet-Weiser asserts that there is no longer a pure and authentic space outside of the forces of neoliberalism and that we should study the ways individuals negotiate the ambivalences of contemporary culture, as individual cultural production overlaps with neoliberal pressures and market forces.[15]

Additionally, my research builds on scholarship that acknowledges the limitations of digital activism but formulates online engagement as highly influential
in encouraging offline, more traditional modes of political participation. In contemporary times, political action shifts away from the organized work of collective unions to individuals forming weaker personal ties through social media.[16]
The latter form of "connective action" incorporates "personalized communication," such as compressing political concerns into phrases that are easy to relate
to, and social media offer the space to circulate these messages.[17] As people
increasingly develop connections through social media and relatable messages,
these activities are difficult to analyze using the traditional logic of collective
political action. Moving beyond the dismissal of social media activities as slacktivism, the distinction of the digital media moment rests in the ability for people
to create connections with and relate to the experiences of others.

Social media create spaces for connective action and community by facilitating what Zizi Papacharissi describes as "feelings of engagement."[18] This sense of
connection has the potential to lead to offline political action and collective
organizing. As Papacharissi explains, "Social media help activate and sustain
latent ties that may be crucial to the mobilization of networked publics."[19] While
not creating social change in and of itself, "[social media] are our means for feeling our way into worlds we cannot experience directly."[20] This affective nature of
social media enables the participants in these cases to connect online around
various issues of social injustices.

Relatedly, digital activities can be understood as "proto-political," as Peter
Dahlgren explains that "online spaces can facilitate offline activity, coordinating
political interventions in 'real-life' spaces."[21] The digital media can serve as spaces
to connect people through shared social experiences, identities, and political
concerns. In these "proto-political domains," Dahlgren states that "politics is not
explicit, but always remains a potential."[22] Specifically for individuals who are
marginalized in traditional political spaces, an engagement with digital work can
be the first step in realizing one's potential to impact larger political causes. In her
work on young people of color and social activism, Lynn Schofield Clark asserts
that "digital activism plays an important role in providing encouragement for
those at the political margins to see themselves as at least potentially part of an
unfolding movement."[23]

Furthermore, activists in social movements are well aware of the limitations
and benefits of using digital media. In her extensive study of contemporary social
movements in several international contexts, Zeynep Tufekci usefully frames
social media as one of many tools that activists can use. Activists understand that
"digital tools and street protests are parts of the same reality."[24] Digital tools
allow protestors to go beyond the limitations of physical spaces and can serve as
sites for gestures that have symbolic power.[25] Similarly, Michela Ardizzoni finds

that current activists often engage with the ambivalent spaces between traditional political protest in offline spaces and emerging interactive digital spaces. She proposes the concept of "matrix activism" to account for "the hybrid nature of new forms of dissent and resistance, as they are located at the intersection of alternative and mainstream, non-profit and corporate, individual and social, production and consumption, online and offline."[26] Activists work within this in-between space, aware of the affordances and limitations of digital media.

For instance, Twitter hashtags might develop a wider audience for a cause but don't necessarily produce social change. In a study of the #MeToo campaign, Rosemary Clark-Parsons finds that participants are aware of the limitations of hashtag feminism. However, contributing to hashtag campaigns allows individuals to participate in "a performative politics of visibility, in which one person's narrative, when shared and connected with many others, makes power visible so that it might be deconstructed and challenged."[27] Along similar lines, Sarah Jackson, Moya Bailey, and Brooke Foucault Welles assert that Twitter hashtags provide a counterpublic space for marginalized groups "to build diverse networks of dissent and shape the cultural and political knowledge fundamental to contemporary identity-based social movements."[28] In all of these cases, marginalized individuals work within the powerful spaces of digital media to assert that their voices, perspectives, experiences, and lives have value. As Stuart Hall so influentially argued, popular culture is a space of struggle over ideology.[29] There is a constant dialectic relationship within popular culture as ideas around gender, race, class, and sexuality are negotiated and contested. Those on the margins are constantly doing the work of chipping away at structures of inequality while working within cultural spaces to foreground their alternative perspectives. The digital media are increasingly the spaces where these cultural debates take shape.

DIGITAL ACTIVISM AND RELIGIOUS IDENTITY

Religious identity adds another layer to this digital activism, as people make claims on their equal value as God-given and inherent. Although there are numerous approaches to studying religion by focusing on beliefs, practices, or communities, my focus in this book is on religious identity as a significant layer or intersection in one's larger identity. The anthropologist Birgit Meyer's understanding of religion as a "bridge" that connects humans to the "transcendental or spiritual force"[30] is a useful formulation because it accounts for how media convey this transcendental and unseen realm through sensory elements. Furthermore, formulating and representing one's religious identity happens in connection to this higher sense of being. Specifically, the projects in this book articulate one's inherent value by appealing to this transcendent realm and countering the shameful feelings of being judged as flawed, impure, and distant from the divine.

Additionally, digital media provide the openness and creativity for young people to formulate their religious identity outside of the influence of dominant religious institutions and mainstream cultural forces. In her edited volume on media, religion, and gender, Mia Lövheim discusses several examples of how digital media become a space to explore religious subjectivity. She writes, "These studies show how digital media spaces can become arenas for the construction of new forms of female subjectivity, where women in a previously male-dominated public sphere act as agents, presenting their own interpretations of religion."[31] For instance, Anna Piela examines how young Muslim women who wear the niqab face veil use online self-portraits to convey their subjectivity as pious Muslim women but also to assert their agency in the face of dehumanizing stereotypes. She writes that these women "are able to exercise their agency by stating 'I exist' on their own terms rather than in the narrow confines of the mainstream media, which not only represent them in a stereotypical way, but exclude their voices, even from discussions of socio-political issues regarding their own lives."[32] A similar project to counteract the stereotypes and marginalization of Muslim women was the #MuslimWomensDay campaign, started by Amani Al-Khatahtbeh, the founder of *Muslim Girl*. As Rosemary Pennington explains, this tag created "an opportunity for Muslim women to tell their own stories in social media" and to "carve space for themselves."[33]

For former and questioning Evangelicals, there is less of a need to address discrimination and dehumanizing stereotypes, since Christianity is a powerful, mainstream aspect of U.S. life. However, those leaving the isolated subcultures of Evangelicalism often seek community and support online. In a discussion about the communities related to podcasts like *Exvangelical* and *The Airing of Grief*, Steven Fekete and Jessica Knippel address the need for online communities of those deconstructing religious identity and meaning: "Through these communities, they embody the radically honest and supportive relationships that they had sought in their previous religious contexts but so often were unable to find."[34] Digital media provide the space and supportive community in which to work out one's identity as a religious misfit. Furthermore, Andrew Herrmann acknowledges the significance of online activism for those coming from traumatic experiences in Evangelical communities. He describes how #ChurchToo (as well as other online hashtag movements) "provides hope, counseling, a reckoning, and most importantly a voice to the women and men who have been sexually, physically, and psychologically abused in fundamental evangelical circles."[35] Digital media activism around hashtags, podcasts, and social media groups enables young people raised in Evangelical subcultures to express the trauma of marginalization and build up supportive communities of other religious misfits.

THE HYBRID, FLEXIBLE, AND PLAYFUL NATURE
OF DIGITAL MEDIA

For the individuals in this study who have not had their voices heard in traditional religious spaces due to structures of inequality, digital media offer spaces
that are flexible, playful, and hybrid to creatively assert their own perspectives.
Rather than focus on certain technological capacities of digital media such as
networks, algorithms, mobile devices, or platforms, this project analyzes the
overlaps between the playful nature of digital culture and the hybrid existence of
religious misfits, who challenge the binary structures of religious institutions.
These various examples of projects to root out misogyny, homophobia, and racism within Islam and Evangelical Christianity illustrate how the in-between fac-
ets of digital culture can be engaged to cleverly articulate marginal perspectives
and necessary critiques.

Throughout this book, I explore how the hybrid and malleable aspects of
digital media complement the unruly, queer, and contradictory activism that is
brewing among young people within more conservative religions. For instance,
the playful use of language in Twitter enables young Evangelicals and former
Evangelicals to celebrate their sexuality by writing under hashtags like #Kiss-
ShameBye, which plays on the popular purity culture book *I Kissed Dating Goodbye*.[36] Similarly, Mona Haydar's music video "Barbarian" transforms the exoticized labels often applied to Muslim American women into identity markers, as
she sings, "We them barbarians / Beautiful and scaring them / Earth shakin' rattling / Be wild out loud again."[37] Along with the lyrics, the video features a multicultural array of Muslim women playing off harem stereotypes: they lounge in
outdoor gardens, eat food with their hands, clap and dance to music with an
Arab beat, and wear garments that represent their diverse cultural backgrounds.
These are just two examples of how young people engage with the creative and
layered aspects of digital media to speak about how they have been misrepresented and spoken for by mostly white men.

Whitney Phillips and Ryan Milner theorize similar aspects of digital culture
in their work on "the ambivalent internet" and the bizarre, satirical projects that
proliferate in certain corners of online media. This playful and ambivalent work
can at times be harmless and at other times become threatening trolling, but it
can also be a creative way to question norms and challenge binaries. While some
of these projects are only "for the lulz" or are completely abhorrent, the authors
see the potential for ambivalent internet work to "provide an outlet for historically underrepresented populations to speak truth to power."[38] Rather than focus
on all the various productive, destructive, and neutral behaviors that are possible
in the ambivalent internet, my goal is to theorize the overlaps between the hybrid
identities, the intersectional concerns of these young people, and the flexible and
interstitial aspects of digital media. How are these individuals who have been

classified as queer, unruly, and impure misfits within their religions embracing the hybrid and playful aspects of digital media in their efforts to find spiritual acceptance and equality?

Without disregarding the valid critiques mentioned above of the limitations of digital media and the prominence of corporate forces, this study focuses on how these individuals, who have consistently been silenced in religious and political institutions, engage with small tactics of resistance within digital media. They write and record hip-hop songs that call out misogyny and colonialism; they contest religious teachings on sexuality through clever but supportive Twitter threads; they post photographs that challenge assumptions about the agency of women in traditional religions; and they create podcasts and cultivate listener communities to deconstruct patriarchal and white supremacist religious teachings. The playfulness, queerness, and hybridity of this work allows these young activists to contest the problematic teachings around sexuality, race, and gender roles, as well as other social injustices that are deeply embedded in traditional religions, while also building supportive spaces to welcome others harmed by religious institutions. This study traces not only the work to call out various injustices and abuse within religious institutions, but also how young people deploy the intimate aspects of digital media to create healing spaces for those recovering from religious trauma and to build up new expressions of faith, centering on the value of unruly souls.

FOUNDATIONAL THEORIES FROM MARGINAL PERSPECTIVES

My analysis of these varied cases of digital activism is built on foundational theories from intersectional feminist, decolonial, and queer perspectives that address how marginal voices find creative modes of contestation. Religious identity adds another layer to this analysis, as the individuals in these cases seek to reform their religious traditions by foregrounding their position as unruly souls. This approach allows me to place contemporary digital advocacy work within the longer history of intersectional feminist activism. The term "intersectionality" comes from the argument of the legal scholar Kimberlé Williams Crenshaw that oppression is compounded when you look at the intersection of racial identity and gender. For instance, if a Black woman brings a case of harassment and discrimination at work, it is difficult from a legal standpoint to determine if the discrimination is based more on her gender or her race.[39] Additional elements like ability, class, education, immigration status, sexuality, and religion would add more intersections of oppression and/or privilege.

Crenshaw follows the extensive tradition of Black women who expressed their particular experiences of injustices. For instance, in Sojourner Truth's "Ain't I a Woman" speech from 1851, she called out the ways that the first wave of feminism ignored her experiences as a formerly enslaved African American woman. Late in the nineteenth century, Ida B. Wells advocated for the rights of African Americans along with participating in the women's suffrage movement. In reaction to how the second wave of feminism in the United States mostly focused on the concerns of middle-class, white women, groups like the Combahee River Collective and the National Black Feminist Organization formed in the 1970s to focus on the specific injustices experienced by Black women, as well as other groups such as queer folks, disabled people, and working-class women. As explained in the Combahee River Collective Statement, Black women have long had "a shared awareness of how their sexual identity combined with their racial identity to make their whole life situation and the focus of their political struggles unique."[40] The intersectional experiences of Black women highlight how gender inequality is tied to racism and capitalism. As the Black feminist activist Frances Beal asserted in the 1970s, a focus only on gender oppression hides larger structures of inequality and incorrectly blames Black men: "Black people are engaged in a life and death struggle with the oppressive forces of this country and the main emphasis of black women must be to combat the capitalist, racist exploitation of black people."[41] Black women have a hard time finding a home in either antiracist work or feminist organizing because of their specific concerns based on race and gender, but intersectionality enables an exploration of how larger forces privilege and oppress different groups in complex ways.

Feminist activism and scholarship didn't use the term "intersectionality" until the 1990s, but feminist thinkers have reflected on how their particular experiences of oppression are complicated by layers of race, gender expression, sexuality, class, ability, religion, and other elements. For example, in *Borderlands/La Frontera: The New Mestiza*, Gloria Anzaldúa writes about her experiences between various identity markers as a queer, Chicana feminist. She uses the example of the border between Mexico and the United States to illustrate this feeling of being caught between binaries.[42] Related to Anzaldúa's groundbreaking work, Lisa Flores discusses how Chicana feminists struggle to find an activist space, since their specific concerns are not welcome in white feminist circles and they face misogyny within masculine Chicano spaces. In response to this feeling of being caught in between, these women develop a discursive "space of their own," in which they can affirm the values of their specific experiences.[43] Writing before the digital revolution, Flores explains the power of reading against the grain in culture: "When Chicana feminists refuse to accept mainstream definitions of themselves and insist that they establish and affirm their own identity, they build a space through discourse."[44] This book explores similar practices of women refusing to be labeled as pure, virginal icons of their religion and resisting by celebrating things like their unruliness, dark skin, queerness, and sexuality.

I find it relevant to build on this theorizing of intersectionality, queerness, and marginality from the pre-digital era because it illustrates how the playfulness exhibited in contemporary culture is certainly aided by digital tools but was not born from the digital moment. Instead, the participants in these projects draw on their hybrid and marginal experiences, while digital media provide the tools and networks to circulate these messages. As Sarah Florini writes in her book on digital activism among Black Americans, "Participation, remediation, and brico-lage, hallmarks of digital cultures, have historically been central to the expressive cultures of Black American communities."[45] People on the margins because of race, class, gender, sexuality, or religion have long relied on creative tactics of resistance that play with categories and blur binaries. Digital media provide new outlets and devices that often allow for playfulness, hybridity, malleability, and circulation.

From the decolonial perspective, the scholar Homi Bhabha discusses the tac-tic of mimicry, in which the colonized subjects (who are caught between the local culture and the culture of the colonizer) are able to subvert the colonizers' power by pointing to the flaws in Western arguments while still borrowing from Western culture in politically productive ways. Bhabha explains this tactic: "The menace of mimicry is its double vision which in disclosing the ambivalence of colonial discourse also disrupts its authority."[46] Muslim women often find this a useful tactic for pointing out the hypocrisy of telling Muslim women to uncover for their safety but then harassing women because of their skimpy clothing.

The playfulness and in-between nature of digital media enables marginalized individuals to more effectively mimic the dominant culture. For example, Indig-enous activists created and circulated memes to support their protests against the Dakota Access Pipeline. As Angel Hinzo and Lynn Schofield Clark assert, these digital memes destabilize the power of the U.S. government through the deployment of the interstitial trickster character, "a spiritual figure who disobeys established rules and conventional behavior, while establishing expectations for humanitarianism."[47] Similar to the concept of mimicry, the use of trickster humor and irony allows Indigenous activists to call out the U.S. government for abhorrent behavior while celebrating their own cultural traditions. As I discuss in chapter 5, Mona Haydar excels at twisting and subverting the stereotypes of Muslims in a playful way that celebrates her culture while criticizing Western society.

Another related tactic is what José Esteban Muñoz terms disidentification, in which those in marginal, queer positions can resist the dominant culture by read-ing against the dominant narrative. Instead of identifying with or resisting domi-nant culture, the marginal subject disidentifies or reads "oneself and one's own life narrative in a moment, object, or subject that is not culturally coded to 'connect' with the disidentifying subject."[48] Disidentification works from within a cultural text to create an alternative and innovative reading from a marginal perspective. In addition to displaying the flaws in the majority culture, disidentification is a way of "representing a disempowered politics or positionality that has been rendered unthinkable by the dominant culture."[49] The political potential of this tactic lies in the ability for subjects to rework the dominant meanings of cultural texts in ways that point out the problems with the text while also incorporating the voices of the marginalized. The anti-purity culture movement, growing among former and current Evangelical Christians, demonstrates disidentification as the participants often engage with purity culture language in their Tweets as a way to dismantle the dominance of this language in their Christian faith.

While the concept of disidentification comes out of queer activism in creative spaces, bell hooks theorizes the oppositional gaze within Black feminist thought. This is the power of being able to look back, even when one is being oppressed. As a Black female spectator of mass culture, hooks describes not seeing herself represented in media forms, so she developed an oppositional gaze, a critical eye that watches films not for pleasure but to point out misogyny, racism, colorism, and so on.[50] Women like hooks who refuse to take pleasure in mainstream culture are what Sara Ahmed calls a "feminist killjoy," one who always brings a critical eye to spaces of enjoyment.[51] Most of the women in these cases take on the role of the feminist killjoy as they refuse to be positive, happy icons of their religions but instead point out deep problems of misogyny, racism, colorism, classism, and harassment within religious communities. These women are not pessimists: they are seeking a deeper joy that comes with equality and justice.

Finally, the digital media offer these women the chance to speak back, to rearticulate the ways that their lives have been framed by others. According to Stuart Hall, articulation is an active process through which hegemonic ideas are linked to certain bodies and thus solidified into common sense, but these connections are not necessarily permanent.[52] Hall uses the example of an English "articulated" truck (called a semitrailer or tractor-trailer in the United States) to demonstrate how articulation connects two distinct elements, but this linkage "is not necessary, determined, absolute and essential for all time."[53] Disarticulation is a way to unlink these connections, which often gain strength through their appearance as natural or common sense, and to rearticulate new links to different meanings.

The work in these cases is an effort at disarticulating connections, such as the assumption that dark-skinned bodies are hypersexual and impure or the assumption that Muslim women wearing a hijab are oppressed and dangerous. These connections become deeply embedded in our cultural understandings to the point that they are often presumed to be inherent and immutable. These digital projects attempt to rearticulate the value and equality of these lives. Similarly, Yarimar Bonilla and Jonathan Rosa discuss how the #BlackLivesMatter digital activism can provide a space for the "revaluation of black materiality."[54] Black youth use Twitter hashtags and digital images to contest how their bodies have been used and abused in the media and physical spaces: "Whereas, in face-to-face interactions, racialized young people like the ones described above might not be able to contest the meanings ascribed to their bodies (or impede the deadly violence exerted on them by the police), through their creative reinterpretations on social media, they are able to rematerialize their bodies in alternative ways. With these creative acts, they seek to document, contest, and ultimately transform their quotidian experiences by simultaneously asserting the fundamental value and the particularity of their embodiment both on- and off-line."[55]

Similar to how young Black men are often fighting against negative labels, the women in these religious communities are either placed in an iconic position of perfect representatives of the religion or dismissed as inherently flawed based on their skin color, body shape, sexuality, gender expression, or appearance. They face both the spiritual wounds of being labeled unholy as well as the social wounds of racism, misogyny, colorism, and homophobia. The flexibility of digital media spaces offers opportunities to rearticulate their inherent value as beautiful souls created by God. This digital work goes beyond playing with categories or challenging dichotomies to formulate a nonbinary interpretation of religious faith. These activists are not simply using digital media to have their voices heard. More importantly, their work critiques the hypocrisy and injustices within religious institutions while presenting a revolutionary understanding of Christianity and Islam that centers queerness, Blackness, imperfections, impurity, and hybridity.

METHODS AND ETHICAL CONCERNS

Conducting a comparative study of digital media activism of feminists within Islam and Evangelical Christianity is admittedly a daunting task, with endless Tweets, web sites, comments, images, podcasts, and videos to study. Rather than focus on a single media space or form, I find it more beneficial to examine the various media spaces and tools that activists use, depending on the particular affordances. Sarah Pink's "multisensory approach" to conducting online research accounts for the intersection of different types of media beyond just images and texts. Pink argues that the internet should be studied as a "multisensory environment" that engages more than just the visual sense.[56] She emphasizes the spatiality of the internet, the interactions between offline and online spaces, and the researcher's location in these spaces. With John Postill, Sarah Pink also recommends that studies of digital communities should look at "social media as a research environment that is dispersed across web platforms, is constantly in progress and changing, and implicates physical as well as digital localities."[57] There is no need to create a barrier between offline and online activities or between different social networks, as most participants rarely are cognizant of this distinction in their daily lives.

To have a more complete view of the various advocacy movements within Islam and Evangelical Christianity, I immersed myself in these diverse digital sites, watching videos, perusing comments, reading articles, looking at photos, and listening to podcasts. My goal was to understand the larger arguments going on in these spaces. I also conducted in-depth interviews with the creators of and participants in these projects. My intent in these interviews was not to use the creators to get a good quote or confirm what I already knew. Instead, I view the interview as a collaborative process of jointly interpreting the work, so that as the researcher I did not have what Katherine Borland calls ultimate "interpretive authority."[58] Most of the participants in this study are public figures who have active online presences, but when I quote from people who are not public leaders in these movements, I follow the Association of Internet Researchers' ethical guidelines in considering the vulnerability of the participants and their expectations of privacy when they post to digital spaces.[59] For instance, people post Tweets in public conversations about purity culture, but they are discussing personal experiences with an assumption that the Tweets will not leave that community. For those Tweets, I used pseudonyms and slightly changed the wording in the posts to avoid revealing the identities of the posters. It is important to bring an ethics of care and compassion to this work, since a lot of the participants in these online projects are sharing traumatic experiences of assault, abuse, discrimination, and emotional harm. I strove to take an empathetic approach by focusing on the experiences of the public-facing activists, who have already shared their stories widely, while amplifying the larger trends that are present in the comment sections and Twitter threads without sensationalizing personal experiences of trauma.

Finally, this work comes out of a personal desire to conduct research rooted in feminist convictions of gender justice and equality. I am aware of the extensive tradition, especially within Western feminism, of speaking for Muslim and nonwhite women and attempting to save them from the oppression of men.[60] Feminist methodology encourages me as a researcher to be aware of the power dynamics inherent in research and my position as a researcher, who is both an insider and an outsider to the communities that I study. As hooks advises, "When we write about the experiences of a group to which we do not belong, we should think about the ethics of our action, considering whether or not our work will be used to reinforce and perpetuate domination."[61] Relatedly, Patricia Zavella argues that the assumption that all women are insiders to other women's experiences leads to the essentialization of female researchers and neglects the real power differences between feminist scholars and their subjects. She urges feminist researchers to reflect on their positions as both insiders and outsiders and on how these positions will impact their research.[62]

As a white, middle-class, educated American woman raised in the Catholic Church, I am unable to relate to certain experiences of the participants in this study. However, I can closely connect to the deep pain of feeling devalued based on misogynistic misinterpretations of Christianity. Along with understanding the spiritual wounds of being defined as inherently inferior, I was exposed to Evangelical teachings around purity culture at a friend's church and in a nonde-nominational Christian club at my public high school. I was also given a purity ring as a teenager. While I was not inundated with abstinence teachings, I did carry feelings of anxiety and shame around sexuality into young adulthood. At the same time, I do not understand the pain of being told that your skin color makes you inferior, your physical body is disgusting and dirty, or your religious beliefs and cultural traditions are exotic and backward. For these experiences of racism, Orientalism, or fatphobia, I focused on the reflections from the partici-pants in their conversations with me, as well as on articles, podcasts, and videos. Based on my experiences, I have a desire to critique and reform the ways that white supremacy, patriarchy, heteronormativity, and American imperialism dis-tort religious teachings and damage the faith of individuals.

BOOK OUTLINE

This book engages with critical scholarship from marginal perspectives (such as Black feminist thought, queer theory, and decolonial theory), using those per-spectives as lenses to understand a variety of creative projects and in turn to draw wider conclusions about the potential of digital media activism. While this book is centered on creative activism and digital media studies, it is relevant to provide background on the religious context from which the projects I discuss emerge. The first chapter in the book provides a historical overview of how reli-gious discourse—specifically Evangelical Christianity in the United States—has been deployed to reinforce white supremacy, patriarchy, and heteronormativity. The unique context of Islam in the United States is also discussed by examining both how Islam is positioned as inferior to Christianity and Western imperialist projects and how Muslim American communities often reinforce similar racist and misogynistic ideologies. Chapter 1 also looks at feminist critiques within Evangelical Christianity and Islam from second-wave activism around women's role in religious spaces to contemporary discussions of racism, sexual abuse, and homophobia. This chapter provides an analysis of the overlaps between feminist activism in Islam and Christianity, while clarifying the unique context of these religious traditions in the United States.

The book proceeds with a series of chapters that examine various instances when Muslim and Christian young people use digital media to offer an intersec-tional feminist critique. Each chapter in the series focuses on the affordances of certain digital media, within the context of analogue media antecedents, while addressing how elements like text, images, fashion, dialogue, music, and gestures enable these activists to demonstrate their inherent value and to dismantle inter-secting forms of oppression. For each case, I engage with theories of how those in marginal and interstitial positions find tactics of resistance by working within dominant culture while asserting alternative perspectives. Each of the chapters focuses on a particular form of religious expression, whether that is Evangelical purity culture, Islamic modesty teachings, Black womanist theology, or Islamic creative culture. The chapters each acknowledge the ways that other religious identities are expressed in these media spaces, but more extensive analysis of the overlaps between religious expressions and activism is featured in the conclusion.

Chapter 2 focuses primarily on textual spaces such as Twitter hashtags, blogs, and online forums, and on how creative language play is foundational to the burgeoning movement against purity culture within Evangelical Christianity. I argue that the clever and hybrid use of language in digital spaces enables the rearticulation of bodies and experiences in ways that celebrate instead of shame sexualities. Young people who feel harmed by problematic teachings around maintaining virginity and proper gender roles express these traumatic feelings through a variety of hashtags, organized Twitter discussions, blogs, and web forums. As the tenets of purity culture have often been conveyed through texts, especially the popular *I Kissed Dating Goodbye*, those harmed by these teachings engage with textual spaces and the language of purity and shame to challenge these misogynistic, homophobic, and racist teachings. Activists against purity culture have created various spaces where others—deemed queer, impure, and unruly based on their sexuality or skin color—can share their experiences and feel supported.

The book then shifts from textual media and Evangelical Christianity. Chapter 3 addresses how dominant ideologies of proper Muslim femininity are perpetuated through Islamic fashion icons online. In contrast to these portrayals of glowing and bubbly Muslim women in flowing, pastel-colored garments, this chapter explores the activist work of several Muslim American women who insert their unruly bodies and vocal political critiques into the bubblegum aesthetic of Muslim influencers on Instagram. These women build on their intersectional experiences to call out the ways that this dominant icon of Muslim femininity defines women as immodest and immoral because of their skin color, body shape, sexuality, intellect, or independence. Through a discussion of the various Instagram projects of Muslim American women such as Leah Vernon, Blair Imani, Zainab bint Younus, and Angelica Lindsey-Ali, I assert that these creators engage with the visual tropes and malleability of Instagram to do more than share beautiful fashion images or dispel stereotypes of Muslim women. Instead, the women discussed in this chapter blend together photography, graphic images, videos, and captions to share relevant intersectional feminist critiques and deconstruct the icon of the pious Muslim woman. These activists transform their Instagram pages into supportive platforms, celebrating Muslims who fail to meet the unachievable standards of the Islamic fashion industry.

Chapter 4 focuses on podcasts as open forums for dialogue on theological interpretations, often from marginalized perspectives. I examine the flexible, intimate, and authentic feel of podcasts and how they enable younger Christians to critique the white supremacist and patriarchal aspects of mainstream churches. After addressing the popularity of podcasts that expand theological boundaries, such as *Exvangelical, Queerology,* and *The Liturgists,* the chapter presents a deeper discussion of *Truth's Table,* featuring three Black women involved in Christian ministry and theology. I assert that podcasting can be a productive medium for celebrating the spirituality of Black women, especially in the context of a society and church communities that diminish these women's voices. The authentic aesthetics of this podcast reinforce the fact that Black women, who may feel displaced in other digital spaces, are welcome to "sit at the table" with the three hosts and talk about theological topics. The fluidity and openness of podcasts allow the hosts to present an oppositional take on Christian theology and to disentangle the legacy of white supremacy and patriarchy from biblical teachings.

After analyzing texts, images, and podcast discussions, I turn in chapter 5 to highlight the convergence of the digital moment through an examination of digital music videos. Not only do these videos engage with the multisensory elements of digital media (such as lyrics, music, colors, gestures, fashion, movement, and fast-paced editing), but the remediation of videos in various online locations emphasizes the accelerated circulation of the digital moment. This chapter argues that these multisensory features and hybrid styles enable Muslim women to creatively insert intersectional feminist critiques into their videos while also demonstrating pride in their religious identity. Haydar engages with tactics of mimicry and rearticulation in her videos to show how Muslim women have been demeaned as backward and exotic. By employing clever lyrics, body movement, bright colors, multicultural styles, and hybrid fashion, the women in Haydar's videos embrace negative labels like barbarian and exotic to rearticulate their inherent value. Similarly, a multiplatform project from the creative collective, Mipsterz, allows Muslim Americans to engage with eclectic fashion styles, visual art, and music to formulate their own vision of a future free from oppressive misrepresentations.

The conclusion analyzes what these cases taken together have to say about the current state of feminist activism, originating within religious communities but expanding into wider society. In many of these cases, activists realize that the oppression they face relates to white, heteronormative, patriarchal structures that extend beyond religious institutions. These dominant structures reinforce women's subordinate position, the interpretation of female and queer sexuality as disordered, and the inferior status of both Black Christians and Black Muslims. By examining the through lines in all of these cases, I conclude that digital media enable collaborative political activism, particularly related to gender-based violence in religious spaces. Beyond these tangible political projects, I analyze the ways that these digital projects cultivate supportive communities for people recovering from religious trauma. Finally, the flexibility and creative tools of digital media encourage the development of faith communities, centered on the inherent value of these unruly souls. The playfulness and unruliness exhibited in hashtags calling out the hypocrisy of purity culture, images that counteract the bubblegum beauty standards of Instagram fashion, podcasts celebrating Black womanist theology, and digital music videos envisioning Muslim futurism are all efforts to chip away at the patriarchal and white supremacist structures of religious institutions and society. These young people are proudly building something new: an intersectional, complex, and nonbinary interpretation of religious faith.

1 · DISMANTLING THE HIERARCHY OF SOULS

All of the creative projects discussed in this book are critiquing in various ways the ideologies that reinforce unequal power structures, such as white supremacy, patriarchy, or heteronormativity. While this book is centered on digital media scholarship and various modes of creative activism that arise in marginalized communities, the religious context to these projects is also significant. To comprehend the resonance of these images, podcasts, videos, and Tweets, it is essential to understand the religious discourse to which these projects are responding. One of my main assertions in this book is that religion is not just another identity label but a significant aspect of one's being and connection to the transcendent. This chapter will lay out the well-established historical and political project to use religion (mainly Christianity) to make claims about who has inherent value based on immutable characteristics, like gender, sexuality, or skin color. As a result of this project, there is a deep injury on one's soul when one is classified as less holy because of one's existence rather than one's actions.

While ideologies related to white supremacy, colonialism, patriarchy, and heteronormativity transcend religious spaces, this chapter addresses how American Evangelical Christianity has been a major vehicle for perpetuating these structures of inequality. These ideologies locate white, straight, American, Christian men as closest to God and thus in powerful social positions. This warped interpretation of Christianity provides theological justification for imperialist projects like the Atlantic slave trade, colonization, and the invasion and occupation of Middle Eastern countries, along with paternalistic policies like the regulation of female sexuality and reproduction. In addition, Islam in the United States presents a unique context because it is positioned as inferior to Christianity and Western imperialist powers, but at the same time, racist and misogynistic ideologies seep into Muslim American communities. Although several of these projects demonstrate the overlaps between Islam and Christianity in terms of anti-Blackness, misogyny, sexual abuse, and homophobia, these religious traditions have distinct contexts and different amounts of political power in the United States.

MAINTAINING WHITE CHRISTIAN PURITY

Evangelical Christianity has often employed rhetoric around purity and maintaining proper roles to promote the superiority of straight white men. Women are seen as inherently inferior to men based on biblical narratives, such as Eve's creation from Adam's rib; Eve's temptation of Adam; God's taking the form of a male, Jesus, who had mostly male disciples; Mary Magdalene's apocryphal legacy as a prostitute; and Paul's letters that reinforce the inherent superiority of men in the early Christian community. For instance, the first letter to Timothy in the New Testament has been used to assert that women are "second in nature and first in sin"[1] and therefore not fit to serve as leaders in the church. Christianity is not alone with the misogynistic elements in religious texts. As Rita Gross explains, "statements that subjugate women to men can be found in the scriptures of all three monotheistic religions."[2] Within Evangelical Christianity in particular, these scripture readings are used to limit the leadership roles that women can hold, promote traditional gender roles in relationships, and view women's sexuality as the source of sexual indiscretion in the wider community.

Evangelical purity culture, which is discussed in chapter 2, arises from anxieties over women's sexuality and nonreproductive sex.[3] Reinforcing clear gender roles and God's design for procreative sex within marriage is a strategy to control women and designate as sinful any expression of sexuality that strays from this narrow path. In the face of wider social acceptance of things like homosexuality, birth control, and women's rights, Evangelical Christian churches promoted abstinence until marriage (which was defined as being between one man and one woman) and policies that restricted women's reproductive rights. Instead of affirming the equality of men and women, Evangelical churches endorsed complementarianism, the belief that men and women have different roles that are meant to complement each other.[4] By returning to biblical roots, Evangelical leaders pointed to scripture passages emphasizing the authority of men. As Deborah Jian Lee explains, "Conservatives argued that because God ordained male leadership and female subordination, any departure from these views assaulted God's creation."[5] Women are to play the roles of wives and mothers; they are not ordained by God to be ministers or leaders in the church or home.

This rhetoric around purity and proper roles also extends to race, as virginal white women became icons of Christianity who must be protected from the defilement of Black men. As Anthea Butler explains, when white women were placed on this pedestal of purity, Black men became threats to this purity, but Black women were free to be "sexualized and sexually abused by white men who deemed them 'loose' or wanton."[6] This positioning of Black men and women, even Christians, as inherently distinct from and inferior to white Christians has been used to justify systematic racial oppression. Christian theology has played a significant role in the perpetuation of white supremacy and projects like the

Atlantic slave trade, the genocide and displacement of Indigenous people, the forced conversion of non-Europeans, and other imperialist projects throughout the world.

Kelly Brown Douglas discusses how the Puritans who left England wanted to build a Protestant Christian nation of white English people. She explains, "In fact, for them, building an Anglo-Saxon nation was virtually synonymous with building a religious nation."[7] Likewise, Jeannine Hill Fletcher notes in her book on the role of religion in the racial project of the United States, "the theology of Christian supremacy gave birth to the ideology of White supremacy."[8] The belief in the superiority of Christianity is interwoven with the belief in the superiority of white people. As Fletcher explains, "when religion is bound up with culture, and where Whiteness has been bound up with culture, and where Whiteness has been bound up with Christianity, the supremacy of Christianity too easily slips into a supremacy of White Christianity."[9] These forces easily converge with and blend into each other so that white Christians are seen as the most superior, above Black Christians and certainly above heathen non-Christians.

Through their theology, white Christians are responsible for creating and perpetuating what Fletcher terms "the witchcraft of White supremacy"—that is, the ideologies that determine the racial hierarchy of the United States.[10] These ideologies were used to justify institutions and legal systems that gave preference to white Christians while oppressing nonwhite people and non-Christians. In Christian spaces, a hierarchy positions white men as superior to all others and closest to God. Whiteness becomes what Douglas terms a "cherished property" that "is the marker of a superior people, if not an exceptional people."[11] This theology subverts Christianity by making whiteness the object of worship. People place their faith in whiteness, Douglas explains, "as the supremacy of whiteness is that which provides the link to exceptionalism and, as we will soon see, the link to God."[12] Therefore, the white Protestants who colonized North America had a higher mission to create a "city on a hill" because they "believed themselves to be as close a human manifestation of God on earth as one could get."[13]

At the same time that white Christians saw themselves as one step away from God in the hierarchy of the universe, they deemed people with darker skin and the heathens who had not been saved by Christ to be inferior and in need of salvation. Because darker skin, as Stephanie Mitchem explains, "was believed to be sign of God's curse against black people,"[14] the enslavement of Black Africans was justified because it fit with what was seen as the natural hierarchy. As Mitchem writes, "Enslavement of black people was viewed as part of a God-given natural, social order, and North Atlantic Christian theology came to justify the misconceptions and unjust treatment of people of color."[15] Katie Cannon asserts that white Christians justified the evil act of enslavement by claiming to be saving Black people from the "spiritual darkness" that had cursed them.[16]

The effects of these theological justifications for slavery are still prominent today in Evangelical Christian churches that continue to promote the view that whiteness is superior, holier, and closer to God. Butler succinctly explains this legacy: "Evangelicalism is synonymous with whiteness. It is not only a cultural whiteness but also a political whiteness."[17] Evangelical Christianity has become a political force that is centered on maintaining the power of white Christian males. For example, the emergence of the religious right in the 1970s and 1980s was built on a foundation of maintaining white supremacy, as Christian institutions like Bob Jones University were threatened with losing their tax-exempt status if they didn't desegregate their schools or allow interracial dating.[18] These political projects also involved the policing of other marginalized communities such as women and queer people through restrictions on reproductive rights, gay marriage, access to resources, and transgender rights. These projects often appeal to language around maintaining purity and following God's design, but this often hides the motivation to protect the superiority of whiteness.

Furthermore, the framing of whiteness as superior and holy through language and images of a white Jesus inflicts a spiritual harm on the souls of Black people. Austin Channing Brown explains that the assumption within many Christian churches is "that white is right: closer to God, holy, chosen, the epitome of being."[19] While the institutions that are perpetuated by white supremacy cause physical and mental harm, what the Black liberation theologian James Cone terms "spiritual death" causes deep hurt for both racists and the oppressed people. As Cone writes, "Through cultural and religious imperialism, Europeans imposed their racist value-system on people of color and thereby forced them to think that the only way to be human and civilized was to be White and Christian."[20] A great deal of work is needed to break away from this white supremacist mind-set and build up a spirituality that recognizes all people as created in the likeness of God. The activists profiled in this book are attempting to center on the value of these marginalized lives in their work.

THE RACIALIZATION OF MUSLIMS AS INFERIOR TO WHITE CHRISTIANS

Within American Evangelical Christianity, Black Christians are positioned as lower than white Christians on the hierarchy of holiness because their skin color is interpreted to mean that they are less pure and more primitive. The presumed inferiority of women to men is also justified through a warped theology that focuses on the strength and masculinity of Jesus and his disciples in contrast to the weak and submissive role of women in the Bible. While Christian women and Black Christians are positioned on a lower rung than white Christian men, those who are not Christian are often viewed as potential converts to or enemies of Evangelical Christianity. With a strong focus on evangelizing, Christians often looked to Islamic regions as potential missionizing fields.[21] At the same time, Islam is frequently positioned as a "political ideology" that must be stamped out through American intervention, such as the wars, occupation, and political involvement in the Middle East over the past several decades.[22] After 9/11, Evangelical Christian leaders resuscitated the language of crusade and holy war to position Islam as a political enemy to white Christian America. President George W. Bush's War on Terror and his binary of good America versus bad Islamic terrorists encouraged Evangelicals "not only to speak of Islam disparagingly but also to deepen their faith's embrace of nationalism and American exceptionalism."[23] This rhetoric easily fit into the larger project of maintaining the supremacy of white, male, Christian Americans.

Rather than being viewed as equal human beings who have chosen a religion that many Christians see as flawed, Muslims are defined as a racially distinct group that is inherently inferior to white Christians. Racialization is a systematic process through which certain "groups are rejected from whiteness," as Saher Selod and David Embrick explain.[24] At the same time, other individuals are granted the power and privileges of possessing what Cheryl Harris terms "whiteness as treasured property."[25] Racialization has very little to do with phenotypical features and is almost exclusively about creating a hierarchy of who has value and power. Amaney Jamal describes the racialization of Muslims as "a process by which the dominant social group claims moral and cultural superiority in the process of producing an essentialized, homogeneous image of Muslim and Arab Americans as non-whites who are naturally, morally, and culturally inferior to whites."[26] This positioning of Muslims as inherently inferior to white Christians provides justification for policies meant to protect white Christian America from Muslim aggressors.

In a similar manner to how white supremacy in the United States is interwoven with Christian supremacy, the racialization of Muslims and anti-Islam rhetoric is tied to the dominance of Christianity. The classification of non-Christians as inferior to white Christians was a key part of European colonization. The Europeans used their presumed superiority as a race and a religious group to justify their political and economic exploitation. As they encountered new cultures, they were obsessed with creating systems to categorize these "others." Their classification systems were based on physical characteristics, but religious beliefs and practices were also significant. Junaid Rana explains that racial differences and religious differences were often conflated in the European imaginary: "For the discoverers, it was precisely their understanding of the religious other and of religious difference that formed the lens through which to understand *racial* difference in the New World."[27]

Selod and Embrick also explain how Europeans categorized non-Christians such as Jews and Muslims as having the "wrong religion" and Indigenous people in Africa and the Americas as having "no religion."[28] According to this formulation, religion was not a choice that one could make openly but rather an identifying characteristic that was closely tied to an individual's race and biology. Religion could not be separated from race in the European hierarchy of society. Therefore, the early colonizers of what would become the United States asserted both their racial and religious superiority over nonwhite Indigenous people and enslaved Africans. Just as anti-Black racism in the United States is closely connected to Christianity, anti-Muslim racism is built on a foundation of the superiority of whiteness and Christianity. As Khyati Joshi succinctly explains, "Whiteness and Christianity came to be not so much conflated as co-existent, the two strands of the double helix of American identity."[29] This interconnection between whiteness and Christianity as the foundation of U.S. culture reinforces a hierarchy that grants social power and privileges to people based not only on race but also on religion. Furthermore, the role of Christianity cannot be ignored when examining white supremacy because of the way an appeal to the divine is used as justification for systematic oppression of women, Black people, and Muslims. In various ways, the creators of the projects featured in this book are working to dismantle this hierarchy of souls and illustrate how this system oppresses an interconnected web of those deemed unruly based on skin color, sexuality, gender, and religion.

THE MUSLIM WOMAN AS POLITICAL ICON

The Muslim creatives profiled in this book are mainly responding to Western cultural representations of Muslims that have often been used to portray Islam as inferior, backward, and repressive. The bodies of Muslim women, in particular, have been used as symbols of the presumed repression and backwardness of Islam. Lila Abu-Lughod argues that after 9/11, the images of burqa-clad women in Afghanistan circulated in U.S. media as symbols of the oppression of Islam. The images of these women became a justification for the Afghanistan War because the American troops would save the women with the introduction of progressive Western culture.[30] This rhetoric of saving, Abu-Lughod argues, locates the United States in a superior position but fails to realize that Western countries have been part of the oppression of women in parts of the world like Afghanistan. The use of these images serves only to reinforce the view that Muslim women are merely icons of larger political struggles. As miriam cooke explains, the women are reduced to the their religious and gendered identity of "Muslimwoman." Marked by the veil, the women become one-dimensional victims of Muslim men.[31] The image of the victimized Muslim woman becomes what Alia Al-Saji calls a "foil or negative mirror" to reflect back the presumed superiority of Western culture.[32] While Islam is seen as inherently repressive and backward, Western culture is portrayed as essentially progressive and forward thinking.

The dominant counterimage to the portrayal of Muslim women as oppressed victims of Islam is the stereotype of Muslim women as hypersexualized and exotic objects of the Western male gaze. Malek Alloula's analysis of harem photography in the early twentieth century showcases how the action of lifting the veil is not a genuine way to liberate Muslim women but only an avenue to access the forbidden space under the veil. The women do not become individuals with their own autonomy; rather, they are liberated to become sexually available to Western men.[33] In her analysis of an American Apparel advertisement called "Made in Bangladesh," Dina Siddiqi clarifies this dichotomy that Muslim women face. The ad featured a topless Bangladeshi woman, along with a story about how she had escaped from the oppression of Bangladesh and Islam. This ad reinforces the ideologies of liberal feminism and secular democracy sweeping in to liberate Muslim women. The model in the ad has only two choices: to remain physically covered and oppressed by Islam or to uncover herself and be sexually liberated by Western culture. Siddiqi explains, "Exercising the 'right' to bare the body signifies an act of empowerment for the Muslim woman whose 'natural' state is understood to be covered and behind the veil."[34] The only way for the woman in the image to embrace the freedoms of the West is to abandon Islam and uncover her body, revealing herself as a sexual object.

In the face of these negative portrayals of Muslim women in Western culture, the women are also pressured from fellow Muslims to always represent Islam in a positive light. Muslim women articulating feminist critiques often feel trapped between what the activist Mona Eltahawy calls "a rock and a hard place." She explains in an article about her work to address sexual assault in Muslim communities: "On one side are Islamophobes and racists who are all too willing to demonize Muslim men by weaponizing my testimony of sexual assault. On the other side is the 'community' of fellow Muslims who are all too willing to defend all Muslim men. . . . Neither side cares about the well-being of Muslim women."[35] Women become icons to represent what is good and bad about Islam, but the serious concerns about gender justice within the religion are ignored. Muslim women are often discouraged from discussing within Muslim American spaces significant issues such as sexual harassment and abuse; the perpetuation of misogyny through modesty culture; and discrimination against certain Muslims based on their skin color, class, or country of origin.

THE HIERARCHY OF PIETY WITHIN ISLAM

Countless studies have documented how Muslims—particularly those who are visibly practicing their faith—face regular discrimination and harassment in the United States.[36] The dominance of cultural narratives that frame Muslims as irrational and backward terrorists encourages support for "the enactment of policies like the PATRIOT Act, the War on Terror, no-fly lists, indefinite detention in

Guantanamo Bay, 'Countering Violent Extremism' CVE programs, and the Muslim Ban."[37] The racialization of Muslims as a threatening "other" is made clear by the experiences of white American converts to Islam, who describe the harassment they face once they are marked as Muslim and lose the privilege of whiteness.[38]

Additionally, Muslims in the United States are an extremely heterogeneous group, with privileges and restrictions granted based on class level, race, ethnicity, immigration status, sexuality, sect, and attire.[39] At the same time that Muslim Americans are classified as inferior to white Christian Americans, Muslims sometimes find it advantageous to participate in the white supremacist project that positions Black Americans as having lesser value. As Su'ad Abdul Khabeer elaborates, "White supremacy produces a racial logic that sets up a grid of associations in which Blackness, in relation to Whiteness, is always and already less-than, in terms of value, history and, most importantly, humanity."[40] Muslims in the United States are often divided into two groups: Black Muslims (both African Americans and recent immigrants from Africa) and Arab and South Asian Muslims. Muslim immigrants from the latter group are often "encouraged to adopt ideologies of anti-Blackness as an immigrant rite of passage."[41]

Arab and South Asian Muslims "have their own complex relationships to Whiteness"[42] because of the racialization of Muslims as foreign and threatening to white Christian America. While Muslims are rarely able to pass as white, they are still incentivized to hold anti-Black views by receiving a small amount of privilege compared to Black Muslims.[43] Arab and South Asian Muslims face a significant amount of discrimination, but they don't have the experience of Black Muslims who are "marked as black twice and placed into a racialized double-bind" in which they face discrimination for being Muslim and Black.[44] South Asian Muslims in particular are more easily able to reach the status of a model minority in the United States by building on their higher socioeconomic status, education, and professional backgrounds.[45]

Within Muslim communities, there is an "ideal of Islam as a religion without racial hierarchy."[46] Muslims often cite the Prophet Muhammad's last sermon, in which he reinforced the radical equality of all Muslims. Contrary to this ideal, Black Muslims in Islamic spaces are often viewed as "lacking religious authority and authenticity" because of their race.[47] This discrimination can be systematic (for example, refusing to allow Black Muslims to hold leadership roles in masjids) or more interpersonal (such as assuming that all Black Muslims recently converted to Islam and have little religious knowledge or believing in stereotypes that Black Muslims are poor and in need of charity).[48] The Muslim Anti-Racism Collaborative (ARC) found in a survey of Muslim Americans that 79 percent of Black, African, or Caribbean Muslims experienced discrimination from other Muslims based on race or ethnicity.[49] As chapters 3 and 5 illustrate, it is often the women who fail to meet the high standards of Islamic piety because of their skin color, sexuality, or attire who offer the strongest criticisms related to issues like misogyny, racism, colorism, classism, and homophobia within Islamic communities.

FOUNDATIONAL RELIGIOUS FEMINISM

At the same time that religious institutions and communities often perpetuate the hierarchical thinking that positions certain people as higher on a chain of value based on gender, race, or sexuality, feminists have offered critiques that point to the radical equality of all people in the eyes of God. The contemporary activists in this book often build on the work of Muslim and Christian feminist scholars who both pointed out the ways that misogyny had warped religious teachings but also incorporated the sacredness of femininity into scripture and rituals. Feminist discussions within Islam often center on the Qur'an and look to the example of the Prophet Muhammad to argue that men and women are created equal by God. As Leila Ahmed writes in her groundbreaking *Women and Gender in Islam*, at its roots Islam promotes justice and equality, but those teachings have been seen through a patriarchal and misogynistic lens and misinterpreted.[50] Scholars like Amina Wadud examine the Qur'an from a feminist perspective to highlight the equality of all people.[51] Female figures in early Muslim communities, such as the Prophet Muhammad's wives Khadijah and Aisha, are revered as strong leaders and exemplars of people living a pious and ethical life.

Early feminist critiques within Christian denominations ran on a parallel track to the larger second-wave critiques of the 1960s and 1970s. This theological work incorporated issues similar to those in the feminist movement, like celebrating the feminine and granting women equal leadership roles. Scholars like Carol Christ promoted the concept of the goddess to celebrate the divine nature of women.[52] Other feminist theologians like Mary Daly challenged the patriarchy imbedded in Christian churches through the institutional structure[53] as well as the theology that promoted a masculine view of God.[54] Some of the mainline Protestant churches began to ordain women and "rewrite traditional liturgies that used masculine language both to describe worshipers and to describe the deity."[55]

Within Evangelical Christianity, as Pamela Cochran explains, a movement called biblical feminism "began among a group of well-educated, upper-middle-class women (and a few men) who believed that women suffered injustices and discrimination because of their sex and that the Bible offered a viable solution."[56] Specifically, the groundbreaking 1974 *All We're Meant to Be*, by Letha Scanzoni and Nancy Hardesty, offers a feminist Evangelical reading of women in the Bible as well as an argument for the equality of women in churches and society. Building on Jesus's message of liberation for all who are oppressed, Scanzoni and Hardesty argue that women, like men, are created in the image of God and have gifts to offer the church and world. Going beyond gender equality, the authors engage with the radical message of Jesus to highlight larger structures of oppression. Scanzoni and Hardesty write, "The essence of sin is not pride but dualistic division and domination, the desire to lord it over one another that we see so graphically displayed in sexism, racism, homophobia, classism, nationalism, and militarism."[57] Strikingly, these Evangelical Christians engage with the Bible to construct a form of feminism that is both intersectional and queer in its resistance to binaries and recognition of complex forms of oppression. Unfortunately, this Evangelical feminist movement mainly reflected the concerns of its members, most of whom were middle-class, educated, straight, white women.

INTERSECTIONAL FEMINIST ACTIVISM WITHIN AND BEYOND RELIGIONS

The current state of intersectional feminist activism within Evangelical Christianity can be gauged by examining the outpouring of grief online over the untimely death of the writer and activist Rachel Held Evans in 2019. After Evans died tragically of an infection at the age of thirty-seven, the Tweets about her legacy illustrated the lasting impact of her work to create a supportive community for those who had been excluded from Christianity. Thousands of people posted reflections on what her life and writings had meant to their own spiritual development as women, queer individuals, and people of color. She was an online leader who advocated for an intersectional critique of conservative Christianity that would welcome all people to the church. As Eliza Griswold explains in an article after Evans's death, "She fiercely insisted that God's love included everyone, and she attempted to offer those who'd been shunned by the church a way to return."[58]

In addition, my conversations with people involved in activism against the purity culture revealed an ever-expanding movement and a wider public interest in this exodus of young Evangelicals. Those I spoke with about the purity culture told me that I was one of several academics researching these progressive movements among Evangelicals, and numerous articles have appeared in the popular press about the purity culture,[59] the death of Evans,[60] the Exvangelical movement,[61] and Chrissy Stroop's Empty the Pews project.[62] In 2018 CBS News ran a thirty-minute national show titled "Deconstructing My Religion," which featured various activist projects criticizing Evangelical subcultures.[63] There is clearly a growing movement of young people leaving white Evangelical Christianity, as white Evangelicals are an aging population with a median age of fifty-five, and only 10 percent of Americans under the age of thirty identify themselves as white Evangelical.[64]

Contemporary online discussions among former or questioning Evangelicals focus on intersectional concerns not only regarding women's rights but also related to inclusion and justice for queer people, nonwhite people, and others

who have been labeled impure and sinful. These concerns stem from the particular experiences of younger generations of Evangelicals, raised in churches that
emphasized sexual purity above all other religious tenants, promoted Republi-
can politicians and antichoice policies, preached about financial prosperity
while ignoring the poor, covered up the roots of white supremacy in American
Christianity, and downplayed the gospel call to love your neighbor and care for
the less fortunate. The popularity of Evans's books[65] about her personal struggles to stay in a religion that she found to be very exclusionary and out of sync
with the gospel demonstrates the desire for these intersectional critiques. In
addition to the feminist lens on scripture, new activists are promoting the queer
perspective on faith.[66]

In the context of a growing social movement to address the legacy of racism
in American institutions, Christian authors such as Austin Channing Brown and
Lenny Duncan examine the roots of white supremacy and anti-Blackness in
Christian churches.[67] Furthermore, these Black Christian activists also call out
racial injustices and inequality in contemporary Christian institutions. For
instance, current church communities may discuss becoming more multiethnic,
but these efforts are often ways to add token diversity without tackling deeper
issues of institutional and historical racism. As Brown shows, the many failed
attempts at racial reconciliation "keep the church feeling good, innocent, maybe
even progressive, all the while preserving the roots of injustice."[68] Young Evangelicals of color work to tackle social justice problems related to poverty, policing, immigration, and prison reform, but as Lee writes, they need to get "white
evangelicals to recognize that institutional racial injustice truly exists."[69]

In terms of intersectional feminist concerns within American Islam, cultural
spaces like films and streaming shows illustrate how young Muslims seek to
expand their image beyond one-dimensional portrayals as loyal and harmless
Americans to dig deeper into social injustices and problems within Muslim
American communities. The Hulu series Ramy, for instance, deals with the typical issues of an immigrant Egyptian Muslim family striving to be accepted in the
United States, but it also offers pointed critiques of homophobia, anti-Blackness,
and misogyny in Muslim communities. Other shows like The Patriot Act, The Bold
Type, or We Are Lady Parts illustrate the concerns of young Muslims about how
their experiences of injustice intersect with other forms of inequality based on
race, gender, sexuality, or class. These cultural products relate to the work of the
Muslim creators discussed in this book, such as Mona Haydar, the Mipsterz collective, Leah Vernon, and Blair Imani, who expand the experiences of Muslims to
explore wider issues of racism, imperialism, misogyny, and homophobia.

Organizations like the Muslim ARC offer speakers, trainings, workshops, and
other educational programs that address racial justice. Although the Muslim ARC
focuses on Muslim American communities, it addresses a range of issues from
interpersonal incidents within Muslim circles to wider institutional racism.[70]

Namira Islam explains that this organizations hosts events that "begin to educate communities about systemic racism, critical anti-Islamophobia activism, and the history of colonialism and global white supremacy."[71] Rather than focusing only on issues related to anti-Black racism, this group analyzes larger forces of white Christian supremacy that have perpetuated intersecting forms of oppression. Similarly, the online collaborative "Islamophobia Is Racism" syllabus expands anti-Muslim hate to see interconnections to other systematic forms of oppression.[72] Both of these projects take a Critical Race Theory approach by examining how hatred against Muslims is not an individual fear but rather a systematic form of oppression that has been supported through laws and policies.[73]

INTERSECTING OPPRESSION IN DISTINCT CONTEXTS

While the activists profiled in this book come from distinct religious backgrounds in Christianity and Islam, they are united by their engagement in progressive causes and their concern about people with a wide diversity of experiences. They seek to dismantle binaries and other categories and are skilled at using the flexibility and playfulness of digital media to accomplish these goals. There are overlaps between their progressive projects, as I discuss in the conclusion, but Muslims and Christians face specific concerns when they examine the three main issues addressed in this book: racism, sexism, and homophobia.

The online discussions around racial injustices in the summer of 2020 illustrate some differences between Christians and Muslims. Among Christians, the conversations focused on how white supremacy corrupts Christianity by promoting the superiority and holiness of whiteness. Among Muslim Americans, issues around racism are more complicated, as discussed above. White supremacy still infuses Muslim spaces and perpetuates ideas of Blackness as less pure than whiteness, but all Muslims are racialized in the United States. This racialization perpetuates the view that Muslims are inferior, backward, and threatening and thus cannot claim the privilege of whiteness. Furthermore, Black Muslims have long been a very visible presence in American Islam, with figures like Muhammad Ali, Kareem Abdul-Jabbar, and Mahershala Ali representing Islam to a wider American audience.[74] Despite the legacy of anti-Black racism in the United States, these Black Muslims have often been familiar and, at times, friendly faces of American Islam.

Issues of misogyny and homophobia are often similar in Evangelical Christianity and Islam, as leaders in both religions promote the view that women have a responsibility to remain pure and modest to protect the holiness of men and the larger religious community. Purity culture in Christianity and modesty teachings in Islam both state that sexual indiscretions are generally the fault of the women for not covering themselves and protecting their sexuality. In addition, both Islam[75] and Evangelical Christianity[76] frequently promote a complementarian approach to gender roles: men and women are equal but have distinct roles that complement each other. These separate roles usually grant men power and authority within the family, religious community, and society, while women play roles within the domestic space. With these unequal power dynamics, instances of gender-based violence and sexual harassment are rampant in both communities, as demonstrated by the similarities in stories shared under #ChurchToo and #MosqueMeToo. Both religions have similar examples of shaming and blaming the female victims for causing sexual assaults or harassment. Finally, progressive activists in Christianity and Islam also have related interests in dismantling binary structures that reinforce gender categories and heteronormativity. Projects like the Mipsterz collective and the *Queerology* podcast illustrate the beauty of queerness and the liberating potential of blurring categories.

Over the past several years, feminist concepts and catchphrases have gained visibility in U.S. cultural, political, and consumer spaces. As Sarah Banet-Weiser asserts, this form of "popular feminism" promotes a neoliberal approach of finding individual solutions through consumption, branding, and entrepreneurship, while ignoring structural inequalities that lead to the oppression of those who fall outside of the white, straight, middle-class, and cisgendered norms.[77] The activists discussed in this book come from perspectives that are often silenced by popular feminists: they are nonwhite, immigrants, queer, fat, unruly, loud, and angry. Rather than seek changes that amount to little more than window dressing within their faith communities, these individuals are rooting out the deep injustices and inequalities within religious institutions. Although the political situations of Muslims and Evangelical Christians in the United States are notably distinct from each other, these prophetic voices call for reform within religions by foregrounding the perspectives of women, people of color, queer individuals, and members of other marginalized groups.

2 · #KISSSHAMEBYE

Textual Critiques of Evangelical Purity Culture

In July 2019, Matthias Roberts, the host of a podcast about queer spirituality, posted on his Twitter page, "I kissed straighting goodbye."[1] The Tweet immediately garnered positive comments, including more than 550 likes, and was retweeted over sixty times. To those who grew up exposed to the purity culture that dominated Evangelical Christianity in the 1990s and early 2000s, this concise but multilayered Tweet called to mind both the prominent *I Kissed Dating Goodbye* book that circulated throughout youth groups at the time and the heteronormative teachings promoted in purity culture texts.[2] Roberts's Tweet exemplifies how humorous language play can be used as a signal to people raised within this subculture while also pointing out the hypocrisy and oppression of purity culture.

Digital media spaces often encourage this playful and creative use of language, which at times can transition into trolling or harassment but can also be used to call attention to the social injustices faced by marginalized communities. Women have often taken to Twitter to point to the absurdity and misogyny of political statements by writing about their experiences under tags like #BindersFullOfWomen, #NastyWoman, #ShePersisted, and #DontMessWithNancy.[3] Muslim Americans have also engaged with humorous hashtags to contradict terrorist tropes such as #MuslimsReportStuff, #MuslimRage, and #RamadanProblems.[4] Similarly, Twitter is often a space for Black Americans to speak about how their lives are consistently devalued in mainstream cultural spaces. As Sarah Florini notes, Black users of Twitter engage in linguistic practices of "signifyin'" to perform racial identity but also to resist dominant political powers.[5] For instance, the engagement with memes like Karen and Becky illustrate how Black people creatively use social media to call out the white supremacy displayed when white people call the police on Black people for doing harmless things like barbecuing, bird-watching, looking at real estate, jogging, and mowing the lawn.

Alongside these projects that display the value and equality of marginalized individuals, this chapter focuses on how those traumatized and ostracized by Evangelical purity culture engage with textual spaces such as Twitter hashtags, blogs, and online forums to creatively articulate their inherent value. Through books such as *I Kissed Dating Goodbye* and *Every Young Man's Battle*,[6] the tenets of purity culture reinforce the idea that only certain women—those who are white, straight, and virginal—can be considered pure and thus pious. Inevitably, these teachings, which position women as the bearers of purity for the whole community, infuse Evangelical Christianity with misogynistic ideas that women are inherently hypersexual, sinful, and flawed. Women and queer people come out of this culture feeling shame and psychological trauma after being repeatedly told that they are intrinsically flawed. In chapter 3, I continue this discussion of sexual purity by analyzing a parallel but distinct project in Islam to promote modesty and piety through fashion and clothing.

In this chapter, I assert that those recovering from the trauma of purity culture creatively engage with textual spaces online to rearticulate their inherent value within a supportive community; celebrate their sexualities; and root out the patriarchal, white supremacist; and heteronormative aspects of Evangelical Christianity. Since the teachings of purity culture have been elevated to near doctrine status among Evangelicals through the prominence of certain books and workshops, people seeking to dismantle these oppressive systems engage with digital textual spaces to develop a new doctrine that reinforces the inherent goodness and equality of all people in the eyes of God. These young activists display sadness and anger as well as humor in their writings, and these digital textual spaces provide supportive connections to help people address the trauma of purity culture.

THE PURITY GENERATION

As the popularity of Roberts's Tweet above indicates, people who came of age in the United States during the 1990s and 2000s were likely to have had some exposure to what is known as purity culture, whether through a Christian youth group, an abstinence seminar at public school, or a paperback memoir about the importance of waiting until marriage to have sex. Although I was exposed to comprehensive sexual education at my public high school that focused on using contraception, I attended a youth event at my friend's Pentecostal church where we all took a pledge to stay virgins until marriage. I remember repeating a line about sex being "worth the wait." In addition to the prominence of purity teachings in church settings, secular versions of purity culture proliferated in public schools and youth centers. Since these workshops and lesson plans were often federally funded, they didn't make explicit religious claims but rather argued for sexual purity to prevent unwanted pregnancies and sexually transmitted diseases.

The development of purity culture was connected with other conservative cultural movements of that time as the religious right and Evangelical Christianity became more socially prominent. Amanda Barbee explains that this was a period of reaction against some of the sexual freedoms of the previous decades: "In the 1980s and 1990s, a decline in the economy, as well as the onset of the AIDS epidemic, caused a cultural shift back toward sexual conservatism. And it was in the midst of this shift that the purity movement was born."[7] Concerned about sexually transmitted diseases and teen pregnancies, Christian congregations and other organizations developed and promoted abstinence programs for young people. True Love Waits was the first such program developed by the Southern Baptist Convention. Launched in 1992, it promoted the signing of abstinence pledges.[8] At a rally on the National Mall in 1994, True Love Waits displayed more than 210,000 signed abstinence pledge cards.[9]

As churches across the country sought to bring these programs into their communities and federal funds were made available for abstinence-only education, an entire "purity industry," as Linda Kay Klein terms it, developed around various speakers, curriculums, workshops, and books. In addition to the speakers and workshops, the purity industry produced and sold "purity-themed rings, bracelets, necklaces, shirts, hats, underwear, books, journals, devotionals, magazines, Bible studies, trainings, guides, DVDs, planners and other products."[10] Purity teachings were so prominent in Evangelical culture that, as Klein explains, "the purity industry gave many adolescents the impression that sexual abstinence before marriage was *the* way for them to live out their faith."[11] The negative consequences of refocusing the Christian faith on sexual purity played out later, when people internalized the shame of impurity.

While several books, workbooks, and pamphlets promoted the tenets of purity culture, one book appears to have the most resonance in the minds of Millennials reflecting back on their teenage years. Originally released in 1997, Joshua Harris's *I Kissed Dating Goodbye: A New Attitude toward Romance and Relationships* has sold over 1.2 million copies. Along with focusing on the importance of saving sex until marriage, Harris promoted formal courtship, approved by one's parents, over casual dating and physical gestures like kissing and holding hands that could lead to sexual intimacy. With its attractive cover (showing a handsome man in a fedora) and written in an accessible style by a twenty-one-year-old raised in the Evangelical Christian homeschooling movement, this relationship advice book quickly circulated among youth groups and Christian schools. As Sarah Stankorb wrote in a *Cosmopolitan* article about purity culture, "Harris instantly made purity 'cool' to young people."[12]

Furthermore, *I Kissed Dating Goodbye* presented what seemed to be a reasonable and modern approach to relationships while remaining abstinent until marriage. As Ruth Graham discussed in a *Slate* article, Harris laid out a clear blueprint for how to protect your virginity to have a more fulfilling marriage later: "There was a reassuring black-and-white quality to that stricture, with the promise of a juicy wedding-night reward for my self-control."[13] Dating and casual relationships would inevitably take young people down a slippery slope, resulting in physical and emotional intimacy that would be a hindrance in marriage. The idea was that when you get married, you want to be able to give your whole body and soul to your spouse without having previous relationships weighing you down. After several years of distancing himself from purity culture, in 2018 Harris recanted the teachings in *I Kissed Dating Goodbye* and follow-up books. While he ordered the publisher to stop printing *I Kissed Dating Goodbye*, copies are still easy to find online.[14] Furthermore, this book is simply one of the most prominent examples of purity culture and the wider industry that promotes sexual abstinence until marriage and concurrently perpetuates misogynistic, homophobic, and anti-Black interpretations of Christian theology.

IDEOLOGIES OF PURITY

Several recent books have outlined the extensive history of the purity industry and its ties to political, cultural, and educational sectors in the United States.[15] I want to focus here on the prominent themes that are repeated in purity culture texts. It is important to understand these key themes and how they reflect dominant ideologies about women and other marginalized subjects before moving into an extensive analysis of how young people use digital activism to dismantle these ideas. These teachings devalue women, not only by objectifying them and transforming them into icons of religious ideals but also by inflicting the deeper injury of labeling women as impure, sinful, and flawed because of their gender, sexuality, skin color, or body shape. This ideology implies that as women, we are intrinsically sinful. We are made with flaws that can never be corrected. Our sexualities and other unruly aspects must be covered up and repressed to maintain the purity of the community. And some individuals—because of their sexual preference, gender expression, skin color, or body shape—have little hope of ever being considered pure.

Icons of Purity

In one of the first texts to identify and investigate purity culture, *The Purity Myth: How America's Obsession with Virginity Is Hurting Young Women*, Jessica Valenti explains that young women who are virgins are placed on a pedestal for all to admire. This is one of the main ideologies perpetuated by purity culture: young women are the bearers of purity for the whole community. However, this high status does not grant pure women any agency. While these women are given value for their virginity, the "purity myth" reinforces the need "to prop up the idea of the perfect woman as a blank slate, as powerless and in need of direction."[16] Therefore, misogynistic and paternalistic policies are needed to control women and restrict their agency.

Within Evangelical Christian circles, virginal young women are often positioned simultaneously as icons of purity and piety and as in need of constant protection to prevent a fall from grace. Thus, many rules police women's behavior, as detailed in an article in *Sojourners*: "Dress modestly (so as not to be a stumbling block), avoid one-on-one interactions with someone of the opposite sex (to avoid sexual temptation), and keep your thoughts 'pure' (because you can be unfaithful even in your mind)."[17] Purity goes beyond not having sex; rather, it encapsulates a larger project of ensuring that women are completely pure. As Amy DeRogatis explains, purity "is a lifestyle that requires scrutinizing all one's innermost thoughts and feelings and working tirelessly to guard oneself from any evidence of improper sexual desires or actions."[18] A pure lifestyle also includes dressing modestly, eating healthy food, exercising, avoiding sexual images, and not using vulgar speech. This work is part of a "complete system of dedicating your body and mind to God."[19]

In addition, if young women stray in any way from this pure lifestyle, then they will damage not only themselves but the whole community. DeRogatis explains how they can harm their personal relationships: "According to purity literature, young women who depart from this path are not only living a sinful life of impurity but are endangering the health and happiness of their future spouses and children."[20] Women take on the role of icons that represent the purity of Christianity, and this purity must be protected.

At the same time that women are designated as bearers of sexual purity for the community, they are also objectified as barriers to male holiness. As Klein so aptly describes it, women are positioned as "stumbling blocks" that prevent male Christians from achieving greatness and piety: "The implication that my friends and I were nothing more than *things* over which men and boys could trip was not lost on me."[21] While women can be put on the pedestal of sexual purity, they are at risk of having their inherent flaws and hypersexual nature take over and harm the whole community.

This sense of being intrinsically flawed and impure produces not just feelings of guilt but also a deep shame. Klein explains that there is a distinction between guilt (over doing something bad) and shame, which is a feeling that "I *am*—or somebody else will *think* I am—bad."[22] The penalty for not maintaining the purity of the community is feeling a deep shame about your inherent failings. DeRogatis writes, "sexual sin is [young women's] responsibility and sexual defilement is their eternal shame."[23] In interviews with people who survived the purity culture, Klein details the various symptoms (like those of post-traumatic stress disorder [PTSD]) that young people feel as a result of this deep shame. She explained in an interview on *The Liturgists* podcast that the "feeling of impurity was so internalized" that it triggered anxiety, fear, and depression for young people in their intimate relationships.[24] These effects of internalized shame are reflected in the Tweets and other digital activism that are the focus of this chapter.

Chewed-Up, Thrown-Out, Damaged Goods

Along with the teaching that young women must protect this precious gift of purity for the larger community, another recurring theme of purity culture is that if virginity is lost outside of marriage, then purity can never be reclaimed. Conveying the concept of jumping into a pit of filth and shame are repeated object lessons that refer to a single drop of coloring in a glass of water, a chewed-up piece of gum, a used piece of tape that has lost its adhesiveness, or a piece of food that has been spit on and dropped on the ground. All of these lessons reinforce the idea that once you have crossed the line of sexual impurity, there is no going back. You can never be clean and pure again. You will never regain your value. Valenti explains that young women are exposed to hypersexualized messages in mainstream culture, but they are also taught that "their only real worth is their virginity and ability to remain 'pure.'"[25] Within purity culture, the loss of purity equates to the loss of inherent value.

In work on purity culture, numerous women talk about feeling "worthless" or "used up,"[26] "as something less than fully human,"[27] or as "disgusting garbage"[28] after they have lost their virginity, even if this happens because of rape. This devaluing of women's bodies and sexualities by defining them as dirty and defiled relates to a branch of Christian theology that positions the body, and in particular women's bodies, as the source of sinfulness. As Barbee explains, "The church's history is full of influential men who have created theologies of gender around the idea of Eve as the cause of the fall and the root of evil."[29] These theologies articulate a binary consisting on the one hand of women who are embodied and sexual and on the other hand of men who are spiritual and celibate. This dichotomy, Barbee explains, devalues women by positioning them "as bodily and sexually problematic."[30] When young women are unable to live up to the high standards of the purity culture, they are degraded by being seen as living out their true debased and corporeal essence.

Emily Joy Allison, one of the leaders in the movement against the purity culture, points to this "anti-body theology" along with theologically justified misogyny as root causes of sexual abuse within the church. She explains that she grew up "believing that my body and my sexuality were the source of everything bad in my life."[31] Similarly, Klein discusses how purity culture promotes a hierarchy that positions the spirit above the mind and the mind above the body. She explains: "The body is this sinful fleshy thing, not in heaven, [that] only exists here in this testing ground that is earth. So, the idea is that we can be most pure by being most separate from our body."[32] A lot of the digital activism for those recovering from purity culture relates to these ideas of articulating the value of the body and sexuality, especially for women and queer people.

Pure as White

Another significant theme of purity culture, which is often unacknowledged, is that only certain women can be placed on this pedestal of pure icons. "The desirable virgin is sexy but not sexual. She's young, white, and skinny," Valenti explains. "She's never a woman of color. She's never a low-income girl or a fat girl. She's never disabled."[33] Because of their skin color, body shape, sexual orientation, or other form of unruliness, certain women can never achieve purity. These unruly women are not seen as in need of protection, like the beautiful, fair virgin; rather, their sexuality must be policed. DeRogatis details how the purity culture literature often uses white characters like fair princesses or deploys metaphors for purity like "lily white" or "stainless" to "relate 'whiteness' to purity, godliness, and beauty."[34] These are not isolated examples. Instead, they illustrate how purity culture reflects the foundation of misogyny, homophobia, and racism within American Evangelicalism.

In a podcast interview, Klein explained the negative connotation of using words like "purity" and "cleansing" in regard to human life: "Often times when we are talking about purity and applying it to a human being what we are trying to do is control them and make them 'like' the common group. Anyone who doesn't fit into the common group is bad, impure, out."[35] Purity culture reflects greater power dynamics that create a hierarchy of who is pure and thus holier in the community. Klein elaborates: "The idea of sexual purity is very connected to white women's sexual purity. And this idea that as a white woman to maintain your whiteness, to maintain your power, you have to fit into this pure, desexualized, or unsexual category to be the good wife. Whereas people of color are never afforded the possibility of purity."[36] Thus, purity is equated with whiteness, and whiteness is equated with being inherently better in the eyes of God. Purity culture perpetuates the idea that people with dark skin are created dirty and can never be pure or holy.

Purity culture causes deep harm to the souls of Black Christians, who don't have the privilege of whiteness. Keisha McKenzie grew up as a Seventh-day Adventist in Jamaica and the United Kingdom but was still exposed to white American Evangelical Christianity and purity culture. Now an activist working to dismantle these structures of oppression, McKenzie is aware of how her experiences as a Black queer woman are devalued within Christian churches. As she explained to me, "Christianity is a way of teaching white supremacist, binary-gendered views of order and value that disadvantaged Black people overall, Black women especially and queer Black people . . . with white, cis, hetero men at the apex of those beliefs."[37] Not only were McKenzie and other Black Christians harmed by the teachings of purity culture, but she also realized that the popular purity culture texts that circulated during her teenage years were not written for her. "I first saw the *I Kissed Dating Goodbye* book when I was in Jamaica. It actually didn't resonate with me at all because I think that its cultural grounding is very obvious to me," she explained. "It felt very white American, very middle America, very middle class, very male centered, which is also the ground from which a lot of the purity culture norms are written."[38] The fact that McKenzie was able to see this text as not written for a Black audience does not dismiss the deep harm caused by these ideologies that equate whiteness with purity and value.

DEVELOPMENT OF AN ANTI-PURITY MOVEMENT ONLINE

As young people raised in Evangelical Christian churches in the 1990s and 2000s entered adulthood and mature relationships in recent years, there has been an explosion of interest in talking about the purity teachings that proliferated during their teenage years. Although the ideologies of purity were ever-present in Evangelical spaces, young people did not always have supportive communities to honesty discuss sexuality. Klein explains that digital spaces opened up these conversations: "All of a sudden with the online community, people are aware of purity culture and are turning to activism."[39] Some of the early online connections were through anonymous message boards or closed Facebook groups. A lot of those closed groups had been formed through connections at Bible colleges, and participants often had to be invited into the groups by someone they knew. Because the tenants of purity culture are often conveyed in textual forms such as books, annotated Bibles, purity pledges, workbooks, and pamphlets, young people often engage with digital textual spaces to counter dominant ideologies and articulate teachings in ways that celebrate instead of shame sexualities and bodies that have been deemed impure.

McKenzie was one of the early participants in these message boards and Facebook groups. She found these platforms provided open spaces to connect with others, discuss various issues, "and more broadly to have spaces to thrash out and talk through the aforementioned categories like doctrine or theology or the new information from science or psychology." McKenzie describes the original Facebook groups as spaces of possibilities for debating topics from a variety of perspectives. "In my sphere at least, we were having really complex and interesting hundred-comment threads on Facebook," she explains. "It didn't feel really hypersurveilled. It felt really fresh and exciting."[40]

Along with providing freedom to discuss topics that were often taboo in Evangelical circles, the internet in its early days was significant to people emerging from the Evangelical subculture. Klein told me that "there is a tremendous amount of fear that people will find out" about these online discussions that critique Evangelical culture. While Evangelicals do not feel physically threatened, they are afraid of being culturally ostracized and harmed by secular culture. Klein explains, "Even though in Evangelical communities, you are still surrounded by secular culture, there is an ideological isolation in which Evangelicals are taught not to trust anybody from outside Evangelicalism."[41] Going online to explore alternative ideas about sexuality is very risky, especially for people raised in a culture that teaches once you have dirtied yourself by entering the sinful space of secular culture, you can never be clean again. Online platforms in the early days provided the open space for exploration and the anonymity that was needed for people to emerge from these subcultural enclaves. Klein explains, "So online, for a lot of my interviewees, has proven to be groundbreaking even before activism around purity culture emerged."[42]

Following these early days of message boards and private Facebook groups, a more public-facing, progressive Christian activism began to emerge in the early 2010s. Valenti's *The Purity Myth* was released in 2009, and while it didn't focus exclusively on Evangelicalism, it was the first major book to directly name purity culture. Additionally, in 2010 the progressive Christian activist Rachel Held Evans began to publish books that provided trenchant critiques of the fault lines in American Evangelicalism. Allison, one of the creators of the #ChurchToo campaign against sexual abuse in churches, discussed with me the early activism online against purity culture: "The progressive Christian Twitter was kind of coalescing at that time. And shortly thereafter—so in 2012, there were all these 'blog-arounds' where all these people found each other from all over the country and all over the world. That's when we started using words like 'purity culture.'"[43] Allison remembers this as the perfect moment when everything came together around various critiques of Evangelical culture: "It felt like the big bang in a way, like the planets started forming."[44]

During this time, several online forums and web sites served as repositories of the various experiences of people raised in purity culture. Lola Prescott began the web site *No Shame Movement* in 2013 as a "platform for people to discuss growing up in conservative Christian environments that were taught abstinence only and 'unlearning' this ideology as adults."[45] The web site lists various resources and articles related to sexuality and recovering from religious trauma. Another web site, *Thank God for Sex*, also began in 2013 as an archive of video, audio, and written stories submitted by people about their experiences with sexuality and religion. It aims to be "an online community of solidarity for people who've experienced religious sexual shame."[46] Additionally, a June 2016 roundtable on *The Toast* about the legacy of *I Kissed Dating Goodbye* brought together several young activists to elaborate on the various ways that Harris's book and purity culture have negatively impacted young Christians.[47] Significantly, this forum featured three Black Christian activists—Prescott, McKenzie, and Verdell Wright—who addressed the prevalence of anti-Blackness and colonialism within purity culture and American Evangelicalism.

FIGURE 1. Screenshot of Twitter announcement of the #KissShameBye discussion.

Twitter discussions around the trauma of purity culture were prominent in the summer of 2016. Through *No Shame Movement*, Prescott facilitated a Twitter chat on July 18, 2016, about *I Kissed Dating Goodbye* and purity culture under the tag #KissShameBye (see figure 1). In response to Harris's going on an apparent apology tour and gathering stories of how his book had negatively affected people, Allison and Hannah Paasch started a web site and Twitter discussion under the tag #IKDGstories as a way to take control of the narrative around purity culture (see figure 2). This hashtag did not seek for people to "perform their trauma," in Allison's words, so Harris and others could feel better about the damage they inflicted.[48] Various other conversations have happened on Twitter around tags like #PurityCulture, #LifeAfterIKDG, #StillPurityCulture, #Break-FreeTogether, and the wider #ChurchToo movement.

The discussions around purity culture have shifted from the early days of mostly private or anonymous conversations that quietly raised concerns about Evangelical Christianity to the current era of activism aimed at dismantling purity culture completely and calling out and removing sexual abusers and their enablers within churches. As Klein explains, digital media activism against purity culture has grown stronger and louder as people feel more empowered to share their own critiques and traumatic experiences. "In order to be paid attention to, you have to say things at the same level to be heard," Klein says.[49] She also explains that there is a need for both activists who are going to boldly bring up these issues and community organizers on the ground who get people to work together for social change. However, she believes that digital media have an important role to play, noting that "I think online media actions are catalytic because they inspire and embolden people to become involved in ways that can change their community."[50] The remainder of this chapter analyzes the ways that textual spaces in digital media have encouraged young people raised in Evangeli-

**#IKDGSTORIES
TONIGHT ON TWITTER
08.03.16
6:00 CST/7:00 EST**

FIGURE 2. Screenshot of Twitter announcement of the #IKDGstories discussion.

cal purity culture to celebrate their sexualities rather than live in anxiety and shame. As the ideologies of purity have been drilled into young minds and souls through various textual sources, these young people engage with written spaces like Twitter, blogs, and online forums to articulate counterdiscourses about the value and equality of their unruly souls.

CHALLENGING THE DOCTRINE OF PURITY

Although there are valid criticisms of the limitations of political action online, recent scholarship has shown that hashtag activism can enable marginalized communities to make visible their particular experiences and the value of their lives. Hashtag campaigns around #BlackLivesMatter[51] or #MuslimWomens-Day[52] may not cause political change on the ground, but they allow marginalized voices to express the values of their lives in contrast to dehumanizing stereotypes. Furthermore, the numerous stories of sexual harassment and assault shared under #MeToo illustrate the political power of personal stories and, as Rosemary Clark-Parsons explains, make "power visible so that it might be deconstructed and challenged."[53] The hashtag campaign is a project to "politicize the personal . . . by making it visible."[54] Twitter hashtags are significant spaces for making visible the experiences of oppression and marginalization and challenging dominant discourses. Muslim Twitter and Black Twitter in particular are supportive communities that often use humor, irony, and language play to creatively demonstrate the value of lives that have too often been dehumanized.

In this chapter, I focus on Evangelical activism on Twitter and other written forums because of the significance of textual spaces such as the Bible, scriptural interpretations, and sermons within Protestant Christianity. Words and phrases like "pure," "shame," "fair princess," "noble prince," "kiss dating goodbye," "courting," "true love waits," "purity ring," and "virginity" have resonance for young people raised in this community. Those harmed by purity culture embrace the playful language that is enabled within the margins of Twitter. The space limitations of a Tweet encourage these young people to use creative strategies as they articulate their inherent value. Since these people have been classified by Evangelical culture as falling outside of the norms of purity, they engage with the language and themes of Evangelical purity culture to disidentify themselves from it and present an alternative reading of sexuality and gender from a marginal, unruly, and impure perspective.

As José Esteban Muñoz explains, "Disidentification is meant to be descriptive of the survival strategies the minority subject practices in order to negotiate a phobic majoritarian public sphere that continuously elides or punishes the existence of subjects who do not conform to the phantasm of normative citizenship."[55] Young people raised in Evangelical communities express the trauma and deep pain of being classified as falling outside of the "phantasm of normative citizenship" that is reinforced through purity culture.[56] Since these individuals can never be classified as pure, they work within the textual language of purity culture to disidentify or present a counternarrative of sexuality and gender. Instead of accepting or completely resisting purity culture, disidentification "is a strategy that tries to transform a cultural logic from within, always laboring to enact permanent structural change while at the same time valuing the importance of local or everyday struggles of resistance."[57] The activism against purity culture often seeks to build a new space that supports and celebrates all types of bodies and sexualities. The "I kissed straighting goodbye" Tweet from the opening of this chapter is the perfect example of how those who are deemed impure (in this case because of being gay) engage with the vocabulary of purity culture to present a counternarrative that celebrates queerness.

For those not raised within American Evangelicalism, it might not be obvious why a paperback relationship advice book by a twenty-something author would be so influential or a purity pledge would have so much power. Yet Christian bookstores and web sites are filled with these scripted stories and memoirs that extol the positive aspects of maintaining virginity until marriage. Klein explained the popularity of purity culture texts this way: "Evangelicalism is purposely non-denominational and not affiliated. As a result, they [Evangelicals] argue that they have no doctrine and everything comes from the Bible. But in reality, those books [in the Christian bookstore] are considered holy. . . . I would say that is their doctrine, those are their holy texts."[58] Allison offered a similar take on Harris's books, telling me that "it's not Bible, but it's close to Bible."[59] When there is no institutional doctrine (and the Bible does not spend a great deal of time discussing sexuality), these personal memoirs and texts on sexual purity take on a doctrine-like status within a lot of Evangelical communities.

As a result, digital projects have a great significance as individuals engage with these sacred texts and ideologies as a way to disidentify or present alternative ideas about sexuality. Klein explained that the pro-purity stories are often used as publicity for Evangelical Christianity, but she noted that "the reality of someone telling their own story that doesn't fit into the marketing, even in small ways, is incredibly empowering."[60] One of the ways that Klein tries to facilitate these alternative narratives is through a postcard project. She hosts Break Free Together gatherings at which people can share experiences of growing up in cultures that promoted sexual shame. As part of these workshops, individuals can share their experiences of purity culture on a postcard. Klein also receives postcards in the mail, which she then shares to an Instagram account.[61] Postcards are physical and anonymous ways to share intimate stories, and these stories can also circulate through digital spaces.

Online textual spaces like Twitter have increasingly become battlegrounds over narratives of purity culture, sexuality, and ultimately the future of Evangelicalism. As an early adopter of Twitter and the cocreator of the #ChurchToo hashtag about sexual abuse within churches, Allison recognizes the power of using Twitter to reclaim people's narratives and have their stories recognized. She told me: "It was a very powerful thing. All it is, if you talk about #ChurchToo or #MeToo, is this feeling like, *me too*, I've also been through this really niche experience that other people don't understand."[62] One of the powerful features of Twitter, according to Allison, is that it is an "equalizer" that enables anyone to share a story with a hashtag, and that story will enter the stream. Scholars have similarly argued that #MeToo provides "solidarity" and "community building that works to alleviate the risk and fear associated with coming forward."[63] In her activism related to calling out sexual abusers and removing them from churches, Allison has observed the power of #ChurchToo, as institutional churches "are desperately trying to wrest back the narrative because for so long they have been in control of the narrative."[64] It is essential that these hashtags remain controlled by the queer and unruly misfits who ultimately seek to dismantle the larger structures of misogyny, heteronormativity, and racism that drive purity culture.

RECLAIMING THE BODY AND CELEBRATING SEXUALITY

In analyzing the movement against purity culture that emerged online in the 2010s, I focused on two Twitter discussions in the summer of 2016: #KissShame-Bye and #IKDGstories. These were two of the most substantial Twitter discussions, each featuring over a thousand posts about the lasting legacy and traumatic experiences of being exposed to purity culture—often through Harris's books. Incorporated into my analysis are some of the related discussions that happened online, such as a roundtable on *The Toast* with some of the leaders in this movement, posts on the group blog "Life after *I Kissed Dating Goodbye*," articles in the popular press about the effects of purity culture, and the postcards and Tweets that have been shared as part of Klein's Break Free Together project.

Some of the Tweets were written by individuals who have become leaders in this movement by sharing their experiences and facilitating these online discussions, such as Allison, Paasch, Samantha Field, Prescott, McKenzie, and Wright. Since these individuals have a wide presence in this movement, I include their names alongside their reflections. For the countless other people who have shared their personal experiences in these online spaces, I have slightly changed the wording of their Tweets to protect their privacy. Even though Twitter is a public space, it is important to protect the safe space that is created for these discussions of highly emotional and intimate topics.

In the following sections of this chapter, I address the ways that these textual spaces enable young people raised with purity teachings both to express the traumatic effects that these teachings had on their sexuality and self-worth and to creatively celebrate the value of their lives within a supportive community. In these Twitter discussions, the participants spend a lot of time addressing the ideologies that are prominent within purity teachings. In addition to revealing the harm of these teachings, participants also alter the language of purity culture as a way to reclaim their agency, celebrate sexuality, and demonstrate their inherent value.

Twitter threads often discuss how purity culture promotes the idea that women's bodies are objects that men control. As Paasch wrote, "My body & reputation belonged to everyone but me."[65] Another writer commented: "I learned that I wasn't able to say no. My body did not belong to me, my body would betray me, and my body was for my husband's enjoyment." Additionally, Field talked about how women are infantilized in *I Kissed Dating Goodbye* and other books and notes that these ideas about women had a negative impact on her marriage.[66] These Tweets are not humorous, but they point to the absurdity of teaching girls that they do not control their own bodies.

In response to these teachings that minimize women's control over their bodies, people write about reclaiming agency. Tweets discuss the importance of healthy relationships, individual autonomy, and exploring agency. Several people repeat messages similar to what Wright wrote: "Main lessons: my body is mine and it's okay to use it for my own pleasure."[67] Another person commented: "I was in my 20s when I first recognized that I controlled myself and owned my body. Not the church or my future spouse. Me. It's so mistaken." These written Tweets can provide a space for young people, raised in a religion that dismissed their agency, to assert powerful control over their own bodies and sexualities. A lot of these Tweets have a caustic edge, as the women write about learning through purity culture that their own body was actually controlled by the church, their father, or their future husband.

Another common theme in the Tweets is how purity teachings cultivate feelings of shame, especially about women's normal sexual desires. Several participants wrote that they felt dirty and sinful for having high sex drives. Field wrote, "my libido is higher than my partner's, tho, and it made him feel like a failure, like he was broken and not good enough."[68] Another person shared experiences with a high sex drive, saying "I have always despised that part of me and felt dirty for what was a normal sex drive." Prescott explained what is so problematic about teaching that sexual desire is dirty: "When you frame a NATURAL HUMAN EMOTION as 'sin' you teach ppl [people] to perpetually hate themselves for not being able to suppress it."[69] Again, these Tweets point out the irony of telling women that their natural emotions and desires are actually sinful. There is a consistent rhetorical style to these Tweets, as the writers simply share what purity culture taught them: women don't control their bodies, and they are flawed if they have sexual desires. By distilling the tenets of purity culture into short Tweets, the posters are able to easily point out the weakness of these arguments. It's absurd to say that women don't have agency over their own bodies and sexualities.

Not only is sexual desire framed as dirty and sinful, especially in women, but sexual intimacy outside of marriage is also framed as shameful. The No Shame Movement's account on Twitter added this comment to the discussion: "#IKDG framed sex as something that 'happened' when you 'slipped' and let lust take over, not an intentional, loving act."[70] One of the consequences of teaching that sex outside of marriage is dangerous and will lead men and women to stumble into sin is that when people get married, it is difficult to automatically shift to seeing sex as a positive, loving activity. People recovering from purity culture often discuss experiencing PTSD-like symptoms when they try to enter a safe and loving sexual relationship. As one person wrote in an anonymous postcard for Klein's Break Free Together project, "I was taught that sex was a way men use women. That pleasuring a man, makes you a whore, they only want to use you & that you do not have the capacity for pleasure as a woman. This has made me have an extreme fear of sex & oral sex because I associate it with hurting me & being used, even if I'm in a loving relationship. It has made me feel powerless."[71] When you are raised to fear stumbling into sexuality and the extremely negative consequences of being deemed impure, then it is difficult to adjust to sexuality as a positive, healthy act just because you are now married.

An important aspect of the online work is to start to reverse some of these shame-based teachings by reinforcing the ideas that sex is positive and that it's great to enjoy sex in all of its forms. In reflections on what they wished they had known about sex when they were coming of age, participants in the Twitter forums share positive messages like "It's fine to enjoy orgasms, even for women," "I'd tell my younger self that sex is fine and that expressing sexual desire is healthy," and "I had to take small steps out of purity culture, like learning that sexuality is not tied to sin, future spouses or *having* sex." These Tweets reflect the intentional work that is needed to reverse the beliefs about the negative aspects of sexuality. As one poster wrote, "I actively have to inspect and discount the deep shame I experience in order to enjoy my sexuality."

One of the main reasons for this deep work to root out purity culture is because these teachings reinforce that women are inherently flawed. For instance, purity teachings focus on the idea that women are solely responsible for maintaining purity and protecting men from sexual failings. As one person wrote, "I was taught that it was my role to stop men from having sexual feelings or thoughts about me." Another person tweeted: "Women must keep relationships pure. Men are not expected to control their desires." These ideas reinforce the belief that men can't help themselves if women are acting in ways that will trigger their sexual desires. One of the anonymous writers of a Break Free Together postcard clearly summed up purity culture: "Sex is bad. Don't talk about it until you're married. Then it'll be perfect. Sexual immorality is always the woman's fault. Even if she wasn't consensually involved at all. She should've covered up more. It's the woman's job to keep men from sinning."[72] This writer uses irony to point to the absurdity of this culture. Sex is portrayed as the most dangerous and sinful action until you get married, and you are told that after that sex will be perfect, with no problems. At the same time, women are always to blame, not because of what they do but because of who they are. They are inherently hypersexual temptresses who will inevitably lead men to sin, just like in the apocryphal story of Adam and Eve.

Along with teachings that reinforce the inherent sinfulness of women, purity culture often determines women's value based on their ability to remain pure. For instance, one person tweeted about being taught that their body was like a car, and they needed to keep low sexual mileage to retain its value. Object lessons like this reinforce the view that women have value only based on their sexual purity. As one person wrote, "Your value and your ability to love another person diminishes with each date and physical interaction." Purity culture teaches that a woman becomes more and more worthless with each moment of intimacy, like a cookie that is licked by multiple people or a flower that loses most of its petals. Even when a person is sexually assaulted and has no control over what happens, they are still treated as valueless. One person wrote about being blamed after having been sexually assaulted, "I was damaged goods since I allowed the sex to happen." These feelings of worthlessness and shame run deep among the activists against purity culture.

A significant part of the work online is to articulate that women have inherent value and are created beautifully in the image of God. The No Shame Movement account shared this message, "PLEASE REMEMBER: you have value, regardless of what you do or don't do with your body. full stop."[73] This reverses the message that a woman's value is tied only to keeping her body pure and remaining a virgin. Value is inherent in the person and not lost or weakened because of sexuality. Another writer reclaimed inherent value and control over the body: "Your body belongs to you. Your body is beautiful and you can choose who to share it with, and if others don't love you, they are the ones who are losing out." These Tweets engage with the language of purity and self-worth but disidentify from purity culture texts by articulating that value is not dependent on actions or external factors.

For some individuals, this reclamation of value comes through a connection to God and the Christian teaching that all people are created in God's image. One of the postcard writers from the Break Free Together project said that this realization of being created in God's image helped in reclaiming one's intrinsic value: "The religious community in which I was raised taught me my body and my use of it was dirty, sexual, wrong. But, my God + my relationship w/him taught me that I am fearfully, and wonderfully made in his image. God is love + so am I. Love for others and love for me. Love embodied + enacted. Physical love + emotional love. Love is not defined by gender or sexuality, and neither am I. I forgive myself for all the years I doubted that."[74] This postcard demonstrates that the textual spaces of purity culture have been used to denigrate individuals for their flawed bodies and impure sexualities, but this writer reclaimed her value by engaging with the Christian teaching that all individuals are created in the image of God. She refers to a theological understanding that God is about love and forgiveness rather than shame, sinfulness, and worthlessness. Sexuality and gender expression do not exist apart from God's love but are intrinsic to one's being, which is created flawlessly by God.

RECOVERING FROM PAIN AND TRAUMA

Alongside this work to reclaim sexual agency and celebrate everyone's inherent value, the online activism against purity culture focuses on the need to develop a supportive community and a space for individuals to recover from these traumatic experiences. While there is a need for activism and support around hashtags like #MeToo that critique institutional misogyny, the activism around purity culture and #ChurchToo reveals the deep pain that is caused by theological teachings about the inherent impurity and sinfulness of women and queer individuals. In my conversation with Allison, she discussed the need for a distinct space for conversations about abuse within Christian communities. Even though misogyny and power imbalances exist in the broader culture and institutions, there is a particular harm caused by this biblically based abuse. "For example, you are not going to find Harvey Weinstein justifying the things that he was doing by using a chapter and verse from the Bible. But you do find pastors doing that and congregants supporting them," Allison explained. "It's one thing for a terrible thing to happen to you, but it's another thing entirely for a terrible thing to happen to you and then [for] somebody else to say this is as God determines. God's fine with this. There's no problem with what has happened to you in the eyes of God."[75] Through references to God and the Bible, these abusive actions and teachings inflict a deeper harm by promoting the idea that women are intrinsically flawed and sinful.

A good portion of the Twitter comments relate to struggles with mental health problems (including those caused by fear, anxiety, self-hatred, and anger) that manifested themselves as people raised with teachings around purity begin to mature and form adult relationships. Many people write about feeling anxiety, fear, and shame as they enter intimate relationships as adults. For example, one person wrote: "Before I had sex for the first time, I was terrified. I worried and obsessed over my choice." Another person wrote that even after being in a happy marriage, she still had a great deal of shame to deal with. Other people wrote about being anxious about dating and starting serious relationships. "Purity teachings created shame, avoiding authentic relationships, and more feelings of shame," one wrote. Another person commented, "It's so hard to initiate dating since the PTSD of IKDG [*I Kissed Dating Goodbye*] makes you feel wrong about dating."

Books like *I Kissed Dating Goodbye* promote the belief that dating is dangerous because it will lead to sexual intimacy and growing close to someone who may not be your lifelong spouse. This slippery slope approach to sexuality makes people worry that any little action might lead them astray. For instance, one person wrote about how they had worn a purity ring until the age of twenty-two and that deciding to take it off was "terrifying." Field talked about how she tried to follow the courtship rules that Harris outlines in his book, but her partner was abusive and assaulted her.[76] Another person wrote that she had friends who suffered psychological problems within marriages and even dealt with vaginismus, a painful tensing of the vaginal muscles that is often caused by stress and anxiety.

Several people wrote about feeling angry over how purity teachings had negatively impacted their relationships and mental health. For example, one commented, "I can't say this enough, it's fine to be angry about IKDG and how it taught women to be passive." Another person wrote: "I want to participate in this discussion around #KissShameBye but I'm already so angry. Purity culture messed me up so badly." Clearly, the impact of purity culture goes far beyond teaching teenagers to avoid sex until they are in a committed relationship. In appealing to the Bible and theology, purity teachings cultivate feelings of worthlessness, shame, and guilt within women and queer people over their bodies and sexual desires. It is difficult for people to put these deep feelings aside when entering intimate relationships as adults.

Twitter and other digital media have become supportive spaces for people who have suffered as a result of these shame-based teachings on sexuality. As Klein noted, Evangelical Christianity is a subculture that promotes an "ideological isolation" so that those raised with these teachings have a deep fear that they will be ostracized and have no support if they abandon or even question these teachings.[77] Similarly, McKenzie wrote, "There's a way in which purity culture isolates us (an attempt to protect?), but isolation is actually harmful."[78] An online discussion space like Twitter can be incredibly supportive for people who feel isolated and alone in their feelings of discontent with purity culture.

Participating in a collective discussion about shame-based sexuality teachings does not minimize individual experiences, but it reaffirms the validity of each person's feelings. A mantra that is repeated throughout the Twitter threads is "you are not alone." Some people say that they aren't ready to share their own experiences but are benefiting from just reading the stories of others and feeling less isolated. One person wrote, "If you have challenges with purity culture, read through the #KissShameBye posts and feel supported in knowing that you are not alone."

A majority of the work that Klein does in her writing and online activism is to help individuals recover from the trauma of being raised in a religious culture that teaches women that they are impure barriers that men trip over. She uses the hashtag #BreakFreeTogether to share stories from people who read her book and to remind people of the need to work together to celebrate sexuality. After reading Klein's book, people share their responses. For instance, one individual wrote about staying up all night to read the book: "I'm sitting here with the understanding that I am not the only one. Thank you, God, that I am not the only one." Another person wrote that they thought Klein was reading from her own teenage diary. Similarly, one writer said that she lost count of how many of Klein's stories connected to her own experiences. Klein often reminds people of the importance of creating this collective support network so everyone can recover from these distinct but connected experiences of trauma.

McKenzie also discussed the importance of working together to overcome these shameful teachings: "One of the biggest ways to #KissShameBye is to break through the emotional isolation we were encouraged to shield ourselves with."[79] Wright explained that they created the #KissShameBye discussion as a "refuge for healing."[80] As a way to extend this safe space for healing, McKenzie and other leaders in the movement write supportive statements and encourage participants to seek help and continue doing recovery work. McKenzie wrote, "If tonight's conversation stirred up old and painful memories for you, it's ok, you're ok, and you're no longer in that place."[81] Since Evangelical teachings on purity often created feelings of isolation and fear of the outside world, a repeated theme in the online activism is that the work to recover from the trauma of purity culture must be done collectively. Several participants wrote about how the discussion threads are "ministering" and "heart-wrenching and healing." Additionally, the playful engagement with the language of purity culture is a way to use humor (for example, see #KissShameBye or Roberts's Tweet above: "I kissed straighting goodbye") to call out the hypocrisies promulgated by those in power while building a healing space for people traumatized by these teachings.

DISMANTLING THE SYSTEMATIC OPPRESSION BEHIND PURITY TEACHINGS

Another important aspect of the online activism against purity culture is to critique the ways that Evangelical Christianity uses teachings on sexual purity to perpetuate misogyny, racism, and homophobia. As individuals call out these oppressive structures that undergird purity teachings, they also work to rearticulate the value and inherent equality of people who have been deemed unruly and impure. In the midst of the activism against purity culture that was prominent in 2016, Allison and Paasch set up a blog titled *Life after "I Kissed Dating Goodbye"* as a space for people to share longer stories about the book and purity culture. The web site has since lost its domain address, but the postings present in-depth critiques of the systematic problems of purity culture. In one reflection, Field clearly stated the problem: "Purity culture is not just 'weird.' It is an oppressive system."[82] Field was responding to a common response from apologists for purity culture, who say that the teachings might have been a little bit strange or gone a little too far but that most people ended up okay as adults in normal relationships. As the online reflections on the impact of purity culture illustrate, these teachings have lasting negative effects on people. These negative repercussions, many activists argue, are the result of purity culture's revealing a deeper rot in American Evangelical churches related to misogyny, white supremacy, colonialism, and heteronormativity.

For example, Allison is very active in the #ChurchToo movement, which seeks justice for those who have been sexually harassed and abused within Christian communities. Allison believes that abuse within churches is not simply an administrative problem that could be solved with better training or reporting procedures. Instead, she sees the stories of #ChurchToo as revealing deeper problems with how sexuality is taught and discussed within churches.[83] In a discussion on the *Queerology* podcast, Allison explained, "You can try to separate this #ChurchToo movement from how the church teaches about sexuality overall, but you can't."[84] The churches are unwilling to look at how teachings about sexuality, which are based in misogyny and homophobia, are only going to perpetuate sexual shame and abuse. Allison stated, "When sexuality is forced into the dark, then I think that a culture of abuse is the natural result of that."[85] Solutions to sexual abuse cannot come through changing policies or running background checks. Instead, churches need to account for how shame-based teachings on sexuality promote a hatred of women and queer people. These teachings justify and perpetuate the abuse of those who are deemed impure.

As a poly queer woman, Vxysin Drake, wrote on the *Life after "I Kissed Dating Goodbye"* blog, purity culture emphasizes "that sex was shameful and not something you talked about openly."[86] After she had sex with a man for the first time, she felt so much self-hatred that she wanted to kill herself. "All those phrases drilled into my head from a young age haunted me: 'you're dirty,' 'you're impure,' 'no man will want you now,' 'you're damaged,' 'you're a slut,'" she wrote. "Purity culture isn't just some cutesy romantic ideal that protects you from pain. It's misogyny cloaked in religious language programmed to make women hate themselves and hate one of the main things that makes them who they are." This blog and the various related Tweets reflect this larger misogynistic system: women are inherently flawed and impure, women are responsible for maintaining purity, and women are viewed as property with value that can be lost through sexual acts.

Related to the perpetuation of the hatred of women, purity teachings also ignore the experiences of nonstraight sexualities and promote fear and hatred of lesbian, gay, bisexual, transgender, and queer (LGBTQ) individuals. On Twitter, several people talked about how their queerness was rarely discussed in purity teachings. McKenzie noted that "non-heterosexual people are entirely absent from IKDG: simply don't exist."[87] Another person wrote that the only people who existed in IKDG were "cis-gender, straight Christians." This dominance of only one expression of gender and sexuality caused feelings of confusion in people who didn't relate to such rigid expressions. "Purity culture is so heteronormative," one person tweeted, "that it wasn't even conceivable that anyone [any female] would be attracted to girls." Another person wrote that they didn't realize their queer identity until late adolescence, saying "I didn't understand that I could even be queer." Again, there is a sense that individuals are somehow flawed or impure because they have sexual desires or gender expressions that fall outside narrow cisgender, heterosexual roles.

Furthermore, purity culture reinforces the dominance and supremacy of whiteness within Christianity by equating purity and holiness with white women. Several Black Christians reflected on how purity texts like *I Kissed Dating Goodbye* were clearly written for white audiences, but Black Christians still weren't exempt from these standards. The No Shame Movement Twitter account explained: "Black women especially stay pressured to conform to a standard that was never meant for them."[88] Purity culture indicates that Evangelical Christianity is often entrenched in a theology of white supremacy and anti-Blackness. As Wright explained in a Twitter discussion, "Purity culture is rooted in Victorian ideals that exclude Black people."[89] These ideals of sexual purity position white bodies as higher in the order of creation than Black bodies and thus closer to God and holiness.

In a roundtable on *The Toast*, McKenzie described purity culture as "religious colonialism" that brings these misguided teachings on sexuality and purity into various cultural traditions.[90] This is part of a larger project of white supremacy, as these ideas are used to control nonwhite people. As Wright explained in the same roundtable, "Even in the Black churches that I attended, this book [*I Kissed Dating Goodbye*] was widely read. In hindsight, it's a bit scary that a white evangelical had that much sway over people whose bodies are already policed by white ideas."[91] Purity culture is a way to control unruly women and queer folks, and its teachings also attempt to police the souls of Black Christians.

In an article on the *Life after "I Kissed Dating Goodbye"* blog, Jameelah Jones reflected on how Harris's books promoted a form of purity that is rarely granted to Black women and girls. "Purity isn't a luxury afforded to Black girls. Purity implies an innocence that the world refuses to recognize within us," Jones wrote. "Enforcing the IKDG model on Black girls is to watch dirt be thrown at us, then yell at us for not keeping our clothes clean."[92] Purity culture is used to shame Black women and blame them for not living up to these unachievable standards of purity. By positioning white women as the pinnacle of purity, these texts reinforce the idea that Black women are intrinsically impure and dirty.

Instead of falling into the self-hatred that comes from these teachings, Jones used the textual space of this blog to reclaim her inherent value. She wrote about how she is working on healing and moving past these harmful teachings about sex and the body. "Most of all, I am working to live my life under the basic assumption that my body is a good, holy thing," Jones wrote. "Even now, all I can think about is little Black girls in their tweens, teens, and early twenties. Praying that they become Black women who love themselves in their fullness. I am praying that they discover a God who looks and sounds like them—who writes for them."[93] Jones clearly stated that the problem with purity culture texts is that they equate purity, holiness, and godliness with white, straight, virginal women. Instead of the radical belief that all people are created in the image of God and reflect holiness and internal beauty, purity teachings build on a distorted view of theology that is based on human-created structures of oppression. These teachings use references to theology and the Bible to justify the belief that straight white men are created as the pinnacle of humanity and thus are closest to God. Online forums and blogs provide extensive spaces for young people to critically reflect on the harm caused by purity culture, while also reinforcing the value of those who have been dismissed as impure and sinful.

ARTICULATING THE VALUE OF UNRULY SOULS

The online activism against purity culture illustrates how concerns over various injustices are converging within religious spaces. When young people sit through a workshop on sexual purity or read a paperback memoir about courting instead of dating, they aren't just being exposed to some strange but harmless teachings. Instead, cultural artifacts like *I Kissed Dating Goodbye*, purity rings, and True Love Waits pledges are emblematic of institutional rot within American Evangelical churches. These teachings reinforce misogynistic, white supremacist, and heteronormative structures of power. The young people who are dismissed as impure and unfit for the holiness of Evangelical purity culture are the ones taking to digital media to call out the flaws in these teachings and, more importantly, in the churches. Similarly, the other cases discussed in this book all focus on how people who have been disregarded as unruly souls because of their gender, sexuality, body shape, skin color, or ability are using digital media spaces to build something new.

In these examples of projects against purity culture, young people use textual spaces such as Twitter, blogs, and forums to create new understandings of sexuality and gender expression. Shame-based sexuality teachings have reached almost doctrine-level status in the Evangelical subcultures through various books and speeches, and textual online sites provide creative spaces for young people to articulate the beauty of their sexuality. These young people are exhausted with trying to live up to unachievable standards. If you are queer, Black, or a straight woman with normal sexual desires, purity culture texts already define you as impure. As Jones wrote in her blog post, it's like having people constantly throwing dirt on you and then criticizing you for always being dirty.

Rather than try to fit into a culture that devalues individuals for their natural expressions of sexuality, these young people use Twitter and other online spaces to build a new understanding of sexuality and gender expression that celebrates the inherent value in all people regardless of their gender, sexuality, race, skin color, ability, and so on. These religious misfits are unable to speak back in Evangelical cultural spaces, but online spaces provide the opportunity to build up a radical theology that celebrates the inherent equality of all people. At the same time, the misfits' Tweets and written reflections dismantle the institutional hierarchies that place certain people in positions closer to God.

Much significant work has examined the role of hashtags and online activism in connection to wider political movements. #MeToo and #BlackLivesMatter address social inequality and injustices, but this book seeks to understand the additional concerns involved when women, Black people, and queer individuals are devalued through appeals to religious teachings—in this case, the Bible and Evangelical theology. In the face of religious teachings claiming that certain people are less holy than others, these young people creatively articulate the inherent value of their bodies and souls by embracing their unruliness. Digital textual sites like Twitter provide a more level playing field on which these young people can speak back and critique the system, especially through the use of humor and irony. Their Tweets cleverly engage with the tenets of purity culture to point to the absurdity of and flaws in these teachings. The following chapters examine how this playfulness and flexibility continues in digital spaces that highlight visual images, spoken dialogue, and music videos.

3 · BOLD AND BEAUTIFUL

Images of Unruly Bodies Destabilize Pious Muslim Icon

Evangelical Christianity in the United States promotes a repressive and misogynistic system of sexuality through an extensive purity culture, and Muslim American communities often endorse similar ideas about the need for young women, in particular, to maintain sexual purity and modesty in their appearance and behavior. Islam does not have as prolific a purity industry as Evangelical Christianity does. However, the growing Islamic fashion industry often serves to reinforce dominant norms around sexuality and gender roles. Unlike in Christianity, where purity teachings are consumed through popular memoirs and public speeches, in Islam the tenets of what makes a properly modest and pious Muslim woman are often conveyed through social media images of attractive but covered up light-skinned women. As Islamic fashion slowly gains recognition in mainstream American culture, modest fashion styles occupy a prominent corner of social media, with YouTube videos of makeup styles, hijab wrapping tutorials, and outfits of the day, as well as Instagram postings of modest styles from some of the top fashionistas. In addition to the modest clothing choices and the prominence of the hijab, a distinct aesthetic style unites most of these Muslim fashion figures. They maintain a positive, bubbly, bright glow in their social media presence. The fabric of their clothing is usually solid pastel colors or floral prints; they often wear flowing but stylish garments; and they post about lighthearted topics like shopping, food, and travel. Additionally, Muslim fashion influencers on social media represent particular beauty ideals: they are flawlessly attractive; cover their thin bodies in modest clothing; and, while not usually of white European origin, have light complexions.

As Islamic fashion spreads through the visual space of Instagram, these images promote a certain icon of Muslim femininity: a woman who reflects Western beauty standards while remaining a positive and passive representative of Islam. Basically, these fashionistas should be seen and not heard, always reflecting the Muslim community in a positive light. These visual images endorse an icon of Islamic piety while also condemning people who fail to meet these standards as impure, flawed, and sinful. At the same time, a growing movement of Muslims who fall short of these unachievable piety standards use visual spaces like Instagram to challenge the way Islamic fashion imagery perpetuates harmful ideals and ignores serious social concerns. Because Instagram was conceived of as a social media space in which to share photos, the theorization of this platform generally focuses on artistic and feminine elements like selfies, fashion, and lifestyle influencers. Furthermore, Instagram has evolved into a social media platform that rewards users with followers and sponsorship money if they can manage to maintain an aesthetic style that is attractive but not too fake or extravagant. Lifestyle influencers have emerged as masters of the Instagram style, as they present a view of their positive and glowing lives, papering over everyday struggles with curated posts about travel, food, luxury items, and fashion styles.

In this chapter, I discuss the Instagram pages of four Muslim American women, each of whom distinctly critiques both the icon of Islamic fashion and the Instagram influencer tropes. All four women successfully engage with the stylistic expectations of Instagram while cleverly challenging the unachievable ideals placed on Muslim American women. Leah Vernon uses her page and her intersectional identity as a fat, Black Muslim woman to visually contest what is accepted as beautiful and consequently whose lives are valued. As one of the most popular Muslim American influencers on Instagram, Blair Imani does unprecedented work to engage her followers in progressive causes as well as her fashion and lifestyle content. Although she has a small number of followers, Zainab bint Younus uses her Instagram page to creatively promote an Islamic aesthetic style without focusing on fashion or the body. Finally, Angelica Lindsey-Ali cultivates a female-driven space on Instagram to share knowledge about women's bodies and sexuality. These Muslim American women all use the visual aesthetics of Instagram to challenge in distinct ways the fashion icon of the pious and demure Muslim woman. At first glance, these Muslim influencers appear to reinforce the problematic beauty standards that proliferate on Instagram, both in Islamic fashion and among secular influencers. Through a closer analysis, this chapter explores how these women add a critical edge to the Instagram influencer culture by inserting their unruly bodies and political calls for justice into this digital culture.

THE COMPLEXITY AND HYBRIDITY OF ISLAMIC FASHION

In contrast to the persistent stereotypes of Muslim women that often present them as either covered and oppressed victims or as sexualized objects of desire, modest fashion styles provide ways for Muslim women to illustrate their complex experiences. Academic and popular discussions on Islamic fashion often focus on how modest fashion offers a flexible space for Muslim women to combine their faith and tenets of modesty with an interest in contemporary fashion trends. A common refrain is that the emergence of modest clothing styles allows Muslim women to interweave fashion and faith. In a study of Canadian converts to Islam, Géraldine Mossière found that the "polysemy and flexibility" of fashion styles allow the women to incorporate "their religious identity as pious and veiled Muslim women as well as their position as modern and Western citizens."[1]

In her book on Islamic fashion in the United Kingdom, Reina Lewis examines how the practices of debating fashion styles online and in person can be a way for young Muslim women to develop their agency as religious subjects. Rather than reject fashion as an inherently negative element of Western neoliberalism, Lewis argues that "the possibilities of Internet commerce and commentary combine with offline practices in modest fashion to foster women's agency in the making of new forms of Muslim habitus."[2] Online spaces allow women to develop the authority to determine how they will incorporate a pious subjectivity into Western neoliberal culture. Similarly, Elizabeth Bucar examines how Muslim women's decisions about what to wear are part of negotiating norms around identity, piety, aesthetics, and consumption: "More than just a veil, this is pious fashion head to toe, which both reflects and creates norms and ideas related to self-identity, moral authority, and consumption."[3] Bucar finds that fashion grants Muslim women some agency within social, political, and religious structures.[4]

Annelies Moors's and Emma Tarlo's work on Islamic fashion is particularly relevant because of their emphasis on how clothing style can be a political statement for Muslim women in Western spaces. Muslim women frequently talk about how they are silenced in public spaces, and fashion provides a way to speak back. While Muslim women are often viewed in terms of stereotypes about their being "dull, downtrodden, oppressed and out of sync with modernity," Moors and Tarlo argue that the public presence of Muslim women in styles that combine their faith and contemporary fashion presents an alternative view.[5] Fashion can provide a productive in-between space that allows women at the intersection of various identity markers, such as Vernon or Imani, to play with various categories in developing their unique styles. Susan Kaiser explains, "Especially compelling are the overlapping or 'in between' spaces, through which fashion subjects exercise agency and articulate more than one subject position simultaneously."[6] The public presence of Muslim women wearing modest attire while participating in modern life is a visual contradiction of the assumptions that Muslim women are oppressed victims or are concerned only with their faith.

IDEOLOGIES OF ISLAMIC FASHION

While Islamic fashion and the playfulness of visual styles can provide Muslim women with a space to negotiate various identity positions and contest dichotomies, the most prominent representatives of Islamic fashion tend to reinforce a certain style and mode of being a pious, modest Muslim woman. Particularly in digital media spaces such as style blogs, YouTube videos, and Instagram shoots, almost all of the dominant women are skinny, attractive, middle class, and light-completed. The top Instagram Muslim fashionistas (such as Amena Khan, Maria Alia, Dian Pelangi, Leena Asad, and Maryam Asadullah) all have hundreds of thousands, if not millions, of followers. If one scrolls through their feeds, a similar color palette emerges: pastels of pink, beige, peach, and lilac. The women are all perfectly gorgeous and have equally attractive husbands. They wear flowing and stylish garments that properly cover their thin bodies, their makeup is impeccable, and their complexions are light.

Furthermore, as Leah Vernon points out in "The Deletion of the Perfect Instagram Hijabi," these flawless Muslim women promote unachievable beauty standards while ignoring real social injustices. Vernon writes, "Dear Instagram Hijabi, YOU make your followers feel as if they aren't good enough, that they aren't Muslim enough."[7] Additionally, Vernon calls out the hijabis for ignoring issues of "sexual abuse, misogyny, racism, and body-shaming." She continues, "Of course, this is because those kinds of topics don't fit into their pastel social media aesthetic filled with fancy doughnuts and lavish trips to Dubai." Not only do these social media feeds promote an ideal of Muslim femininity that is unachievable for most women, but the women also focus only on positive and trivial topics like travel, food, fashion, and makeup. For example, in the midst of strict lockdowns and travel restrictions during the COVID-19 pandemic, the British Muslim fashion influencer Amena Khan posted pictures of her family's extravagant trip to Dubai.[8] These influencers often present an alternative reality in which no one struggles financially, deals with health concerns, or faces the repercussions of racist and sexist systems.

The dominance of these pastel Muslim fashion leaders online promotes white supremacist, colonialist, and misogynist concepts of proper femininity, and it encourages a Western, neoliberal focus on perfecting the self through consumption. Instagram images from Muslim women like Vernon or Lindsey-Ali interrupt the bubbly, positive glow of these Islamic fashion images to point out that dark-skinned and differently shaped bodies are not welcome in these spaces. Furthermore, the prominence of thin white women illustrates racist, colonialist, and misogynist beliefs about the inherent superiority of light skin and bodies without curves. In a reflection on the work of plus-sized fashion leaders like Vernon, Lewis addresses the white supremacist and imperialist beliefs that reinforce the intrinsic immodesty of larger, dark-skinned bodies.[9] Specifically, Vernon's work calls out the hypocrisy of these beliefs circulating within Islamic circles, especially since these ideas run counter to the Islamic belief in the radical equality of people.

While Islamic teachings do promote the value of beauty, both inside and out, the images and commentary from the women discussed in this chapter show that the beauty dominating social media influencer spaces is not a deep beauty but rather a superficial focus on unachievable standards, often based on white European and American norms. These young women use the creative and visual tactics of Instagram to demonstrate a way of being a Muslim woman in the Western context that is not hypersexual or oppressed and that does not abandon the critical edge of Islamic values. The focus on the perfect modest icon of Islam places inherent value on the exterior appearance of Muslim women and makes value judgments based on racist and misogynist ideals of beauty. By inserting their unruly bodies, Islamic aesthetic styles, and political commentary into this glowing display of Islamic fashion influencers on Instagram, the Muslim creators discussed in this chapter complicate the icon of the pious, modest Muslim woman. More significantly, their work points to the greater harm caused in the Muslim American community by the misconception that piety is correlated with exterior beauty.

INSTAGRAM AND INFLUENCERS

Although a good portion of people's time on social media sites is now spent swiping through pictures, posting daily photos, watching videos, or sharing memes and GIFs, the digital scholarship on visual content still lags behind the extensive studies of discussion forums, Twitter threads, algorithms, and networks. Social media pages like Instagram don't simply promote lighthearted or self-absorbed content. Rather, as Tim Highfield and Tama Leaver argue, "visual social media content can highlight affect, political views, reactions, key information, and scenes of importance."[10] In this chapter, I explore how Instagram images have been a significant site for the negotiation of Muslim American identity, as well as for the coordination of intersectional feminist activism among young people.

In one of the few academic books to focus on Instagram, Leaver, Highfield, and Crystal Abidin discuss how the site was initially one of several mobile apps that allowed users to create "a retro take on mobile phone photography" by adding highly aestheticized filters.[11] Eventually, Instagram emerged as the leading social media site for sharing a broad range of images, from fashion styles and travel selfies to culinary creations and curated domestic spaces. While Instagram features a variety of visual styles, most of the profile pages have a similar sense of capturing everyday moments. Leaver, Highfield, and Abidin write, "creating photographic art on the [mobile phone], and distributing it on the networked spaces connected through the same device, means that the visual and the everyday, the mobile and the now are heavily intertwined, available to anyone with the same technology."[12] In other words, Instagram not only is a site with pretty pictures but also is embedded in users' daily lives as they regularly take pictures, share visual content, and scroll through images. The Instagram platform further evolved from the initial square images that resembled Polaroids to support different dimensions of images; short videos; slide shows with multiple images; and the Stories feature that often involves the overlaying of filters, captions, stickers, or animations.[13] In direct response to the popularity of Snapchat, Stories are vertically oriented posts meant to be consumed on a mobile phone. They have an ephemeral quality, disappearing after twenty-four hours unless the user decides to archive them on their page.[14]

Because of the visual aspect of Instagram, it has become a platform with, as Brooke Duffy and Emily Hund note, "a user experience focused on curated images and, increasingly, opportunities to shop."[15] With Instagram providing a platform for coordinating a particular lifestyle through consumption, so-called influencers emerged to promote fashion styles, makeup products, nutrition, exercise regimens, and various lifestyle brands. As Hund observes, these influencers act as "mediators between consumers and companies."[16] They have an impact on their audience that can be measured through view counts and other data, while also offering followers an authentic glimpse into their lives and honest advice.[17] Abidin explains that these influencers are "everyday, ordinary Internet users who accumulate a relatively large following on blogs and social media through the textual and visual narration of their personal lives and lifestyles."[18] They are able to monetize their social media content by skillfully inserting product promotions, often framed as a recommendation from a close friend. A delicate balance must be maintained between appearing to be too perfect and hence fake and appearing to be too flawed and thus not worthy of the influencer moniker. Duffy and Hund discuss how female influencers in particular are confronted with a "visibility mandate," as they are expected to present their authentic lives through Instagram images but still face public scrutiny and often risk harassment.[19]

Social media influencers are often most successful when they avoid political issues and don't challenge Western beauty norms. In examining some of the popular Instagram influencers, Hund finds that they maintain a "measured beauty," as their social media pages display "the savvy navigation of an increasingly image-first, metrics-dominant digital culture, the aesthetic of a nonthreatening global lifestyle, and the general fitting-in to dominant beauty frameworks."[20] Along the same lines, many social media influencers achieve success and cultivate a community of followers by promoting the view that social issues can be tackled on the individual level through consumption. If you feel ugly because of your skin color, body shape, hair texture, or facial features, the solution can be found in buying skin care products; spending money on hair treatments; finding the perfect clothing for your body shape or; better yet, starting an exercise regime and diet program to fit into the most attractive clothing. Cultural ideologies promoting the idea that only certain types of women and bodies can be considered beautiful remain uninterrogated in most social media influencer spaces. Moreover, the online influencer industry depends on the income that comes from influencers' authentically promoting various products as solutions. The promotion of political activism doesn't usually bring in extra income.

The Muslim creators discussed in this chapter are not immune from financial pressures, but their Instagram pages illustrate how they complicate the social media influencer style as well as the Islamic fashion icon. Vernon promotes body positivity messages and talks openly of mental health and financial struggles, rather than pushing sponsored content. While Imani does promote her own books and various products, most of her page is dedicated to educating followers on the historical roots of social injustices like racism and misogyny. Bint Younus cultivates a joyful and comforting domestic style on Instagram by celebrating Islamic art and values. Finally, Lindsey-Ali shares Islamic teachings related to sexuality, relationships, and feminist issues in an Instagram space reminiscent of female-only sacred spaces. All of these young Muslim women engage with the creative tactics and aesthetic styles of Instagram, but they also playfully subvert the expectations of Instagram by challenging the Western beauty standards and refusing to be turned into a silent and stilted icon of a modest Muslim woman.

FAT, BLACK, AND MUSLIM

Directly confronting what she calls the "pastel social media aesthetic" of Islamic fashion influencers,[21] Vernon bursts onto the Islamic fashion scene with her loud, boisterous, and bold fashion style, along with her fat and dark-skinned body. In response to constantly being told not to draw attention to her body and to remain on the periphery, Vernon uses her fashion style to make herself the center of attention. She explains, "My style is definitely a statement and a testament to, I'm gonna rock the boat and do the most."[22] Vernon uses her fashion images on Instagram along with her written commentary to interrupt the dominant positive glow of Muslim fashion leaders on social media. Her writings point to the psychological damage caused by the promotion of mainly light-skinned, thin, and attractive Muslim fashionistas online. Vernon grew up in Detroit and began blogging about style in 2013 in part because she wanted to expand the fashion images circulating online. Due to her own struggles with body dysmorphia, mental health, and eating disorders, she wanted to create a space where "'all' bodied women feel worthy despite their culture or size."[23] On her Instagram page, she posts images and short videos almost daily for her more than sixty thousand followers, and most of her posts get over a thousand likes and sometimes garner hundreds of comments. Additionally, in the fall of 2019 Vernon published a book about her experiences, titled *Unashamed: Musings of a Fat, Black Muslim*.[24]

Vernon embraces a fashion style that is loud and hypervisible, reflecting her large personality. In a conversation with me, Vernon confidently asserted that she "look[s] good in anything," but that she chooses to wear colorful outfits

FIGURE 3. This photo showcases Leah Vernon's bold clothing style and facial expressions. Used with permission of Leah Vernon @Lvernon2000.

that will place her at the center of attention.[25] Most of these outfits feature bold colors like red, yellow, and blue, with the occasional bright purple or pink. She sometimes wears floral patterns, polka dots, or animal prints, but she rarely wears earthy tones (see figure 3). She also wears ensembles of black, white, and gray. If she is wearing a more casual outfit of jeans and a T-shirt, the shirt often sports a political message like "Black Lives Matter," "fearless" or "black & fat &

perfect." In one photo, she stands in the middle of a street with both hands making the peace sign over her head in a celebratory gesture.[26] She is wearing bright red trousers, a red polka-dotted blouse, and a red hijab. Her big smile is accented with bright red lipstick. She's clearly a person not to be missed on a city street. Vernon's accessories (such as her shoes, jewelry, hats, and handbags) and makeup, are also quite loud, visible, and colorful. Her outfits are noticeably different from the common North American Muslim fashion styles, which often feature fabrics in pastel or earthy colors, long tunics or baggy sweaters over leggings, maxi skirts or dresses, or flowing layers of material.

Vernon blends different aspects of her identity, her particular aesthetic preferences, and cuts and fabrics to accentuate her body's positive attributes. For example, in a photo from February 19, 2019, she incorporates an African American style of tying a headscarf to make a turban, along with a choker featuring yellow beads that is reflective of Indigenous styles.[27] She also employs bold colors, with a bright red dress, yellow fingernail polish, the yellow-beaded necklace, a multicolored turban, red lipstick, and red and blue eye shadow. While Vernon wears a modest outfit that covers her chest, body, and hair, the cut of the dress highlights her curvaceous middle in a way that celebrates the beauty of her body. The fashion styles in this image perfectly illustrate Vernon's embrace of her hybrid identity: the colors and patterns highlight African and African American styles, the headscarf and modest clothing point to her religion, and the cut of the dress and bright colors draw attention to her curves rather than making her invisible. Her fashion welcomes other women who fall outside of the impossible ideals of Muslim femininity based on their skin color, body shape, fashion styles, class, ethnicity, or political opinions.

Vernon's work is groundbreaking in the way she interrupts the impeccable and glowing Instagram feeds of fashion influencers by inserting her unruly body and boisterous fashion style to subvert assumptions about what constitutes beauty. She often directly confronts the uncomfortable feelings that her images induce in viewers. For example, a post from January 19, 2019, features Vernon wearing a gold turban, leopard-skin blouse, and bright red pants. Noticeably, she stands sideways and wears tight-fitting pants that emphasize her large hips and backside, while also revealing her fat and the lines of her underwear. She directly addresses the viewers in her comment: "Does this image make you uncomfortable? Does it challenge your standards of beauty, acceptance? If it does, ask yourself why. Then ask, would you still feel the same discomfort if it was a thinner woman in the same pose. Less back rolls, less thigh cellulite? Maybe even a woman who wasn't Muslim."[28] Instead of hiding the parts of her body that mainstream beauty standards define as ugly or rejecting fashion as a space that doesn't welcome women like her, Vernon embraces Instagram fashion trends while contesting dominant assumptions of who can be accepted as stylish and attractive. In another Instagram post (see figure 4), Vernon wears the same tight-fitting red

FIGURE 4. Leah Vernon standing tall with her left hand on her hip and staring down the camera. Used with permission of Leah Vernon @Lvernon2000.

pants and stands sideways with one hand on her hip.[29] The focal point of the image is the curves of her body, while her position—with her wide stance, the hand on her hip, her chin up, and her stare at the camera—convey confidence and poise.

Furthermore, Vernon works within the space of Instagram to provide a supportive community where other marginalized individuals can find acceptance.

Instead of the emerging term of social media "influencer," Vernon prefers the term "inclusive content creator" because it allows her to use the connections of social media for greater social good. Referring to her goal of creating a supportive community for others, she says: "It's creating a forum, and people are also sharing their own stories and sharing stories is healing. We're kinda doing healing, talking to each other, meeting other people, they are supporting me. I'm trying to support them."[30] At the end of almost all of her posts, she asks a series of questions to spark discussions among her followers and open up the conversations to other issues that she may not address in her posts. Rather than perpetuate the common practice of social media influencers' promoting unachievable ideals of perfect beauty, Vernon posts beautifully composed pictures that accentuate what many would consider flaws. She is also open about her struggles with body image and creates a supportive space for others to discuss and contest beauty standards.

FASHION PLUS POLITICAL COMMENTARY

Because of her embodied experience of intersecting forms of oppression, Vernon does not have the option of ignoring injustices that impact people's daily lives. Related to bell hooks's discussion of the oppositional gaze, Vernon is unwilling to remain silent about the daily experiences of oppression as a fat, Black Muslim woman.[31] She refuses to take pleasure in posting and circulating fashion images that perpetuate racist and misogynist ideals of beauty. Refusing to post attractive fashion images with positive and bubbly comments about her clothing or makeup, Vernon resembles what Sara Ahmed terms a "feminist killjoy," as she brings up biting critiques of the fashion industry, Muslim American communities, and Instagram influencers.[32] While Instagram fashion images often convey positive and happy feelings of conspicuous consumption and ideal beauty standards, Vernon's comments address topics that are rarely mentioned in other Instagram accounts—for example, racism, colorism, economic struggles, mental health, body image, and fat shaming.

In an Instagram post on March 20, 2019, Vernon discusses how she started fashion blogging out of a simple interest in clothing styles: "I never set out to be political. I wanted to be sent clothes and invited to events and be pretty with the nicely edited photos like the others."[33] Instead, she ran into many barriers: from Muslims who said she wasn't modest enough, fashion bloggers who said she was promoting obesity, and clothing companies who said she wasn't attractive enough. In the face of this pressure, Vernon decided to embrace who she is and live unapologetically. She writes in the same post, "I became political once I started to outwardly be myself." Vernon places her unruly body—a body that brings up unhappy political issues of racism, colorism, and misogyny—in a space that regularly exhibits great beauty and positivity. This particular post illustrates how Vernon engages with the beautiful visual style of Instagram, as she posts a gorgeous close-up photo of her face with impeccable makeup, but this attractive image pulls viewers into the political commentary in the caption.

In a post of Vernon dancing to a Lizzo song, she writes that her work is political because she breaks down beauty standards. "My body in motion—with all its jiggles and lumps and curves and bumps—is an act of rebellion. It's political," Vernon writes. "Why? Because it's not what you see on mainstream media. It's not what you see as elevated as something great, something magnificent, something normalized."[34] Being unapologetically herself within her body is a political act to elevate what has been denigrated. In this post and many others, Vernon emphasizes her boisterous body with its black skin, curves, and folds of fat. Furthermore, her posts emphasize that because her body marks her as "other," she doesn't have the privilege of being able to ignore political issues. For instance, in a post accompanying an image of Vernon wearing a Black Lives Matter shirt, she writes: "I wondered how it was to live in such a safe sheltered Caucasian bubble, to live not in fear of your life, afraid to call the cops that end in deaths of young men and women. I often wondered how it felt to not be judged based on your color, stereotyped and typecast as ghetto, loud, aggressive or uneducated. Lazy. Hyper sexual. A monkey. A slave. I try so hard not to be that angry Black Muslim lady but I am constantly reminded that I am not equal."[35] Rather than accompany her pretty fashion images with empty platitudes about empowerment, Vernon brings up the embodied and psychological experiences of racism and social injustices. She forces her followers to confront the daily experiences of living as a fat, Black Muslim woman, providing content that goes beyond an empty political catchphrase.

In some posts, Vernon discusses the racism and colorism that are often deeply embedded in Muslim American communities. Alongside an Instagram video of Vernon dancing, she discusses how Muslims often post comments that question whether she is the most appropriate representative of Islam. In the caption, she discusses the limited representation of Muslim women: "Usually bodies who are Middle-Eastern, bodies that are white passing, bodies that are thin and able. The narratives of Black Muslims, disabled Muslims, and queer Muslims are erased."[36] The physical presence of Vernon's body in the space of Instagram fashion influencers challenges the icon of the perfect Muslim woman, but her written commentary also celebrates the inherent beauty of so many Muslims who fail to meet these narrow ideals.

Vernon also discusses the anti-Muslim sentiment that impacts her life as a visible Muslim woman. Fear and hatred are often applied to her body because of her hijab: "My hijab makes people uncomfortable. They no longer see my body as human. I am 'other'. I am dehumanized."[37] Vernon is doubly persecuted in public because of her race and her visibility as a Muslim. In response to the 2019 mass shooting at a mosque in New Zealand, Vernon posted a raw and honest caption next to an image of her with her eyes closed in prayer. She talked about the physical threats after 9/11: "We have had pig's heads place[d] at our door-steps. Mosques burnt down. Told to go back to where we came from because a Muslim couldn't possibly be American. We have had our hijabs ripped off. Punched in the face. Stabbed. Pressured into segregation, pressured into keeping our faith quiet. Murdered."[38] Again, Vernon shares a beautifully composed fash-ion image but refuses to paper over her daily experiences of harassment with saccharine influencer content. It is striking how Muslim influencers have attracted large followings for their modest fashion styles, yet they rarely discuss the public harassment and even assaults that Muslim women in hijab often face.

Finally, Vernon's work stands out for her honesty about the psychological, physical, and financial struggles of living as an online fashion influencer. While Instagram fashion images generally push positive messages, Vernon does signifi-cant work in discussing mental health and how her own mental health struggles are compounded by the trauma of racism and economic concerns. In one post, she opens up about her diagnosis as having borderline personality disorder and the challenge of being an Instagram leader when she struggles with her own identity. She ends her post by encouraging her followers to share their stories to "normalize conversations about mental illness."[39] This confessional post comes from her own experiences, but it also facilitates important conversations. In a post on March 22, 2019, she writes about feeling burned out and physically exhausted:

> A lot of people think my day consists of playing in makeup and wearing cute clothes. That is very far from the truth. That is a small part of my job. You may be wondering why I feel the need to work harder than most. As a fat Black Muslim entrepreneur, I can't afford to not be at the top of my game. Remember, for me, I have [to] work three times as hard as a white person or a man to get half of the rewards. I can't afford to slack off. If I don't work then I don't eat. I do not have a plan B or a savings [account] or a family to fall back on.[40]

In this post, Vernon highlights the enormous pressures placed on her as a fat, Black Muslim fashion leader on Instagram. She is constantly faced with racism, misogyny, and Islamophobia from all sides while struggling to make a living in this gig economy and dealing with mental health concerns that arise. Many people may come to Instagram to see glowing photos of beautiful women in stylish garments. Vernon provides beautifully composed, high-quality photos with cutting-edge fashion, but she doesn't hide the real-life struggles and inter-sectional forms of oppression that she faces. This aesthetically pleasing style allows her images to fit into the overall look and feel of Instagram fashion images while at the same time challenging beauty standards and inserting social critiques.

FASHION, LIFESTYLE, AND POLITICAL WOKENESS

Alongside Vernon's unprecedented work in calling out the hypocrisy and harm caused by the perfect Islamic fashion influencer on Instagram, other unruly Muslim American women engage with the space of Instagram to go beyond fashion styles and influencer posts. While Vernon incorporates political messages into her captions, Imani uses graphic images, captions, Instagram Stories, and videos to share overt political messages, such as those related to activist work for racial justice and queer rights, election information, and expressions of solidarity with other marginalized groups. In contrast to Vernon's fashion-centered approach, Imani's Instagram page combines fashion images and photos of daily life with colorful inspirational quotes and short slide shows about topics like institutional racism and gender justice.

Imani's posts represent a growing trend on Instagram of what I term tap-through wokeness, or posts that share progressive political messages but are presented in the click-through visual style of Instagram. Rather than share traditional selfies with longer messages in the captions, Instagram influencers engage with followers who are perusing their phones during the day and looking for quick and easy-to-digest messages. An image with a long caption may be brushed over, but an inspirational quote or a tidbit of information conveyed within the Instagram image frame and not the caption can be quickly read on the phone and then possibly shared to more followers. In the summer of 2020 when racial justice activism reached a peak, information about various instances of police violence circulated through Instagram, especially the Stories slide shows. These images usually have a simple but attractive design. For example, Imani uses a rainbow of colors along with a font that looks like handwriting to share her messages. Her slide shows about topics such as institutional racism, discrimination based on age or ability, gender expression, and cultural appropriation are perfectly composed to be tapped through on a phone and then shared.

Since an uncomfortable interview when she came out as queer on Tucker Carlson's TV show in 2017, Imani has cultivated a growing online following connected to her status as Black, bisexual, and Muslim. She converted to Islam in 2015, and as stated on her website, she uses her online platform "to organize and create awareness about injustices in her communities."[41] She does this advocacy work mainly by building on her undergraduate degree in history to share information on the historical roots of social inequality through slide shows, videos, and interviews with other experts on Instagram. For instance, in one post she explains why terms like "inner city," "homosexual," and "minority" are outdated by discussing the origins of the words and how the words can be offensive.[42]

Imani's advocacy online is quite popular (she has over 450,000 followers on Instagram), and her concern about issues related to racism, sexuality, gender expression, and Islam connects with a variety of people. As an unruly soul, Imani repeatedly challenges social injustices, features the voices of those who have been silenced, and addresses institutional forms of inequality. She illustrates intersectionality, as she considers her Blackness and queerness to be just as significant as her Islamic faith. At the same time, the aesthetics of her Instagram feed are blissfully easy to digest. These posts of tap-through wokeness are very satisfying to consume: the slides have beautiful images, an easy-to-read design, and powerful (but not too challenging) messages. There is a sense of accomplishment in reading through a post about institutional racism, for instance, feeling moved for a moment, learning a tidbit of information, and posting it to your own social media page. It's the more recent version of clicking "like" on a post, but with more aesthetically attractive styles and slightly more challenging content.

In addition, the photos that Imani shares on her Instagram page often reinforce the pastel social media aesthetic that Vernon criticizes in her writings. Imani's fashion style features both soft colors like peach, teal, and yellow and bright colors like purple, red, and pink along with loose-fitting and flowing designs. For instance, in one photo (see figure 5), Imani wears a fuchsia headscarf, along with a similar colored blouse that loosely covers her arms and upper chest. She is making a kissing gesture toward the camera and has on light pink eye shadow and lipstick. She even posts an image that is part of a larger style trend, #Cottagecore, which she explains in the caption is a style "that usually features pastel colors, nature, and other bucolic elements."[43] In this photo, Imani appears in a light teal, prairie-style dress and a lilac-colored hijab. She is leaning against a tree, with green leaves in the background. While Imani's profile explains that she represents the intersection of Blackness, queerness, and Muslimness, her visual style and fashion sense do not challenge dominant beauty standards in the same way that Vernon confronts viewers with her fatness, Blackness, and bold style. Imani's written posts celebrate a variety of experiences, particularly at the intersection of her identity as a Black, bisexual Muslim, but her fashion images inevitably promote more Western and white ideologies of beauty since Imani is thin, light-skinned, and femme. Her postings and commentary may challenge the expectations that Muslim women will remain silent and tranquil, but her visual images are often indistinguishable from the pastel hijabi aesthetic that Vernon and others find so problematic.

Finally, Imani is open about how she positions herself as a social media influencer who advocates for progressive causes through sharing information. In a post celebrating her reaching 250,000 followers, Imani writes, "I *never* thought that I would be able to be an educator and an influencer *at the same time*."[44] Notably, the content on her Instagram page is evenly split between educational posts (such as infographics, quotes, and videos) and traditional fashion influencer photos (which usually include product promotion). She includes marketing for brands of items like scarves, jewelry, acne cream, makeup, clothing, shoes, and hats. She also does promotions for products not related to lifestyle. For example,

FIGURE 5. Blair Imani making a kissing expression with her hands on her cheeks. Photo by Kaelan Barowsky.

one post encourages followers to get their flu shot at Walgreens, and another caption promotes Adobe software. It's not unusual for Imani to rely on sponsored content and self-branding, since most successful social media influencers need this type of marketing for income. However, it is difficult at times to reconcile Imani's inspirational quotes about mental health and self-love—such as a post that states, "You should be the absolute last person sh*t talking yourself"[45]— with other posts that include promotions for beauty products to improve physical appearances.

Through her Instagram page, Imani addresses a variety of social issues that are often silenced in Muslim American communities, especially issues related to racism and homophobia. Just as Vernon's work taps into wider advocacy related to body positivity and Blackness, Imani's Instagram work connects with people outside of Islam who are also Black, queer, or interested in any of the progressive causes that she espouses. Imani engages with the popular trends of Instagram—

such as Stories, infographics, video commentaries, and visualizations of written content—to educate followers about institutional forms of oppression and motivate young people to participate in larger political action. While Imani's fashion posts may not challenge people to think differently about the problematic aspects of Islamic fashion culture and dominant beauty standards, her educational posts and videos spread important progressive messages and attempt to motivate political action. Imani clearly doesn't live in the alternative reality of most Instagram influencers, who cover up the injustices and struggles of everyday life with shallow, pleasurable content.

CELEBRATING ISLAMIC STYLES ON INSTAGRAM

While Vernon and Imani use the aesthetic elements of Instagram to challenge expectations that Muslim women must be modest in their appearance and silent about political issues, notably their Instagram posts rarely feature deep discussions of their religious faith. In contrast to these unrulier Islamic fashion influencers, bint Younus, a blogger and Muslim feminist activist, curates her Instagram page to celebrate Islamic aesthetic styles. Rather than paying vapid and sexualized attention to the human body in fashion spreads, bint Younus uses the styles and tools of Instagram to focus on her faith and highlight the deep beauty of Islamic art and culture. Her work relates to the decolonial tactic of mimicry, which Homi Bhabha describes as a way for the colonized subject to engage with the resources of the dominant culture while still pointing out the flaws at the root of that culture.[46] Bint Younus effortlessly embraces the Western visual aesthetics of Instagram influencers, as she shares domestic posts about cooking, travel, reading, and decorative items in her home. At the same time, her posts reject Western values and instead celebrate the superiority of Islamic aesthetic styles and religious values.

In a previous internet life, bint Younus maintained a blog that was popular among more traditional Muslim women. On the blog—*The Salafi Feminist*, which ran from 2006 to 2018—she discussed famous Muslim women in history and the Qur'an, issues related to women and Islamic teachings (including divorce, sexuality, and child rearing), and a revitalization of the feminist aspects of Islam. In 2015, *Wired* named bint Younus one of five women who are "quashing preconceptions about Islam on social media."[47] Bint Younus often emphasizes the contradictions of her identity as a traditional Salafi Muslim who wears the niqab face veil, a Canadian of South Asian background, and a feminist writer who advocates for gender justice from a decolonializing perspective. In 2015, she wrote a series of articles arguing that Muslim women like herself who wear the niqab face veil are individuals with agency who live happy and fulfilling lives.[48]

In recent years, bint Younus has shifted away from writing biting and critical posts about gender equality in Islam on her blog and facilitating contentious discussions on Twitter and Facebook. After browsing content on Instagram, she found that a lot of Muslim women whom she followed on other platforms were using Instagram in more substantial ways. Bint Younus is an active participant in the Muslim Bookstagram community, where people share reviews of books related to Islam and Muslims. She's also connected with communities like Muslim mom bloggers, visual artists, activists, and female scholars posting sermons or Qur'anic recitations. Bint Younus has around five thousand Instagram followers, and her posts emphasize Islamic ethics and aesthetics. Notably, she embraces the highly visual aspects of Instagram to create a stylish and attractive page, but she rejects the social media convention of focusing on the self through self-portraits.

For several years, the portrayal of Muslim women on Instagram was primarily focused on fashion influencers or "hijabistas," as bint Younus terms the Islamic fashion leaders she criticizes for being too focused on appearances and Western beauty standards. "There are *very* little connections to faith," bint Younus noted to me about the hijabista accounts. "Like here's a scarf and I am a Muslim woman, but you are also sexualizing yourself, you are also playing into the exact same beauty standards as everyone else, even as you are talking about body positivity."[49] Even though people like Vernon talk about different standards of beauty, bint Younus is still critical of the hypersexualization of their accounts. "You are literally giving us butt shots and camel toe shots and talking about flaunting your body," bint Younus told me. "This is completely contrary to the ethics of hijab and the ethics of being a Muslim woman."

Bint Younus sees promise in Muslim women who use Instagram in "countercultural" ways that reinforce their faith. This Instagram community, she explains, "is very visual, obviously, but the images used are not necessarily of the women themselves. It's about the content. It's about the substance."[50] She sees the captions as a space to reinforce Islamic values and provide deeper meaning. In one post, alongside an image of a purple journal and a purple and white blanket, bint Younus reflects on why she gets so much enjoyment and pleasure from her home and the objects that she shares on Instagram. She notes that she is "curating joy" in her home by surrounding herself with plants, books, artwork, jewelry, candles, lights, and other items that bring her comfort. "Every item is a reminder to me of my Lord's blessings," she writes. "It is necessary, especially on the saddest days and the angstiest nights, to sit with oneself and remember how much these small joys mean, and how truly amazing it is that we have a Lord who loves to grant us this joy."[51] Rather than simply posting images of more and more stuff that she is accumulating, she cultivates joy in her home by surrounding herself with things that remind her of God's blessings and make her grateful.

This approach is distinctly different from that of an influencer hawking the latest beauty product or accessory that will bring temporary happiness. Bint Younus engages with this common Instagram practice of sharing images of the domestic space and consumer products, but she reminds her followers of the greater and deeper joy that comes from God. Her Instagram page reflects a cozy domestic space, with images of houseplants, shelves full of books, mugs of tea, fresh-baked items, soft blankets, and Islamic artwork. The style of the page, as bint Younus describes it, reflects "finding joy and happiness in the little things in life."[52] Again, this isn't simply about consuming items to create a fleeting feeling of happiness: rather, the captions reinforce a deeper sense of joy. For example, in a post with an image of a small plant and several painted rocks, bint Younus reflects on a verse in the Qur'an that speaks about dealing with hardship and anxiety.[53] Another image highlights the prayer space in bint Younus's home with a Qur'an and Islamic art that features Arabic calligraphy and geometric designs. The caption states, "Curate faith, and beauty, and joy, in your home and your heart. . . . Indeed, Allah is the Most Beautiful, and loves beauty."[54] This caption reinforces how bint Younus uses the visual space of Instagram to promote the deep beauty in art and culture that reflects God instead of the shallow beauty of the physical body or endless consumption.

As a voracious reader, bint Younus devotes a good portion of her Instagram page to sharing the covers of books that she has recently read, along with reviews of the books. The books she discusses feature Muslim women and include novels, poetry, memoirs, graphic books, and academic works. She uses the Stories feature to create longer reviews of books, since in each slide she can share pictures of the book pages with her own captions for the images. From off-camera, she also records her reaction to and impressions of the book. The Stories tool allows bint Younus to focus on certain passages and really engage with the texts, some of which present deep discussions of Islamic scholarship and the Qur'an. She also uses her book reviews to discuss questions of spirituality and celebrate the creativity of Muslim authors.

Along with her slide show reviews, bint Younus writes book reviews in the captions next to beautifully composed images of books. For example, she reviews *The City of Brass* by S. A. Chakraborty, part of a Muslim fantasy series (see figure 6). Since the cover of the book features an intricate geometric drawing with gold and brass elements, bint Younus places the book alongside items with similar colors and styles: a dark brown lantern; a carved wooden tray; a gold candle; and two gold, geometric trivets. She often places book covers in front of backgrounds that feature related colors and patterns.[55] Within the caption review of *The City of Brass*, bint Younus focuses on the ways that the book addresses Islamic issues and provides spiritual guidance. She writes that the books in this series "are the one place where we will ever find a truly outstanding Muslim male character who represents the best of what it is to be a Muslim man - not rigid & unyielding, but beautifully & tenderly rendered."[56] Her reviews often focus on how Muslim characters are portrayed and the religious values of the books. Although bint Younus does not have nearly the number of followers that most Islamic fashion influencers attract, she represents a larger community

FIGURE 6. Bookstagram review of *The City of Brass*. Photo by Zainab bint Younus.

of Muslim women who use the tools and aesthetic styles of Instagram to dig deeper into religious faith and celebrate the beauty of Islamic art and culture.

ALLAH WANTS WOMEN TO EXPERIENCE SEXUAL PLEASURE

Just as bint Younus uses Instagram to celebrate Islamic aesthetics and values beyond fashion, Lindsey-Ali uses it to provide Islamic information about sex and relationships for young women. She consistently reminds her more than 48,000 followers that it is not immodest or sinful to talk about healthy sexuality within a marriage relationship or to emphasize women's pleasure. Lindsey-Ali, a Black convert to Islam and the mother of four children, uses the moniker The Village Auntie online, as she takes on the traditional role of a woman in an African village who shares information about sex, relationships, and childbirth with other women. Like the young people in the anti–purity culture movement of Evangelical Christianity, Lindsey-Ali seeks to move away from shame. She writes in a post: "Sex is not something we have to shy away from. Our beloved Rasulallah . . . [the Prophet Muhammad] taught us to not have shame when learning about our deen [faith]. Sex is a part of life."[57] As a certified sex health educator, Lindsey-Ali incorporates her professional training with Islamic teachings, as well as West and East African traditions. Before the COVID-19 pandemic,

Lindsey-Ali hosted workshops and classes for women in person, but she began to offer online courses in 2020.

The Village Auntie Instagram page reflects the beautiful, natural, comforting style of women-only spaces. Lindsey-Ali's page has a vibe similar to that of a midwife practice or a birthing center. Earthy colors of brown, orange, and yellow fill the space, along with images of flowers, fruits, and jewelry that resemble female genitalia. Lindsey-Ali also posts images of natural items like flowers, plants, vegetables, spices, and tea. Alongside these beautifully composed still-lifes, she shares a mix of close-up self-portraits in African-style fabrics, images of her hands with henna tattoos and rings, inspirational quotes, and photos of other women and children. Notably, she almost exclusively features Black women and girls. Her images highlight the natural beauty of Black women of all shapes and skin tones.

Similar to Vernon's fashion advocacy, Lindsey-Ali's Instagram postings critique dominant beauty standards and celebrate the beauty of each person. In a selfie, taken in a car with the folds of her neck visible in the center of the image, Lindsey-Ali comments on fatphobia and body image in American culture. She writes in the caption, "In some West African countries like Mauritania, when a woman has rings around her neck, it's a sign of beauty. It means she is plump and well-fed. Fullness indicates both attractiveness and fertility. In America, I think it just means I'm fat. Alhamdulillah [Praise to God]."[58] In this post, Lindsey-Ali is pointing to the ways that beauty standards are culturally based and don't represent a person's actual value. Similarly, in an Instagram Story "who is TVA?," she discusses how your body and physical appearance are not what matters, especially if you are trying to live a faithful Muslim life. She writes: "Baby girl, being beautiful isn't the end goal. Being clean of heart and sincere in your spirit is #goals. Sis, your hip to waist ratio isn't the main measurement that counts. How will your scale be measured on that day when we all will have our reckoning? . . . The right people, your people, they see your heart and your soul, not what you look like on the outside. Make sure you are cultivating something truly beautiful."[59] Lindsey-Ali emphasizes here that dominant beauty standards may categorize certain people as ugly, immodest, or fat because of exterior appearances, but this judgment does not impact one's inherent value in the eyes of God.

The main purpose of the Village Auntie Instagram page is to cultivate a supportive space for Muslim women to discuss sexuality and feminine experiences from an Islamic perspective. The hosts of the podcast *Truth's Table*, which is discussed in the next chapter, build on the womanist tradition of creating a space for Black women to have a dialogue. Similarly, Lindsey-Ali explains that the Village Auntie space is created by and for women. In the "who is TVA?" Story, one slide explains, "The Village Auntie is for women, by women. There is no associated brand. There is no parallel movement. It is truly for us, by us."[60] She acknowledges that men may view her content, but she reminds them that the space is created for women. While her posts can be relevant to a non-Muslim audience and she acknowledges that Christians have found her work helpful,[61] she bases her teachings on Islamic scholarship.

Lindsey-Ali uses the Instagram video feature to share short educational videos about topics like vaginal hygiene, the ritual cleansing practice of *ghusl* in Islam, mental health, and penis sizes' correlation to sexual pleasure. While some critics would say that talking about sex and female pleasure is an immodest practice for Muslim women, Lindsey-Ali clearly explains that she is sharing information that is "grounded in [her] faith"[62] and that talking about sexuality is not a forbidden act for Muslims, especially women. In an article, Lindsey-Ali notes that "in Islam, sex is a sacred act."[63] Muslims will have healthier marriages if they think of sex as a sacred act of intimacy and mutual pleasure. Additionally, Lindsey-Ali advocates for sex education for young people that is rooted in Islamic teachings about the sacredness of sexual intimacy.

Through visual images that celebrate the natural beauty of Black Muslim women and videos that encourage healthy sexuality and mutual relationships, Lindsey-Ali cultivates a beautiful and supportive community of Muslim women on her Instagram page. Her images counteract the dominant Islamic fashion influencers on Instagram by illustrating the inherent value of all Muslim women, regardless of their physical appearance. Furthermore, she challenges the assumptions within Islamic communities that proper modest Muslim women are silent and demure. Instead, Lindsey-Ali uses her videos and images to share relevant information and assert that speaking about sexuality is not haram or immodest. She writes in a post: "I will not be quiet. It is not in me to do so. I could have chosen a safer path. But I chose to disrupt for a reason. Being safe does not allow the reach that we need to get information to the people who need it."[64] Lindsey-Ali displays her unruliness and her inability to remain silent about issues related to women's experiences that are too often stifled in Muslim communities. When women are better educated about sexuality and their bodies, they will be more empowered in their relationships to assert their rights and intrinsic value.

INSERTING CRITIQUES INTO THE INSTAGRAM INFLUENCER AESTHETIC

In academic circles and the popular press, many articles and books have focused on the prominent visibility of Muslim American women in public spaces, as they embrace Western cultural items like fashion, pop culture, and social media. While there are certainly valid discussions of the ways that fashion helps Muslim women negotiate their identities in Western cultural spaces, some of this work falls into the trap of obsessing over the appearance of Muslim women. These discussions reinforce the long-standing dichotomy of Muslim women as either covered and oppressed by Islam or unveiled and liberated by Western fashion and progressive values. This emphasis on the appearance of Muslim women also minimizes complex life experiences and transforms women into a simple icon of the religion.

The digital advocacy work of Vernon, Imani, bint Younus, and Lindsey-Ali displays the experiences of women who are left out of this new obsession with Islamic fashion and the elevation of certain modest women to a pious icon. These bold and hypervisible bodies, along with the women's vocal critiques of social injustices in Islam and Western society, are unwelcome in mainstream spaces. In their own distinct ways, these four women use the creative tools and aesthetic expectations of Instagram to critique the icon of the pious Muslim woman. The women curate beautiful Instagram pages that fit into trends of online influencers and Islamic fashion leaders, but at the same time they insert their unruly bodies and marginalized perspectives. Vernon interrupts the pastel, bubblegum style of Islamic fashion influencers with her bold fashion and curvaceous, dark-skinned body to illustrate the value of all Muslims and facilitate discussions about the struggles of those who fail to meet the ideals of Islamic fashion. Imani successfully incorporates an effervescent form of political activism and a revolutionized social history into the influencer style. Bint Younus brings an Islamic ethical perspective to her Instagram book reviews and photos of her cozy domestic life. Finally, Lindsey-Ali cultivates a communal, feminine space on Instagram for Muslim women to share knowledge about sexuality and relationships.

These women use their bodies and visual styles to challenge Islamic ideals of the pious, modest subject while simultaneously dismantling Western beauty standards. These Instagram images and captions point to the problems with promoting a beautiful, perfect, modest, and passive icon of Islam. Such an ideal icon reinforces white supremacist concepts that beauty is tied to light skin and European features, a misogynistic focus on the perfection of women's bodies for the male gaze, and a neoliberal emphasis on self-work and branding within social media spaces. These visual projects call out social inequality in society and Islamic circles in terms of race, gender, ethnicity, class, and sexuality. While some male Muslim leaders may attempt to silence Muslim women by placing them on the pedestal of the pious Muslim subject, the women in these examples loudly assert their rights to have their experiences and opinions valued. Being a modest and pious Muslim woman does not mean that you cannot speak about how your faith intersects with issues of injustice, sexuality, or politics.

It seems notably that the two chapters that focus more on Muslim women (this one on photos and chapter 5 on digital music videos) both discuss visual media. This appears to reflect the obsession in Western culture with the visual appearance of Muslim women—both anxiety over the public presence of covered Muslim women and sexual fantasies about the harem space behind the veil. In contrast, issues related to sexism and racism in Christian communities are often discussed in dialogic spaces of online threads or podcasts. Although this breakdown of the chapters does highlight the Western fascination with images of Muslim women, this doesn't mean that Muslims are less capable than the Christian activists discussed in this book of articulating their critiques through writing. On the contrary, the clever and complex images that the Muslim creatives share are accompanied by captions and articles that add layers of meaning to their visual messages. The images often serve to draw viewers into more complicated arguments about social issues.

Finally, this work connects to the other digital projects discussed in this book, since all of these activists are doing deep work not only to articulate the values of their individual lives in the context of racism, sexism, Islamophobia, or homophobia in society but also (and more importantly) to demonstrate the inherent value of their lives in the eyes of God. Vernon explained to me the deep pain of racism within the Muslim American community: "I'm not less of a Muslim because I'm Black. He's not less of a Muslim because he's a convert. She's not less of a Muslim because she doesn't speak Arabic."[65] The promotion of only certain Muslim women to the iconic status of pious, modest femininity does existential damage to the majority of Muslim women who don't meet these standards because of their skin color, body shape, ethnicity, way of dressing, independence, vocal critiques, and so on. While these perspectives are often ignored in offline Muslim communities, the Muslim women discussed in this chapter use digital spaces to assert the value of their lives and build a radically equal community of other Muslim misfits. Chapter 4 examines the dialogic space of podcasts and the work centered on the value of those forced to the margins of Christian spaces because of their race and gender.

4 · A SEAT AT THE TABLE

Podcasts Facilitate Dialogue
for Marginalized Christian Perspectives

As the social concerns over the COVID-19 pandemic and the demands for racial justice converged in the summer of 2020, podcasts became a significant space for in-depth discussions and efforts to make sense of these unprecedented times. Notably, podcasts with a focus on faith and spirituality featured episodes on grief in the era of COVID-19, police brutality, health disparities based on race and class, the prevalence of anti-Blackness in Christian churches, and support in dealing with various mental health issues. For instance, *Queerology*, a podcast that focuses on the intersections of faith, spirituality, and queer identities, featured a panel discussion on June 2, 2020, with activists in the fight for racial justice and equality.[1] Another podcast targeted at former Evangelical Christians, *Exvangelical*, rereleased an interview with Austin Channing Brown, the author of a book on Black dignity and racism within Christianity.[2] Another popular podcast among young people questioning their Christian upbringing, *The Liturgists*, featured several episodes during the pandemic on mental health concerns such as dealing with pain, trauma, and grief. Finally, *Truth's Table*, a podcast hosted by three Black Christian women, included multiple episodes on the ways that the twin crises of the pandemic and racial injustice impact marginalized communities.

These examples of podcast episodes represent a larger trend as young people, seeking a deeper engagement with their faith and a stronger connection between religious teachings and social activism, engage with podcasts to discuss various issues and motivate social action. While these podcasts represent a range of theological interpretations of Christianity, they all provide open forums for dialogue on religious teachings and spirituality from perspectives that are marginalized and silenced in traditional religious spaces. The episodes in response to the expansive social concerns of 2020 are not abnormal blips. Rather, they are representative of the issues that have been discussed in these podcasts, which are created and supported by those who are often misfits within U.S. Christian churches. These podcasts critique how Christianity promotes white supremacy, anti-Blackness, misogyny, and heteronormativity at the institutional level. For many people deemed to be unruly souls and left out of traditional Christian spaces, podcasts create a community to build a new understanding of spirituality that values marginalized experiences and works for justice and equality.

While the work that is happening in these podcasts is similar to the textual efforts against purity culture and the visual projects of Muslim activists, this chapter foregrounds the medium of podcasts as an open space of dialogue, particularly within U.S. Christianity. In this chapter, I examine how the flexible, intimate, and authentic feel of podcasts enable marginalized Christians to build new expressions of faith that celebrate the value of these unruly souls and to critique the social injustices perpetuated by Christian churches. After a discussion of some of the popular podcasts among former and questioning Evangelical Christians, the remainder of the chapter focuses on the groundbreaking work of *Truth's Table*. All of these podcasts offer significant critiques of social inequality within Christian churches, but the work of the hosts on *Truth's Table* illustrates how the intimate and flexible nature of podcasts encourages dialogue and promotes the significance of Black women's experiences.

PODCASTS AMONG THE FAITHFUL AND THE QUESTIONING

Now a fairly everyday medium among Millennials and Gen-Xers, podcasts trace their origins to 2004, when technology first enabled the distribution of audio programs through RSS feeds. Apple iTunes launched a directory for podcasts in 2005, making it easier to browse shows and download episodes to iPods.[3] In the fall of 2014 podcasts first reached a mass audience, through the popularity of *Serial*—a journalistic show that investigated a murder from the 1990s.[4] Podcasting originally reflected the two elements of its portmanteau name, which was coined by Ben Hammersley in the *Guardian* in February 2004.[5] These were audio recordings that resembled broadcast radio but could be listened to on a mobile device like an iPod. But by the mid-2010s, podcasting had become a unique medium that was popular and profitable, with content from both amateurs and professionals. The style of podcasts is extremely varied, including traditional news programs, long interviews, chat shows about particular topics, experimental artistic productions, true crime reporting, fictional dramas, and personal narrative programs.

Technologically, podcasts constitute an unprecedented medium that allows listeners to subscribe to a particular feed and have the audio content automatically delivered to their mobile devices. While some podcasts resemble radio programing in structure (with episodes, series, and set schedules), they also allow for "time-shifting," so listeners can play the content whenever they want.[6] Podcasting is also, as Martin Spinelli and Lance Dann describe it, "a mobile medium": "podcasts move with the human body and are consumed in urban spaces, while in transit, in the streets and in other public places."[7] Furthermore, the audience has more control, being able to seek out podcasts rather than simply happening upon programming like in the days of broadcast radio. Because of the limitless options of shows and the desire of audiences for specific content, podcasts are created for a variety of niche audiences. There are countless examples of how podcasts, especially because of their close connection to social media spaces, facilitate international connections related to specific interests and experiences.[8]

A quick search of a podcast application reveals a plethora of offerings to match almost every interest or subcultural group. It's no surprise to find countless podcasts about religion from official religious communities like the Church of Jesus Christ of Latter-day Saints; popular figures such as the Dalai Lama or Joel Osteen; or specific groups within religions, such as Latino Catholics or Sufi Muslims. There are also numerous podcasts on topics related to spirituality, such as mindfulness, self-help, wellness, meditation, yoga, astrology, and fitness. Notably, some of the most popular podcasts are hosted by wellness and self-improvement figures like Brené Brown, Oprah Winfrey, and Gwyneth Paltrow.

Within Evangelical Christianity, podcasts from churches and pastors cater to a wider audience, while specific podcasts are targeted toward subgroups. Podcasts are created for kids, single young adults, married women, married men, Black Christians, Latino Christians, Asian Christians, and so on. These podcasts may provide religious inspiration tailored to particular subgroups, but for people who are questioning elements of Evangelical Christianity, podcasts offer space to discuss contentious faith issues outside of religious institutions. Similar to the individuals who use textual spaces like Twitter to question church teachings on purity culture, members of podcast communities expand theological boundaries by talking about gender expression, sexuality beyond purity teachings, racism within Christianity, and other intersecting forms of oppression that are often perpetuated by white Evangelical Christianity in the United States.

Similarly, podcasts create a home for unruly experiences within Islam. For example, *Identity Politics* celebrates Black Muslim American experiences, and the now completed *Good Muslim/Bad Muslim* intentionally played with categories of what it means to be Muslim American. Podcasts such as *Exvangelical*, *Queerology*, and *The Liturgists* also work to create a supportive space for those who are misfits within traditional religious spaces, but these shows also attempt to expand theological boundaries. Building on the experiences of those marginalized within church spaces because of their gender, sexuality, or race, these podcasts offer critical outsiders' perspectives on problems in U.S. Christianity. Similar to the activist projects discussed throughout this book, these podcasts construct meaning and articulate value based on the unique experiences of these unruly souls.

Additionally, these podcasts and the corresponding social media sites provide necessary communities for people leaving traditional religious congregations. As Steven Fekete and Jessica Knippel discuss in their study of young people leaving Evangelical faith communities, "there is a need for and benefit to a similar community when one is going through a process of critiquing or exiting from their existing faith tradition."[9] The digital communities created through podcasts and social media platforms become "spaces for asking questions and telling truths without fear of shame, and for building long-term bonds with others."[10] Through sharing their stories, individuals leaving powerful religious institutions feel supported and less alone.

THE INTIMACY, MALLEABILITY, AND AUTHENTICITY OF PODCASTING

In this chapter, I explore how podcasts provide an intimate space to dig deep into issues of spirituality and faith. Participants share personal experiences in an open space of dialogue and supportive discussion. Although critical academic scholarship on podcasts is fairly sparse, the intimacy and authenticity of podcasts are often discussed in it. Listening to a podcast tends to be a more intimate experience than watching a TV show or reading a Twitter thread because you usually listen to a podcast with earbuds inside your ear as you go about your daily life. As Spinelli and Dann discuss in their list of podcasts' features, "consumption on earbuds encourages an interior and intimate mode of listening."[11] There is a closeness as the hosts speak into your ears while you do chores, get ready in the morning, work, or go for a walk. Because of their mobile nature, podcasts create a soundscape while people are out in the world, commuting to work or running errands. As Richard Berry explains, listening to podcasts through earbuds creates a protective barrier from the busy urban world, and listeners cultivate "a privatized and personalized auditory experience."[12] While some media are more intimate than others, Berry asserts that listening to podcasts conveys a sense of "hyper-intimacy" because it brings together both the physical intimacy of listening with earbuds and an intimate form of communication of listening to human speech.[13] Additionally, Berry explains, "podcasts are presented by people from within a listener's own community of interest or by people she/he may already have a relationship with via social media and are frequently recorded in a podcaster's own personal or domestic space."[14] All of these elements contribute to developing an intimate medium through which people in small communities are able to connect with each other. As Spinelli and Dann observe, the intimacy of podcasts encourages empathy on many different levels: "When we talk about podcast intimacy we refer to efforts to create and reveal emotional experiences and personal connections in a comfortable space between interviewers and interview subjects, between the producers themselves, and between listeners, producers, and subjects."[15] There are many layers of intimate connections forged through podcasts, and these feelings of connection and empathy can be harnessed for activist causes.

In addition to the closeness of podcasts, the hosts also use a genuine style to connect with the listeners. The barriers to becoming a podcast host are much lower than those to becoming a host on a mainstream media platform. Cultivating an authentic style and a genuine community is essential for podcasters, since listeners often seek out this close connection in podcasts. As Sarah Florini explains in her work on Black podcasters, the open structure of podcasts encourages authentic conversations that are free from commercial and other outside influences: "Many of the podcasters assert [that] podcasting allows them to provide content unconstrained by corporate gatekeepers and that they and their listeners consider less contrived and more authentic."[16] Podcasts, particularly the interview- and conversation-style shows, cultivate small communities of listeners through the sharing of personal experiences and deep emotions.

Intimate and Authentic Conversations about Faith

The hosts of podcasts that examine highly personal topics, like faith and religious trauma, use an intimate and authentic style to create connections and trust with the listener community. In response to a growing movement of young people questioning their upbringing in Evangelical Christian churches, Blake Chastain started the *Exvangelical* podcast in 2016—notably, around the same time as the activism against the purity culture was growing. His website in 2020 stated that the podcast is "dedicated to personal stories about living in, leaving, and coming to terms with the messed up subculture of evangelicalism–and exploring the wide world of faith, belief, and disbelief outside of it."[17] This podcast is part of a larger movement of deconstructing the ways that the Evangelical subculture deeply affects those raised in the faith. Chastain writes: "The Evangelical worldview . . . forms your social, cultural, political, sexual, and gender identities. To reject it is to reject your entire sense of self and society. This is no small thing."[18] The podcast uses in-depth interviews with people whose lives have intersected with the Evangelical subculture in some way, with the hope that these stories will resonate with listeners.

Chastain creates an intimacy in the podcast through his soothing, quiet style. Instead of using an opening song, the podcasts begin with Chastain's minimal "hey everybody" greeting and a low-key overview of the specific episode. Then a short musical passage is played before the interview. Usually, Chastain begins an interview with a question about the person's relationship to Evangelicalism. The show is clearly created for people raised in the Evangelical subculture since participants use terms like "PK" (for "pastor's kid"), discuss Christian colleges and homeschooling, and mention theological concepts. Most importantly, the long interview format and Chastain's calm style produce in-depth discussions about personal issues related to sexuality, mental health, racism, and faith struggles.

In *Queerology*, Matthias Roberts also uses intimacy and authenticity, but his style is upbeat and friendly. Each episode begins with music and an energetic "hey friends!" greeting. While *Exvangelical* is explicitly geared toward those who have left Evangelical Christian churches, *Queerology* has a wider goal: reaching Christians (not only Evangelicals) and those from other religious traditions who are seeking to reconcile queer identity with faith. Rather than abandoning Christianity, Roberts seeks to dig deeper into Christian theology to revitalize the faith so that it not only accepts queer individuals but also celebrates what queerness adds to Christianity. As a licensed mental health counselor, Roberts incorporates his own expertise and the knowledge of his guests to provide support for his listeners. As he states on his website, "I create resources to help people fight bad theology so that we might live confident and fulfilling lives."[19] Roberts explained to me that he envisions *Queerology* as a "welcoming space," especially for queer folks who have a lot of hurt and resentment toward religious institutions.[20]

In each episode, Roberts develops a close relationship with his listeners by engaging with his interviewees and delves into deep discussions about religious issues, faith, identity, and mental health. He starts the interviews by asking the guests to talk about how they identify themselves and how their faith helped them form their identity. This opening question helps shape the conversation and focus on how various forms of identity relate to faith and meaning making. Other interview podcasts use lists of questions prepared ahead of time. In contrast, Roberts embraces the intimate and informal conversation style of podcasting. "There is something about having a one-on-one conversation about these really big concepts that I think allows for more expansion, more comfort, more safety in some ways," Roberts told me. "I just know that sitting down with a friend over coffee or over a drink and having these conversations—stuff comes out in that. I think that happens in interviews on podcasts as well."[21] Furthermore, Roberts finds that listening to podcasts can provide an intimate space for queer youth to explore these questions. He explained to me: "With podcasting you just plug in, and no one has to know what you are listening to. I know there are tons of kids and youth who listen to my show who have no other access to that kind of content." Through these honest discussions of personal faith experiences, podcasts like *Queerology* and *Exvangelical* work to cultivate a close community of followers and provide spiritual support that might not be as readily available in traditional religious spaces.

The Experimental Flexibility of Podcasts

Not only do podcasts provide a sense of intimacy and genuineness, but they also enable more flexibility in terms of format, style, length, and focus. Spinelli and Dann document in their book that while podcasting builds on radio broadcasting, it is a medium that is more open and offers new "possibilities in style, content, and engagement."[22] Similarly, Berry notes that podcasts initially came out of radio, but the creative possibilities of podcasting allowed the medium to develop "aesthetics that are notably different to linear radio."[23] This malleability of podcasts encourages not only a wide variety of styles of shows, but it also promotes a more open conversation style among the podcast hosts. This chapter focuses particularly on interview and chat shows, which are less restrained by traditional media formats. As Florini discusses in her work on Black podcasters, these conversation-style shows often "embrace . . . a free-flowing, flexible, and conversational approach."[24] A typical TV talk show, for instance, could address social topics like racism or misogyny, but the show would be constrained by time, commercial breaks, regulations on language, and restrictions imposed by advertisers and other gatekeepers meant to keep out marginal voices. Podcasts are free from a lot of these restrictions, which allows them to include deep conversations about issues that are often censored in other spaces.

Queerology and *Exvangelical* consist mostly of in-depth interviews. In contrast, *The Liturgists* tends to use a more experimental and eclectic style. *The Liturgists* and its related alternative religious community were created by Michael Gungor and Mike McHargue, friends who both were raised in conservative Christian churches. In response to what they saw as "the anti-science and socially regressive stances of mainstream American Christianity," they created community in 2014 to be a home for those who felt misplaced in churches and organized religions.[25] Similar to the other digital projects for unruly souls detailed in this book, *The Liturgists* has the goal of "creating space for those recovering from spiritual trauma, and lifting up traditionally marginalized people as full and equal members of humanity."[26]

The podcast hosts strive to do this work for an audience of listeners from across a broad religious and nonreligious spectrum through episodes that focus on certain themes. Instead of presenting interviews or discussions, the hosts embrace the flexibility of podcasts to create unique episodes on set themes that relate in some way to faith, meaning, science, or culture. For each episode, the hosts incorporate interviews with experts and authors, reflections from listeners, music, and other audio clips. *The Liturgists* covers a wide range of topics beyond religion, such as grief, body image, disability, happiness, hopelessness, sexuality, and antiracism. Because podcasts have little oversight that structures their format, there is a lot of openness in terms of the style, format, length, and topics discussed. *The Liturgists* illustrates how podcasts can delve deeply into topics and take advantage of the experimental potential of the medium. The experience of listening to *The Liturgists* is akin to entering a ritualistic, liminal space of reflection and possibility.

Space for Religious Misfits

The intimate spaces, authentic styles, and flexibility of podcasting create a digital media site that is relevant to religious misfits, particularly those marginalized in Christian churches. *Exvangelical, Queerology,* and *The Liturgists* are open spaces where people can talk authentically and in depth about topics that are often not discussed in organized religions. Podcasts both create the opportunity to present significant critiques of how Christian churches perpetuate social injustices and also provide breadth and depth in discussions of issues related to faith and identity. These podcasts each support communities of young people who feel left out of Christian spaces that promote regressive ideas about sexuality, gender, and social justice.

For the remainder of this chapter, I explore *Truth's Table*, a podcast that has a particular mission of cultivating a supportive space of dialogue among Black Christian women. Because of their intersectional identity as Black women, the three hosts of the podcast often discuss how they are left out of white Christian spaces and not given a voice in Black churches that tend to privilege male leaders. As a result of being doubly marginalized from institutional religious spaces, the women use their podcast to create what Lisa Flores terms a discursive "space of their own" that is built on the foundation of their specific experiences.[27] The hosts open each episode by inviting listeners to sit at their table "that is built by Black women and for Black women." As I discuss through a detailed analysis of various episodes, the three hosts use *Truth's Table* to dialogue about theology and faith, speak about how their voices have been dismissed, and produce new knowledge that centers on the experiences of Black Christian women. *Truth's Table* serves as an example of how podcasts, with their intimacy, authentic style, and flexibility, encourage productive conversations and critical work from the margins of organized religions.

PULL UP A SEAT AT THE TABLE

The hosts of *Truth's Table*, Michelle Higgins, Christina Edmondson, and Ekemini Uwan, employ the authentic and intimate aspects of podcasts to dialogue about issues that impact other Black Christian women. They use the metaphor of the table, encouraging listeners to pull up a chair, listen, and share in the discussion. At the beginning of most episodes, one of the hosts will state, "This table is built by Black women, for Black women. So welcome to the table, sisters!" The women often talk about having tea together with the listeners, and the graphic images on their website and podcast feature drawings of the three women drinking from large cups of tea (see figure 7).

This symbolic space of dialogue and speaking out about personal experiences relates to a longer history of Black women finding room for discussion, espe-

FIGURE 7. Podcast icon for *Truth's Table*.

cially in a world that has silenced their voices. As bell hooks explains in her observation of Black women's speech as a child, "dialogue—the sharing of speech and recognition—took place not between mother and child or mother and male authority figure but among Black women. I can remember watching fascinated as our mother talked with her mother, sisters, and women friends. The intimacy and intensity of their speech—the satisfaction they received from talking to one another, the pleasure, the joy."[28] Dialogue is not speech between people of disparate power positions but rather, in this case, "among Black women" who are on a level playing field. These equal power dynamics enable what hooks explains as speech that is intimate and goes into the depth of Black women's experiences. According to hooks, "true speaking is not solely an expression of creative power; it is an act of resistance, a political gesture that challenges politics of domination that would render us nameless and voiceless."[29] These acts of dialogue and speaking back empower Black women by moving them "from object to subject."[30] Through collaborative discussion, the women claim agency in their own stories and articulate their value.

In addition, there is a long tradition of Black Christian women developing spaces of dialogue outside institutional churches. Womanist theology is a branch of liberation theology that celebrates the daily experiences of Black women, and these experiences often fall outside of formal religious spaces. Womanist scholars like Patricia-Anne Johnson discuss the importance of using secular spaces outside of churches, such as this podcast, to spiritually liberate Black women.[31] Similarly, Stephanie Mitchem writes about the importance of informal spaces to gather and dialogue, noting that "Black women's spiritual and religious understandings are culturally transmitted" within homes and friendship circles.[32]

These alternative spaces of dialogue are also built on a longer tradition of enslaved Africans in the Americas developing their own revolutionary theology through secretive dialogic spaces like hush harbors (spaces for spiritual expression that were hidden from slave masters) and coded language. As the womanist scholar Katie Cannon explains, "In spite of every form of institutional constraint, Afro-American slaves were able to create another world, a counterculture within the White-defined world, complete with their own folklore, spirituals, and religious practices."[33] During and after enslavement, cultural spaces provided opportunities to discuss religious issues and articulate the inherent value of Black lives in the face of white Christianity promoting the inferiority of Black people. It is essential to have these separate spaces, not only for the celebration of Black souls but also to worship God away from white supremacy.

Like these alternative spaces of dialogue beyond the dominating gaze of white Christianity, Truth's Table has become a place for honest discussion among Black Christian women. At the same time, this is an informal community that is built around the friendship of the three hosts. As Higgins states in one episode, they are friends in real life and are "turning our group text into a podcast."[34] Truth's Table is a casual and friendly space for sharing lighthearted conversations about topics like movies and food, as well as discussions of serious issues like racial violence and reparations. In an episode about their experiences as podcast hosts, Edmondson comments that the podcast is not meant to be a formal space of religious education: "Our intention was not to be an explicit teaching tool but rather to create a space of community."[35]

While listeners may come from diverse backgrounds in terms of their understanding of theological topics, Truth's Table is primarily created to be a space of support for and connection with other Black Christian women. The hosts regularly refer to listeners as "sisters" and use phrases and language to acknowledge the listeners and bring them into the conversation. Notably, the hosts don't code-switch but rather create an intimate space that welcomes Black women. The podcast features language like "ain't," "cuz," "y'all," "CP [Colored people] time," and "praise the Lord." Furthermore, a communal feel is created through the conversational style that includes laughter and upbeat affirmations such as "that's right," "amen," "all right," "wow," "love it," and "that's real." A common refrain is for Higgins to sing a short response like "Weell!" or for Uwan to encourage the speaker with a "c'mon now!" Then the whole group often breaks into laughter. The close friendship of the hosts is shown when they refer to each other as "E" for Ekemini, "C" for Christina, and "M" for Michelle. This intimacy and the community feel of the show is reflected in a live episode when they use their catchphrases and the crowd cheers and laughs, well aware of the in-group jokes and friendly spirit.[36]

Additionally, a lot of the reviews of the show on iTunes reflect the ways that the hosts develop the metaphorical table where listeners are able to pull up a seat and join the conversation. One listener writes, "It feels like I am sitting down with good girlfriends."[37] Another says, "I feel like I'm sitting at a table with women speaking words and ideas that I've been thinking about for a long time."[38] Still another listener notes that she feels connected to the hosts since she is also a "Black, Reformed woman." She writes, "this podcast has been balm for my soul. I find myself so often thinking, 'That's how I feel too!' that I feel as though I've made new friends."[39] Listeners frequently comment on the authenticity of the hosts' friendship and the deep wisdom that they share. "You can hear and feel their friendship and truth and passion," one person writes.[40] Another says, "this podcast is informative, authentic, challenging, while being relaxed and not contrived."[41] The authentic and intimate style of the podcasts cultivates these connections between the hosts and their Black Christian female listeners.

As Florini finds in her study of several podcasts created within the Black community, the discussion space of podcasts often resembles offline Black social spaces like churches, the beauty shop, or the barbershop, where Black people can discuss issues without a need to code-switch or fit into the dominant white culture. Florini writes, "These podcasters largely eschew the 'polished' and tightly formatted character of most mainstream corporate media, opting instead for an informal, flexible approach that allows for free-form conversation and embraces a range of Black vernaculars and regional accents."[42] Especially for Black listeners who don't have easy access to Black social spaces in their daily lives, Florini argues that these podcasts can create an "aural cocoon" that allows Black listeners to protect "themselves in the sounds of Black sociality as they navigate a hegemony that constitutes white culture as normative."[43] The hosts of *Truth's Table* use the vernacular language of the Black church and attempt to re-create the social space of a kitchen table, surrounded by Black women sipping tea and dishing on the latest news. In a review, one listener writes that *Truth's Table* creates a space to honor the perspectives of Black Christian women, noting that "as an African American woman, who currently doesn't have many interactions with Black folks, I love hearing their voices and laughter, mixed with wisdom and knowledge[,] fill my home."[44] This review illustrates the ways that *Truth's Table* creates an "aural cocoon" for listeners who desire deep conversations with other Black Christian women.

The hosts frequently discuss how they want *Truth's Table* to be a safe space for Black women to share both their joyful moments and their struggles. "There's a lot of unity that we experience in being Black and women together," Higgins states in one episode, reflecting the womanist tradition of building on Black women's unique life stories. "This is a cool glass of water for our sisters."[45] The hosts also discuss the intimacy of podcasting and note that listeners come up to them and share very personal stories of how the show helped them. In one episode, Uwan reflects on the way listeners create a meaningful community: "For me, I'm honored that they would turn on our podcast for a good 30–40 minutes and weep and laugh and cackle with their teacup in hand. Or start a ritual where they are just cleaning their house while listening to *Truth's Table*. That to me is a very sacred time for Black women in particular, cleaning up the house on a Saturday morning. That's an honor."[46] The hosts of *Truth's Table* build a sacred, ritualistic space of dialogue about their faith outside of institutional religious spaces. One listener noted in her review of the show that she listens to it during her "Saturday morning me time."[47] Another listener wrote: "I enjoyed you on my walk. I enjoy listening while sipping a cup of coffee."[48] These theological dialogues happen in the midst of the daily lives of Black women, as they share a cup of coffee or complete household chores. As I show in the discussion of specific episodes, the hosts of *Truth's Table* build meaning and value from these daily experiences of Black womanhood.

For listeners, it can be a deep, spiritual ritual to listen to a podcast about the specific experiences of Black Christian women. As Florini observes, "the sense of being immersed in sound allows listeners to feel transported into the conversation they are listening to."[49] The hosts of *Truth's Table* recognize how meaningful the act of listening to their podcast can be for Black women. In an episode in the midst of the COVID-19 pandemic, the hosts discuss how the podcast is safe community that loves and values Black women in face of a larger society of misogynoir.[50] As Higgins states:

> That's why this table, as least for me, is about some kind of solace in being able to tell the truth and to not have to code-switch about it and to not be afraid that the people we are trying to minister to will only be able to accept our love, our appreciation, our mercy, and yes, our ministry—that they will only be able to appreciate it in the dark. I'm out here about let's bring our sisters into the light and let's show them love. And by showing them love, it means demanding that their lives have value.[51]

This podcast is a place where young Black Christian women can be unapologetic about their faith and their struggles. They can dialogue about various issues without fear that their perspectives will be dismissed, and they can gain new knowledge that celebrates the inherent value of Black women.

CENTERING THE EXPERIENCES OF BLACK CHRISTIAN WOMEN

In contrast to the long history of Christian theology being deployed to justify anti-Blackness and misogyny, Higgins, Edmondson, and Uwan use *Truth's Table* to celebrate the everyday spirituality of Black Christian women. Podcasts provide an open and flexible space to develop this womanist practice of centering the experiences of Black women. The hosts also engage in dialogue and critique as a way to, as Cannon writes, "break away from the oppressive ideologies and belief systems that presume to define their reality."[52] Traditional religious spaces rarely welcome criticism from the margins, so digital spaces like Twitter, Instagram, podcasts, and digital videos offer creative outlets for these significant critiques. Specifically, the open structure and intimacy of podcasts enable the hosts to have in-depth conversations about topics that are very relevant to the lives of Black Christian women, such as colorism, hairstyles, and the sexualization of Black bodies.

In a podcast episode on resistance, Edmondson discusses the "womanist vantage point theory," which addresses how an individual's position in society allows her to see oppression in different ways and from different angles. Consequently, Black women are not unique, Edmondson explains, but "they have, through God's providence, a particular vantage point which has nurtured a social wisdom."[53] *Truth's Table* offers a perspective on Christianity that is often silenced in mainstream church spaces. As one listener states, "As a black Christian woman, it means so much to me to see women who look like me boldly speaking the truth in love."[54]

The emergence of womanist theology in the 1980s and 1990s builds on Alice Walker's celebration of Black womanhood in her four-part definition of a "womanist."[55] In response to liberation theology that centered on Blackness and to feminist theology that focused on the divine femininity, Black female theologians articulate a spirituality, as Cannon states, "with the experience of Black women at center stage."[56] Along with centering the experiences of Black women, this approach celebrates the value of Black women. As Linda Thomas writes, "Womanist theology is critical reflection upon black women's place in the world that God has created and takes seriously black women's experience as human beings who are made in the image of God."[57] While Black women are often portrayed as the source of all problems in the church and society, womanist theology revalorizes Black women and the beauty of their souls.

The hosts of *Truth's Table* do the work of revalorizing Black women in a series of episodes titled "Embodied Blackness." Throughout the episodes, they frequently talk about "decolonizing" their own minds and the minds of the listeners to eliminate white supremacist ideologies that promote the idea that darker skin and textured hair are not beautiful. In one episode, "Crowns of Glory," the hosts share their own stories about the different hairstyles they have had and how dominant beauty standards have influenced them. Uwan notes that she tried to assimilate as a young girl by using popular hairstyles, and she had to learn to love her natural hair: "It was a long process of decolonizing my mind from the European standards of beauty that I had imbibed and taken in."[58] The hosts frequently discuss the importance of celebrating the beauty of all types of Black women's hair and dismantling beauty standards that are meant to divide women.

Furthermore, the hosts reiterate what Uwan says at the end of the episode, "What God has called good is great."[59] Edmondson describes the decision of how to wear her hair as a spiritual expression: "I think that what God did is good. And God is still doing these good things in the world and our bodies can be a representation of that." Similarly, Higgins discusses how Black women use their bodies to convey God's image to the world. "We are writing our story of Blackness, of womanhood, and we are doing this with our bodies," Higgins says. "We are already little epistles, writing His story on our bodies, by showing us, to show the world that His image is fly." Uwan, Edmondson, and Higgins all engage with their faith to assert the value of their lives, especially in the face of Christian churches that promote the inferiority of Black lives. These discussions remind listeners that God creates all people as beautiful, because everyone is created in the image of God.

In another episode of the same series, "Embodied Blackness: Colorism," the hosts take on issues of anti-Blackness within the Black community. The hosts share their experiences with this contentious topic from their different vantage points. As a light-complected Black woman, Edmondson discusses how people encouraged her to appear as more like white people when she worked in professional settings. Higgins says that her family members told her that she "lucked out" by having a medium skin tone. They would say things like, "You're obviously Black but not so dark that you are scary."[60] Uwan discusses how she feels "hypervisible" because of her darker skin. When she was a child, she even found it disgusting that her skin resembled the color of excrement. Having discussed how views of hairstyles harm Black Christians, the hosts show that Black Christians are also hurt by associating value with skin color.

The discussions in the "Embodied Blackness" series follow similar patterns, with each host sharing her personal experiences with beauty standards. As they discuss stories of growing up and learning about what is considered to be good hair or seeing the advantages of having lighter skin tones, the women offer support, like the affirming "ah-ha" or "hmm," small chuckles, and knowing sighs. Since podcasts have fewer limitations in terms of time or pressures to curate a perfect performance, the women have an open space among supportive friends to dig into the messy topic of how white supremacy causes self-hatred among Black Christians. This is a safe space away from critical outsiders for honest dialogues about issues, so the hosts also address how anti-Blackness is manifested in their own families and communities. The women do not hide the ways that white supremacy even infuses Black Christian churches, with their portrayals of a white Jesus and connections of whiteness to purity and holiness. After each woman is given space to share her personal experiences, the hosts turn to scripture and Black intellectuals to connect their individual stories to wider discussions about these issues. The structure of these episodes creates an entry point for listeners to connect to the confessions of the hosts, followed by dialogues about how to transcend the evil of white supremacy.

In the iTunes reviews of the show, several listeners comment that it is unprecedented, as the hosts center womanist theology and the issues that Black women face in religious spaces and larger society. "They [the hosts] provide a resounding positive voice to the joys and struggles to the journey that so many are on," one listener writes.[61] Several people comment that they feel empowered as their experiences as Black Christian women are heard and validated. "I love that black women are being HEARD!" one commenter writes. "This is what I do for self-care with the white idolatry of our world."[62] This podcast is needed to show the ways that white supremacy has infiltrated American Christianity. Another listener reflects on how the hosts bring up significant critiques: "Hard truths are spoken with candor and grace at this table. The voices of these women are exactly the voices the church in America needs to hear!"[63] The listeners appreciate the ways that the hosts use the experiences of Black Christian women to critique white supremacy and social injustices.

"MIDWIVES OF GRACE AND TRUTH"

Since most churches are not going to value Black women, *Truth's Table* constitutes a significant community to do this work of celebrating the spiritual lives of Black women. As the hosts often say at the beginning of the show, they become "midwives of grace and truth," bringing support and spiritual comfort to the community of Black women who listen to the show. In work similar to that of other individuals discussed in this book, the hosts use the podcast to create a healing space for people who have been harmed by teachings that define them as impure, unruly, sinful, or inferior. One listener discusses the ways that *Truth's Table* creates this space of healing and comfort. "As Solange said so eloquently, I am weary with the ways of this world. A world where I often feel unheard, misrepresented, misunderstood, and unappreciated," the listener notes in her iTunes review. "The women of Truth's Table have created a safe space for me to explore and process my own thoughts, questions, struggles, joys, fears, and identity as a Christ fearing and following Black woman."[64] The hosts use the podcast to validate the experiences of Black women and provide comfort against the daily onslaught of racism and misogyny.

As Uwan discusses in an episode on resistance in the Bible, Black women "embody this resistance" because of the way they are always resisting labels and are never quite enough.[65] Instead of serving as silent and pious icons of religion, all of the activists discussed in this book resist by calling religious institutions and communities back to the justice and equality that are central to Christianity and Islam. In the case of *Truth's Table*, the hosts do not promote personal, feel-good religious teachings but rather resist and challenge the oppression within religious spaces. As Uwan states, "we have to get rid of this domesticated Jesus" to address the real problems and power imbalances in society. In this powerful statement, she reminds listeners that Jesus is a marginalized figure who is not meant to comfort those in power by reinforcing the supremacy of whiteness. Instead, Jesus brings divine justice and love to those who have been oppressed.

In one episode, "Operation 'Sunken Place' Rescue," Edmondson, Higgins, and Uwan attempt to provide healing for listeners from a society that promotes white supremacy. The hosts use the concept of the "sunken place" from the film *Get Out* to discuss how Black people often internalize racism and believe the false ideology of white supremacy. Uwan discusses the global phenomenon of whiteness being seen as superior and how this promotes beauty trends that involve activities like skin whitening and hair straightening. The hosts also call out American Christian churches for promoting whiteness as the norm in Christianity when, as Edmondson points out, the scriptures were not written by white Americans. Furthermore, Uwan addresses how the iconography in churches promotes internalized racism when Jesus, Mary, and the saints are usually portrayed as white. This often leads to people imagining the Bible as full of white characters, but as Uwan exclaims, "There's not a white person in the Bible!"[66] This powerful exclamation demonstrates the work of this podcast to shake people out of a space of self-hatred. The hosts use such passionate statements to remind listeners of their inherent value. As Edmondson states, "We can't obey God's law to love each other well if we don't love ourselves." Again, the hosts use a structure of opening up about their own struggles with the forces of white supremacy and offer affirmation when each person speaks. Then the women build off each other's experiences as they use Jesus's revolutionary messages in scripture to provide comfort and healing.

In addition to bringing to light the ways that Black Christian spaces often reinforce the supremacy of whiteness through images of a white Jesus and valuing white European physical features, Edmondson, Uwan, and Higgins use the podcast as a space to discuss misogyny and patriarchy within religious communities. In an episode titled "Gender Apartheid," the hosts discuss how many Black Protestant churches do not view women as equal to men or give them the same authority to be leaders or preach. As Uwan reflects on the inequality of allowing only men to hold positions of influence, she sharply states that people need a "penis in order to be heard."[67] The hosts argue that just as racial reconciliation starts with hearing the experiences of nonwhite people, male church leaders need to realize the importance of listening to the experiences of women in the church. Black churches understand the harm of racism but are often unwilling to interrogate the ways in which patriarchy is embedded in the church.

In the episode "Embodied Blackness: Blackness as Being," the hosts build on their intersectional experiences to assert that the Black church needs to work toward social justice beyond racial issues. Black churches cannot ignore patriarchy and homophobia, for example, when they work to combat racism. In this episode Higgins discusses how "the Black struggle is intrinsic to how we pursue justice," which means that Black Americans must find ways to empathize with other marginalized communities.[68] For instance, Higgins recollects how during the initial days of the AIDS epidemic, very little information and few resources were devoted to this illness because it was seen as impacting only gay men. This experience helped Higgins understand the ways that she could use her experiences of social injustices because of her race and gender to collaborate with others who face structural oppression. Just as the hosts honestly discuss anti-Blackness within Black communities, they use the open space of the podcast to dialogue about injustices within Black Christian churches.

Finally, the hosts of *Truth's Table* frequently promote a mode of racial reconciliation within U.S. Christian churches that builds on theological teachings of repentance and forgiveness. While people in church spaces don't talk about radical ideas of racial reconciliation, the hosts use the podcast to argue for reparations, both material and spiritual. In one episode, the hosts refer to biblical examples of reparations to argue for racial reconciliation within churches that is built on repentance. Edmondson explains that reparations are not a negative concept like punishment, but in this case are about repairing a church that is broken because of the sins of racism. "Reparations is an expression of grace," Edmondson states. "It's making right as best as we can ... that which is broken or that which we benefit from being broken."[69] Christianity offers a spiritual example of what Uwan terms "eternal reparations," through which all people, who are sinners, seek to repent their misdeeds and make things right with God.

The hosts spend the remainder of the episode discussing how white Evangelical Christians need to come to terms with the legacy of slavery and white supremacy within their churches. Edmondson asserts that Christian leaders need to address the ways that white supremacy "warps" theology and creates hypocrisies.[70] For instance, Evangelical churches have to address "the contradictions of a pro-life movement that says nothing about racism," Edmondson states. As this podcast episode points out, U.S. Christians don't see racism or white supremacy as sins that need to be repented of, but rather as something of which they feel slightly guilty or ashamed. They don't see racism as a sin that needs to be uprooted from American Christianity. As the hosts share their stories and theological reflections at their metaphorical table, they call for spiritual reform that is rooted in the faith of Black Christian women.

SPIRITUAL COMFORT AND DIVINE JUSTICE

While justice for Black lives may not be sought in wider society or even in Christian churches, Uwan, Higgins, and Edmondson use their podcast as a prayerful space to appeal to God's justice and center on their spiritual experiences as Black Christian women. In a powerful episode titled "Strange Fruit," the hosts discuss the injustice of police shootings of Black people, specifically after the acquittal of the police officer who shot Philando Castile in his car. The hosts talk about their sadness at the devaluing of Black lives. "How much bravery is required to be Black," Higgins states. "We have to have us because ain't nobody got us."[71] Edmondson expresses her deep sadness: "I don't have enough energy to be angry." While Uwan points out that Jesus will come back to bring higher justice, she notes that it is still painful to live in a world of such injustice. She states, "God's character is not reflected in this broken and bunked system that we have here." The women take their time to work through their deep feelings of grief and raw emotions as they hear about another example of the way that racism is deeply embedded in American society.

In the "Strange Fruit" episode, Edmondson explains that most Christians have a "spiritual blindness" to the way white supremacy is entrenched in American churches and Evangelical theology. This failure to acknowledge white supremacy creates a deep rot in American Christianity. Edmondson explains, "People really eternally die when they have decided that the sin of racism is actually not a sin but rather the cornerstone of their theology."[72] She observes that white supremacy has become an idol that many Christian churches worship, and this idolatry seems to be confirmed by the white images of Jesus and other biblical figures, the silence on racism in church spaces, racial apartheid in Evangelical churches, and the association between Blackness and sin. For example, the hosts discuss how Christian churches rarely address the social injustices faced by nonwhite people and refuse to acknowledge that the churches are often racist and unwelcoming places. Edmondson's pain and frustration seep into the listener's ears as she explains: "There's something really wrong with American Evangelicalism when the first response that you get from people who claim that they love God is a lack of compassion and retraumatizing language and dehumanizing of people. And the fact that they will chuck their own doctrines in order to not have any sympathy. Wait a minute, I thought that you believed in total depravity but racism doesn't count? Oh, I see. It is so deeply disturbing and wicked." In this quote, Edmondson is directly calling out Evangelical Christians for failing to see racism as a sin that comes from humans' evil nature. She makes a strong theological argument—pointing to the Protestant belief that comes from John

Calvin—that humans are depraved and can be saved only through God's grace. Racism is not some ephemeral force that exists in secular society. Rather, it must be acknowledged as a sin that arises from our flawed human nature.

This emotionally moving episode resembles a religious ritual in which Black female listeners participate in this project to revalorize their lives in the face of society and churches that muddle the scriptures' revolutionary messages. "We don't value Black life in this country. It angers me to no end. Because we are made in the image of God," Uwan states. "That's why we really have to derive our worth from the scriptures, from Jesus Christ himself, because the state ain't gonna give it to us, the media ain't gonna give it to us, the church isn't going to give it to us."[73] Higgins builds on this message of the value of Black lives, saying that "the truth is that we are treated as fruit that can be plucked at any time, rather than the beautiful fruit of God's creative mind." This episode illustrates this work of revaluing the lives of Black women through a direct appeal to God's message that all people are created equal and in God's image. The show ends with Higgins reading the poem by Abel Meeropol titled "Strange Fruit," which is about lynching victims and relates to the larger theme of violence against Black lives. Then Edmondson reads a scripture passage about the fruits of the spirit, reminding listeners that they are not fruit to be plucked but have been given beautiful talents by God. Finally, Uwan ends the episode by reading the names of victims of police violence and states, "Black lives matter, they matter to God." This particular episode illustrates the larger work of *Truth's Table* to revalorize Black woman by appealing to their radical equality in the eyes of God, as well as the podcast's efforts to build new knowledge and theology based on the experiences of Black women.

CELEBRATING UNRULY SOULS BEYOND THE PODCASTS

On June 19, 2020, the hosts of *Truth's Table* celebrated the Juneteenth holiday of the liberation of all enslaved African Americans with a day-long prayer event on social media. Every hour from 8:00 A.M. to 7:00 P.M., different religious figures offered their reflections on a Bible passage in streaming platforms like Instagram Live or Facebook Live. The hundreds of participants who joined throughout the day prayed along and commented with the praying hands emoticon or expressions of praise. The final prayer event was hosted by Uwan and Edmondson and has been viewed over four thousand times since it was posted. In the post announcing the prayer event, the women explain that Juneteenth is often a day of prayer and celebration of liberation. They write in the post, "We are grateful to God for the liberation He wrought on behalf of our ancestors as we continue to fight for earthly justice that points to the divine justice that God will establish for us upon Jesus' return."[74] The digital spaces of Instagram and Facebook extend the communal space and prayer experiences of *Truth's Table*, as this event facilitates healing and points toward the hope for divine justice.

This event reflects the wider project of *Truth's Table*, as digital sites like podcasts and social media create a prayerful space and a supportive community away from the forces of white supremacy and misogyny. The conversations that happen in this podcast are dialogues that build on the womanist tradition of formulating spirituality from the daily experiences and friendships of Black women. While *Truth's Table* does work similar to that of other projects discussed in this book by providing an outlet for people marginalized in traditional religious sites, podcasting provides a distinct platform for these women to have extensive and authentic dialogues that dig deep into messy topics within a supportive, close-knit community of friends. The hosts of *Truth's Table*—along with the creators of shows like *Exvangelical, Queerology,* and *The Liturgists*—use their podcast conversations to call out American Christians for misconstruing the messages of Jesus. These podcasts critique Christian churches and leaders for worshipping at the altar of white supremacy, dismissing queer Christians as intrinsically flawed, and silencing the voices of women. Speaking from the position of unruly souls, marginalized in traditional religious spaces, these individuals use podcast episodes to celebrate the figure of Jesus as a holy misfit who challenged the status quo and called out social injustices. With few restrictions on time, style, or content, podcasts allow for productive dialogues that build new faith traditions centered on the experiences of Black women, queer individuals, and all other religious outcasts.

5 · "WE THEM BARBARIANS"
Digital Videos Creatively Rearticulate Muslim Identity

In the early days of hip-hop, releasing a music video was one of the most effective ways for new artists to get their work out to listeners. In December 1989, for example, a teenage emcee (MC) named Queen Latifah exploded onto the scene with a video for her song "Ladies First," a feminist anthem that celebrates Black women. "For me, in my heart, it was anthemic. It was made to say, ladies, treat yourself like number one," Queen Latifah explains in a documentary about the song. "We just wanted to show unity, love."[1] The video for "Ladies First" illustrates the ability of music videos to convey layered meanings. As Robin Roberts explains, videos allow "one message to be communicated through the lyrics while a complementary message is carried through images."[2] Through the blending of symbols of Black pride, the visuals of women rapping together, the images of racial injustices across the globe, and the lyrics reinforcing the idea of "ladies first," Queen Latifah created an intersectional feminist anthem that contradicts the misogyny of hip-hop culture and critiques the racism and sexism of American society.

More than three decades later, music videos remain a powerful, creative space to layer various elements on top of each other, and the distribution of these videos has spread thanks to the ability of digital spaces to circulate and remediate them. In March 2017, a new hip-hop queen emerged on the stage when Mona Haydar, an Arab American Muslim from Flint, Michigan, released her first song on YouTube. Similar to "Ladies First," Haydar's video for "Hijabi (Wrap my Hijab)" serves as an anthem of pride, celebrating and uplifting Muslim women. "The goal of the video was to bring the medicine, to bring a kind of balm," Haydar explained to me. "And to say that I see you. Whoever you are, whatever your struggle is, covered up or not, I see you."[3] When Queen Latifah released "Ladies First," there was a need for an anthem that would unite female rappers against the misogyny of the industry as well as celebrating their inherent value. Haydar sees "Hijabi (Wrap my Hijab)" as taking on a similar anthemic role: "I wanted to put out a radically affirming call to love for everybody everywhere who ever had somebody tell them that they couldn't do something simply because a man said so."[4]

Continuing the tradition of hip-hop videos, Haydar's video layers various elements, such as music beats, lyrics, visuals, editing, camera angles, gestures, fashion, and lighting, to convey a message of love and acceptance of all—especially people marginalized or deemed unruly. Young Black women in the early 1990s would go around singing "ladies first, ladies first" to express pride and unity, and young Muslim women similarly circulate Haydar's videos now through digital media channels. "Hijabi (Wrap my Hijab)" has been viewed over eight million times on YouTube. In this chapter, I shift my focus to the multilayered space of digital music videos, which illustrate the convergence of the digital moment with the blending of visuals, music, fashion, and online spread. While the chapter addresses how hip-hop has been a productive space for the exploration of various religious identities and spirituality, it will focus on the Muslim American rapper Haydar and the Muslim art collective Mipsterz. As I discuss throughout the chapter, there are several overlaps between some of the early Black female rappers like Queen Latifah, MC Lyte, and Salt-N-Pepa and contemporary Muslim American women. Both groups are placed in an intersectional position, facing misogyny within their cultural communities while fighting racism and sexism in the wider society. Both groups find a productive space in hip-hop music videos to unapologetically express their complex identities and experiences. Although Christian spirituality has often been discussed in hip-hop music, this chapter mainly focuses on Muslim Americans, since they more easily relate to hip-hop culture and its focus on marginalized and unruly experiences than Christians do.

Since their emergence from urban American spaces, hip-hop culture and rap music have been theorized as modes of resistance for marginalized voices. Building on the foundational work of hip-hop scholarship, this chapter examines how digital media enhance the creative resistance of hip-hop music. Through an in-depth analysis of several of Haydar's videos and "ALHAMDU," the Mipsterz' multimedia project, this chapter focuses on the multisensory, layered, hybrid, flexible, and playful nature of digital music videos. These multisensory features and hybrid styles enable Muslim Americans to creatively and playfully insert intersectional feminist critiques into their videos while also celebrating their religious identity, which is so often denigrated. At the same time, these digital video projects do more than illustrate the normality of Muslim Americans, contradicting the dehumanizing stereotypes. Rather than always responding to misrepresentations, the projects enable Muslim Americans to imagine, as stated on the "ALHAMDU" Kickstarter page, "a vibrant and joyous future where Muslims exist unapologetically."[5] The digital videos provide healing and supportive spaces for Muslim Americans to imagine a future that centers on the inherent value of Muslim lives.

VOICES FROM THE MARGINS

Growing up in the 1980s and 1990s in Flint, Haydar observed how hip-hop and the spoken word could be used as part of social justice work and, as she says, "a tool for liberation."[6] She found a cultural home where she had a voice to express herself. At the same time, she explained to me, "I was also taught that I had a responsibility to that voice. And I had a responsibility to tell the truth and to speak about justice and social issues and to work for the more beautiful world through whatever means I had available to me." Haydar sees herself as part of a longer lineage of people using hip-hop as a tool for justice and liberation, while she acknowledges the ways that capitalist forces have often co-opted the industry to promote more lucrative music about sex, drugs, violence, and greed.

As hip-hop music emerged in American cities in the 1980s, it addressed a wide range of topics that often reflected the experiences of racial injustice and economic oppression. As Tricia Rose writes in her groundbreaking book on hip-hop culture, *Black Noise*, "Rap's stories continue to articulate the shifting terms of black marginality in contemporary American culture."[7] Even as rap music becomes more popular in mainstream American culture, Rose explains that the music still has a contradictory relationship to American culture. She writes that rap music "is at once part of the dominant text and, yet, always on the margins of this text; relying on and commenting on the text's center and always aware of its proximity to the border."[8] Hip-hop artists often find themselves both in the center of American culture and addressing the continued marginality and oppression of Black Americans.

While hip-hop music often addresses political issues related to social injustices, there is not always a clear-cut distinction between political music and commercial music about more lurid and illicit topics. For instance, Nancy Guevara discusses how rap music can focus on "themes of sex, money, and power," but this is often a way for Black Americans to struggle with and contest their subjugation in white-dominated society.[9] As S. Craig Watkins writes, hip-hop music and culture enables young people in particular "to find their voice and place in the world."[10] The music can provide a space for young people to express themselves and develop their consciousness of wider political issues. Daniel White Hodge explains that "Hip Hop was, and still is, a way to construct thought, question authority and express anger, frustration, hate, revolutionary world-views and rebellious spirits."[11] While not all hip-hop music promotes political activism, at its essence this music is a cultural form that addresses the experiences of people who are oppressed and marginalized in society. Hodge writes, "Hip Hop at its core—not the commercialization and commodity it has become in certain respects—rejects dominant forms of culture and society and seeks to increase a social consciousness along with a racial/ethnic pride."[12] Although hip-hop is especially popular among African Americans, it has also taken root in other communities because it offers a productive space to speak from the margins while celebrating the value of lives that are too often denigrated.

Especially for women and girls, hip-hop music and videos offer creative ways to challenge their objectification. As Mary Celeste Kearney explains, hip-hop culture often attracted "non-conformist female youth" who were seeking a space of creative resistance.[13] She writes, "Thus, much like punk, hip-hop provided an alternative place for girls' resistance to both patriarchal and feminist constructions of femininity during the 1970s, as well as a space for their more active engagement in cultural production."[14] Hip-hop culture provides a space for the articulation of a variety of experiences of marginality. Despite the prevalence of misogyny in rap lyrics and the hypersexualization of women in hip-hop videos, William Eric Perkins argues that women rappers challenge "hip hop's culture and its attitude of male centeredness" by "turning women from object into subject."[15] From the early days of hip-hop music, women have always been involved as MCs and DJs, but the corporatization of the music often pushed the women into the background as dancers or pressed the female rappers to use their sexuality to sell records. Despite this pressure, some female rappers challenged the misogyny and racism that they experienced in their daily lives. For example, Sister Souljah adopted the label "raptivist," using hip-hop "to promote the causes of the African world while healing its wounds and scars."[16] As shown in Queen Latifah's work with "Ladies First," hip-hop music can provide a healing space of unity and self-love.

Rose points out that female rappers often use music to negotiate "social contradictions and ambiguities," especially in terms of their sexualities.[17] Therefore, it's not the case that all Black male rappers are sexist and all female rappers are feminists.[18] In exploring the work of early Black female rappers, Rose finds that they "provide for themselves a relatively safe free-play zone where they creatively address questions of sexual power, the reality of truncated economic opportunity, and the pain of racism and sexism."[19] Black women often face oppression and critiques from multiple sides. For example, Black women deal with the threat of sexual violence as well as with misogyny from Black men. At the same time, the women don't want to hide their sexualities or be used as examples of the problems with Black men. Just as Muslim women are often positioned as victims of Muslim men, Black women are often viewed as icons of the problems with Black male rappers who appear as overly violent and sexual. As Rose explains, "these female rappers felt that they were being used as a political baton to beat male rappers over the head, rather than being affirmed as women who could open up public dialogue to interrogate sexism and its effects on young black women."[20] Therefore, hip-hop music provides an important space for dialogue and critique about the complexities of women's experiences.

Adding the visual layer of a music video to hip-hop music enables a more substantial exploration of marginalized experiences. Beyoncé's groundbreaking visual album, *Lemonade*, illustrates the potential of this medium, especially to celebrate the spirituality of Black women. Rooted in the womanist tradition, *Lemonade* visually celebrates, as Yolanda Pierce explains, "how black women know and understand the sacred and participate in God-talk."[21] While Black women are rarely given a voice in religious spaces and are frequently disparaged in mainstream culture, creative spaces of art, music, dance, and visuals enable them to articulate their value. Pierce explains that although Black women might not see themselves in church spaces, the lyrics and visuals in *Lemonade* serve as reminders to these women that "they are still reflected in the divine."[22] The videos incorporate Christian symbolism like the water of baptism, along with aspects of African diasporic spirituality like Yoruba dieties as a way of celebrating the divine nature of Black women. As Tamara Henry writes, "Beyoncé uses religious symbolism and rituals within *Lemonade* alongside images of black women as means of re-presenting the sacred through black women's lives."[23] The visual album allows Beyoncé to celebrate the spiritual lives of Black women while also addressing their experiences of oppression. As I discuss in the rest of this chapter, Muslim American artists also engage with the creative potential of digital videos and hip-hop lyrics to articulate that Muslims of all shapes, skin colors, sexualities, and backgrounds are made in the image of God.

CREATIVE RESISTANCE IN DIGITAL MEDIA

Along with the potential of hip-hop music to give voice to people on the margins of society, the flexibility of new media spaces adds more layers of creative resistance. The artistic projects of Haydar and the Mipsterz build on a long tradition of those ostracized from mainstream culture finding productive modes of expression in alternative media spaces. For instance, in her foundational work on girls' media production, Kearney discusses how teenage girls use media spaces to respond to the ways that their concerns are ignored or misconstrued in mainstream cultural spaces. She explains that "many girl media producers rely on the practices of appropriation and *détournement* to reconfigure commercial cultural artifacts into personalized creations that speak more directly to their concerns, needs, fantasies, and pleasures."[24] Through an engagement with bell hooks's concept of "talking back,"[25] Kearney discusses how young women use media spaces like zines and independent magazines to move from object into subject as they represent themselves and discuss issues that are relevant to them. Similarly, in her music videos Haydar discusses issues relevant to Muslim women that are generally unaddressed in mainstream culture or Islamic communities.

Additionally, the creativity of alternative media spaces like zines and blogs offers a space for young women to explore what Kearney calls "unruly identities that subvert traditional notions of girlhood."[26] She gives punk feminism as one example of how individuals deploy unruly and carnivalesque aesthetics as a form of activism. For instance, the practice of *détournement* works by "appropriating objects, text, and the images from their original contexts and placing them in different contexts, often by juxtaposing them with other material that seems unrelated."[27] This confrontational style of activism deploys "jarring, confrontational aesthetics in order to prevent audiences from making traditional meanings and to force them into seeing new connections between disparate objects, ideas, and experiences."[28] Similar work can be seen in the productions of hip-hop artists like Haydar and the Mipsterz, who embrace labels like "barbarian," flip representations on their heads, bring together disparate elements like Islam and futurism, and ultimately celebrate unruliness and disorder. As Haydar states at the beginning of her song "Barbarian," "If they're civilized, then I'd rather stay savage."[29] If such labels continue to be attached to these bodies, then people will eventually embrace the labels and turn them into something productive.

"KEEP SWAGGIN' MY HIJABIS"

While pregnant with her second child in early 2017, Haydar traveled to the Standing Rock Reservation in North Dakota to protest the building of a pipeline on tribal land. She was participating as part of a decolonial liturgy project for her graduate work in Christian ethics at Union Theological Seminary, in New York City. Since she was seven months pregnant, Haydar was uncertain how she could fully contribute to the activist work against the building of the Dakota Access Pipeline. As she approached the camp where protestors were staying, a woman water protector who identified herself to Haydar as Lakota touched Haydar's belly and exclaimed that she had "brought the good medicine."[30] Haydar spent the rest of her time at the camp helping cook for the activists on the front lines and bringing the "medicine" of the new life growing inside her.

Haydar had been waiting to deliver her baby and lose the baby weight before shooting a video for the song "Hijabi (Wrap my Hijab)," but this experience inspired her not to wait. She flew back to Detroit, Michigan, to record the video. While at Standing Rock, she had received a vision for the video and wanted to "bring the medicine" to a wider audience and celebrate the beauty of "women of every shadin'," as the song states.[31] "What I was trying to do was to center my nonstandard body type, the body of a pregnant woman, which isn't something necessarily celebrated and is almost deemed strange, shameful, and not appropriate for something like a music video," Haydar explained to me. "I had to challenge my own beliefs about my body and see the body I had at that time as being worthy of being center stage."[32] The video celebrates the beauty of all types of body shapes, skin colors, clothing styles, and modesty coverings. Most importantly, it was intended to be a "balm" or a healing space for women, Muslim or not, who are criticized, harassed, or oppressed because of who they are or the choices they make. As the song repeats, "All around the world / Love women every shading / be so liberated." With her round pregnant belly prominent on screen, Haydar raps, "I still wrap my hijab" and "keep swaggin' my hijabis."[33] The lyrics are a healing source of love, pride, and unity, specifically for Muslim women who face harassment and prejudice in daily life while also fighting racism and colorism within Muslim communities.

Since "Hijabi (Wrap my Hijab)" was Haydar's first music video, it is relevant to examine the layering within the video. In her early work on rap music, Rose discusses how music videos add additional elements of meaning to the music: "Music video is a collaboration in the production of popular music; revises meanings, provides preferred interpretations of lyrics, creates a stylistic and physical context for reception; and valorizes the iconic presence of the artist."[34] First, the layering of the visual style in the video reinforces the messages in the lyrics. The video features a mix of young women from different ethnic groups wearing different styles of headscarves. In some scenes the women surround Haydar while she raps, and in other scenes they dance and sing along. Haydar told me that the video producers put out an open call in the Detroit area for participants in the video.[35] The visual presence of an eclectic group of Muslim women reinforces the lyrics that celebrate the beauty of women of all shapes, colors, ethnicities, and faith traditions.

Second, this video showcases the layering of political meaning inherent in the bodies of these women, who are often deemed unruly. Haydar describes to me how her body is often politicized, especially when she appears as a pregnant Muslim woman of color in "Hijabi (Wrap my Hijab)." Haydar and the other participants in the video embrace the ways that their bodies are layered with political meaning, but they also demonstrate pride in their complex and intersecting identities. "I definitely thought about all of the layers of how I could best use what was available to me, what I had access to, which is first and foremost my own body, and secondly my talents," Haydar told me. "Additionally, I had a community consisting of friends and friends of friends who had cameras and videography skills. All this was put towards the goal of presenting ourselves in a narrative that we felt was true and real, versus in a narrative that feels racist and wrong, which is what we would often see in mainstream media."[36] It is a powerful gesture for Haydar and the other participants to present their bodies as they are and to celebrate their layers and intersections. As Haydar explains to me, "All of that is a coming together and layering that is a beautiful representation of a diverse community that is organic to people of color [POC] and specifically to the artist POC community."

Haydar's first video not only centers the bodies of a diverse group of hijabis. It also layers fashion, gesture, background scenery, and music styles to reinforce this celebration of the diverse styles of Muslim women. Almost thirty years before "Hijabi (Wrap my Hijab)" was released, Queen Latifah similarly used a layering of styles and meaning in her video for "Ladies First" to cultivate pride and unity among Black women. As Rose writes, "Latifah positions herself as part of a rich legacy of black women's activism, racial commitment, and cultural pride."[37] Latifah accomplishes this through the stylistic aspects of the video, such as wearing a general's jacket, accented with African patterns, along with an African head wrap that resembles a crown. Latifah also appears standing strong and tall alongside other women in the video, displaying both her strength and her unity with other women. A group of women dance and sing the refrain "Ohh, ladies first, ladies first." Finally, in some scenes Latifah raps with images of famous Black women leaders, such as Harriet Tubman and Rosa Parks, projected behind her. The visual images connect Latifah to other strong Black women in history, while her fashion styles reinforce her power and leadership. At the same time, the presence of other women illustrates the strength of women when they come together.

The video for "Hijabi (Wrap my Hijab)" employs parallel stylistic elements to emphasize the pride and unity of Muslim women. Haydar appears in several scenes surrounded by other Muslim women who sing or dance to the song. While the women wrap their headscarves in different styles, they all wear loose, flowing clothing in soft colors—pinks, mauves, and tans. The background in a lot of the scenes is a tan stairway, while other scenes are filmed in a dimly lit room that appears to be under renovation. Another backdrop features a wall paneled in dark wood and resembling a Gothic chapel. A few scenes reflect an Islamic aesthetic style, such as the one in which Haydar appears in front of a wall ornately painted with Arabic script and scenes in front of a blue and orange floral mosaic. The more neutral backgrounds and color palettes of the outfits emphasize the unity of the women and accentuate their distinct body shapes, skin colors, and hijab styles. Similar to how all the women sing "ladies first" in Queen Latifah's breakout video, Haydar is surrounded by other Muslim hijabis who support her as they sing "wrap my hijab" and do a coordinated hand motion of wrapping their headscarves. While strength and pride in Black femininity is reflected in Queen Latifah's use of African fashion styles and gestures such as holding her head high, Haydar's video uses Islamic fashion and aesthetic styles in the backdrops along with a prominent Arab musical riff behind her rapping to celebrate the beauty of non-Western styles.

In addition to writing about adding layers of meaning to rap lyrics, Rose discusses how the music video "valorizes the iconic presence of the artist." Perhaps more than other musical genres, the videos for hip-hop songs often help individual artists reach the status of queen or king. While often misinterpreted as examples of the narcissism, arrogance, and greed of hip-hop culture, these gestures of pride and symbols of status are actions that radically assert the value of lives that are too often marginalized. In the face of a culture that denigrates Black women, Queen Latifah raps in "Ladies First" that she is "divine" and a "perfect specimen." She also takes on the moniker "Queen," wears a hair wrap as a crown, and holds her head high to convey that she is an assertive leader.

Additionally, Rose notes that music videos often establish a rapper's location within a particular community: "Nothing is more central to rap's music video narratives than situating the rapper in his or her milieu and among one's crew or posse."[38] The videos give young rappers, coming from economically disadvantaged areas the power to "have their territories acknowledged, recognized, and celebrated."[39] Music videos give marginalized voices a chance to speak for themselves and have their concerns and experiences recognized. "In rap videos, young mostly male residents speak for themselves and for the community, they speak when and how they wish about subjects of their choosing," Rose writes. "These local turf scenes are not isolated voices; they are voices from a variety of social margins that are in dialogue with one another."[40] While most of the early rap videos that Rose discusses feature young Black male rappers speaking from urban locations, the video for "Hijabi (Wrap my Hijab)" does similar work, establishing Haydar's credentials by positioning her in her hometown among her fellow hijabis. For instance, several scenes in the video feature Haydar and her round pregnant belly in the center of the frame, surrounded by her posse of hijabis. Haydar is presented as a figure of strength and agency, even though she occupies a body that is often misconstrued as weak and helpless.

Along with establishing the power and significance of Muslim women through the common hip-hop video techniques of filming in your own locale among your crew, Haydar and the women in the video intentionally use an oppositional gaze in "Hijabi (Wrap my Hijab)" to reject the Western male gaze and to assert their agency. In many of the scenes, Haydar and the other women appear without strong facial expressions. Haydar specifically directed the women to use a "deadpan" expression.[41] Some viewers criticized the women in the video for not smiling or looking happy, but Haydar wasn't trying to please the viewer. "I'm not pandering to the male gaze or any gaze. I'm not asking for adoration. I'm not asking for validation. I'm not trying to win anyone over with that video," Haydar told me. "I'm saying, here I am. Like it or not we survive, and we continue to create art. It was definitely an intentional exercise in subverting the male gaze and in saying, 'We are not using our bodies to either repel or attract anyone. We are just here.'" This video was created to inspire pride and self-love in Muslim women and other women who have been marginalized. While some scenes feature the women dancing, smiling, and enjoying themselves, these gestures are for the pleasure of the women within this community and not for the sexualized or exoticized gaze of someone outside of the community. The women refuse to return the gaze of the viewer, but they find enjoyment among themselves as they laugh and smile while gazing at each other.

The "Hijabi (Wrap my Hijab)" video is notably distinct from feminist rap anthems of the past because of how the video spread online, as people commented on it, expressed their support for and approval of the women in it, shared images and GIFs from it, and posted their favorite lines from the song on social media. Not only did people share links to the video on social media pages, but news sites and culture websites all over the world published articles on the song. The video has been viewed on YouTube over eight million times and garnered over thirty thousand comments. Haydar's original post announcing the video on Twitter got over 3,000 likes and 2,400 retweets, while her Instagram preview of the video was viewed 97,000 times. A glance at the Tweets from the first month after the video's release illustrates support for the video coming from Muslims and non-Muslims in English as well as Arabic, Turkish, French, Spanish, and German. While some Tweets criticized the style of music, attacked the video because of its political message, or trolled the comment thread with anti-Islam content, the majority of the comments offered approval and support.

The digital spread of "Hijabi (Wrap my Hijab)" allows Muslim women, both those who wear the hijab and those who don't, to share in this expression of pride and unity. On Twitter, people often share their favorite lines from the song, such as "Keep swaggin' my hijabis" and "So even if you hate it, I still wrap my hijab." Sharing these lines expresses pride in being a Muslim woman who wears the hijab, even amid harassment and stereotypes. People also post fire or heart emojis along with positive feedback such as "this song is dope ... beat so lit too."[42] Other people comment on how "amazing"[43] the video is or say how much they "love"[44] it or that it is "beyond perfection."[45] Fans on social media discuss how they have been singing along to the catchy song as they go about their daily life, as also happened with the "ladies first" mantra from Queen Latifah. One person tweeted, "this is my anthem now I feel like singing this all around campus."[46] Another fan of the video made short GIFs that highlight the moments when the women are really expressive with their gestures. These GIFs were then retweeted with approving comments, adding layers of meaning and allowing other people to connect to the unifying message of the video. The digital tools have enabled this video to spread and allowed viewers to add their own reflections as they help create this larger hijabi community.

"YOU'RE A DOG AT NIGHT"

Although viewers may have initially interpreted Haydar's work as a bubbly, positive portrayal of hijabis to counter stereotypes, one of her next videos, "Dog," clearly solidified her position as an unruly soul who seeks to call out injustices, especially within religious communities. This music video is a biting critique of male leaders in Muslim communities who constantly criticize Muslim women for not being modest enough in their public dress and behavior and then harass and assault women behind closed doors. Haydar leans into her unruliness in this video and refuses to be a sweet, quiet, and passive Muslim woman. As I discussed in chapters 2 and 3, women in religions like Islam and Evangelical Christianity that promote conservative standards of modesty and sexuality often place women in an impossible position: they are told to cover themselves and be passive toward men, but they are still faced with sexual harassment and are blamed if they are sexually assaulted.

Haydar uses the video for "Dog" to address these hypocrisies and call for reform in Islamic circles as well as larger society. The problem does not come out of religious spaces, she explained to me: "We have a patriarchy problem. We have a 'men in power who are sexually violent,' problem. I am not against patriarchy as a concept on its own. I am against oppression and how patriarchy is too often weaponized against women."[47] Haydar sees her work as fitting into a larger tradition of religious misfits and artists who call out systematic oppression like misogyny, racism, and capitalism. "The work of an artist is to lean into that which is challenging, to identify that which is wrong, and to tell stories and make art which help society enter into a more just, equitable, beautiful, and peaceful world," Haydar told me.

The music video for "Dog" illustrates how Haydar uses the assertive, playful, and humorous aspects of hip-hop music to present a stinging critique of misogyny while also creating a supportive space for people recovering from sexual trauma. Hip-hop culture is often associated with masculine power or "male swagger and self-boasting," as Watkins writes.[48] But while that culture is criticized for promoting egotism, bragging, and excess, especially among men, female artists have been able to use it to make their voices heard. As Roberts discusses, female rappers have long used the form to "make explicit assertions of female strength and autonomy. Since rap revolves around self-promotion, female rappers are able to use the form without appearing to be unduly narcissistic."[49] Throughout the video for "Dog," Haydar makes confident gestures with her hands and body that reinforce the critique in her lyrics. For instance, she raps while staring straight into the camera, sometimes with a blank expression and sometimes rolling her eyes in frustration. To demonstrate authority, she also uses common hip-hop gestures of moving her hands around to occupy a wide space and signal her control over her body. At other points, she wags her finger in disappointment, waves her hand over her nose to signal a foul smell, puts her hands together as if in prayer, and dramatically waves goodbye. The camera angles also reinforce Haydar's authority. She is often shown straight on or from a lower camera angle, which Watkins explains is a common hip-hop technique used to make rappers appear "larger than life."[50] These gestures highlight Haydar's authority, but they also signal that this video is a caustic takedown of these "dogs," or men who harass and assault women. Haydar rattles off the indiscretions of these men while her facial expressions and body movements express her complete exasperation with them.

Another common hip-hop video technique that Haydar deploys in "Dog" is to rap in front of a backup crew. She raps by herself in about half of the video, but several scenes feature the actress Jackie Cruz, who dances behind her and sings along with the chorus, "Say you can save my spirit / But you're a dog at night."[51] In another scene later in the video, Haydar raps in front of a carousel, and a posse of about eight women stand behind her. A larger group of women can be heard echoing the song's refrain, "He's a dog." Having this crew of other women backing Haydar up both on screen and in the song demonstrates the support and unity of the women. With such a harsh critique in the song, it is important for Haydar to build a barrier against the misogynistic counterattacks that she is bound to face.

Along with her assertive visual gestures in the video, Haydar uses the playful style of rap lyrics to point to the hypocrisy of the men who claim religious authority but are so disgusting and offensive in their interactions with women. The opening line clearly illustrates this language play: "Sheikhs on the DL / sheikhs in my DM / begging me to shake it on my cam in the PM."[52] These lines point to the duplicity when a "sheikh" or religious scholar or leader constantly criticizes women for not being modest and pious enough but then goes on the DL (down low) and into the DMs (direct messages) to harass women or ask for sexual favors. This playfulness with language continues when Haydar raps, "Say my voice is haram / Cuz you getting turned on / Boy you might need Qur'an." Later in the song, she states, "Emotional terrorist / Thinking that you're errorless / But you need a therapist / Boy you need an exorcist." These lines illustrate how these male religious leaders repeatedly blame women for their sexual indiscretions rather than acknowledging their own sinfulness.

Playing with language by layering multiple meanings on top of each other and using coded language is part of an established hip-hop tradition. As Rose writes, hip-hop music "uses cloaked speech and disguised cultural codes to comment on and challenge aspects of current power inequalities."[53] By using language from her particular religious culture (such as "sheikhs," "haram," and "Qur'an") along with terms from American culture (like "terrorist," "therapist," "exorcist," "on the DL," and "in my DM"), Haydar is able to more effectively critique inequalities and contradictions. She states in the opening of her video, "If you think this song is about you, I don't know what to tell you." Then the song uses hyperspecific cultural language to directly address the men who claim to be pious religious leaders while harming and harassing women.

The video and lyrics for "Dog" often refer to Islamic teachings and even specific Arabic phrases, which Haydar raps in Arabic while the English translation appears on the screen. For instance, one scene refers to Qur'anic teachings when Haydar raps in Arabic, translated as: "Better watch out for your enemy. If you please, lower your gaze. / If you please, fear your Lord." The use of Arabic here is both a way for Haydar to continue to have fun with language by using phrasing with the best flow but also to demonstrate her religious authority to speak about these topics. Haydar is well aware of the teachings that are constantly repeated to young women to get them to dress and behave modestly. Again, she flips these teachings on their head to point out that men also bear responsibility for maintaining piety in the community. The male leaders need to practice what they preach and acknowledge their own sinfulness.

While hip-hop music videos have often been critiqued for including sexist lyrics and using women as eye candy, some of the earlier female rappers engaged with humor to critique men and claim a space in hip-hop culture. As Rose discusses, these female artists use their music to respond to misogyny in hip-hop culture, but more importantly this discursive work "must also entail the development of sustained, strong female voices which stake claim to public space generally."[54] Haydar's song "Dog" is part of a long tradition of female MCs aggressively taking men down by labeling them dogs or tramps, as Salt-N-Pepa do in the song, "Tramp." These songs, Rose writes, "are caustic, witty and aggressive warnings directed at men and at other women who might be seduced by them in the future."[55] The songs assertively eviscerate these men while also reinforcing the agency and what Rose calls the "self-possession" of the women.[56]

Along with the layering of language, Haydar employs caustic humor to further critique these men while celebrating the strength and unity of women in the face of this misogyny. A common strategy in her humorous lyrics is to point out how these men fail to live up to their boasts. For instance, she raps, "A teacher? A guru? / Mm, you just some doo-doo / Said I own the whole souk / But you just sell produce / Boy you ain't got no juice / Boy you drive an old coup."[57] In other sections, she insults the men with lines like "But you work at Chuckie Cheese" and "Sorry I have allergies / Allergic to your salary." In all of these examples, Haydar plays off the boasts that these Muslim men make: they are religious teachers, have high-paying jobs, run their own businesses, or drive fancy cars. Her insults are fairly juvenile, comparing the men to excrement or saying they work in minimum-wage jobs. At the same time, her sarcastic style in the lyrics and gestures indicates that she actually doesn't care about these boasts. She's less concerned with where the men work or what kind of car they drive than she is with how they treat women. In the final scene, this caustic humor is in full force when Haydar raps, "Oh my God, you need God" in a high-pitched voice. She shrugs her shoulders in exasperation at these men, and then she walks away while raising her hands in a gesture of celebration.

Although "Dog" uses humor and playfulness to produce a harsh critique, Haydar also uses the video to celebrate the strength of women, especially those victimized by men, and to facilitate a space of healing and comfort. As she raps a common refrain in Arab feminist circles—"*Sawtil mar'a thawra* (A woman's voice is revolution)"—female listeners feel united and empowered. In our conversation, Haydar discussed how she found that using humor is an easier way to attract more people to your message. In the case of "Dog," humor allows Haydar not only to cleverly critique misogyny within Islamic spaces but also to create an uplifting video for women. She doesn't disregard the trauma and suffering in the world, which she is aware of as a Muslim American with roots in Syria. However, at the same time, she finds that humor and laughter help to lighten the suffering:

> My music has been a channel for me to talk about difficult things in ways that are uplifting and healing and loving rather than ways that are retraumatizing. So many of the people who listen to and like my music come from colonized or enslaved histories, and I seek to create art that challenges the narrative that we are nothing more than traumatized people. I hope to create a way for healing and moving forward, not a way of lingering in victimhood, because I was taught by my elders that I shape my reality and that my reality is one of agency. We take our pain and transform it into beauty. This is alchemy. When we are able to laugh in spite of our pain, and I know this isn't easy, it can be so healing. Lightheartedness, gentleness, simplicity, and generosity of spirit are all tools at an artist's disposal for healing.[58]

Haydar's words reflect a common thread throughout the examples in this book: the use of humor, hybridity, and playfulness to cleverly take down people in positions of power while at the same time creating healing spaces for individuals traumatized by exclusionary religious teachings. As Haydar explains, "Dog" tackles topics that are extremely upsetting and related to sexual assault and harassment in religious communities. "I knew I needed to write a song about this, but I wasn't sure I could do it in a healing way, in a way that wasn't going to just trigger people and traumatize people," Haydar told me. "I wanted to talk about it in a way that could help make people feel seen while also celebrating our resilience."[59] The video for "Dog" illustrates the potential of digital music videos not only to bring to light the issues of sexual assault and harassment in religious spaces but also to cultivate a feeling among victims that they are not alone and not sinful, impure, or flawed. The layered aspects and flexible style of digital music videos enable Haydar to convey this multivalent message of political critique and emotional support.

"SAY IT AGAIN, BEAUTIFUL BARBARIANS"

Since her emergence with "Hijabi (Wrap my Hijab)" in the spring of 2017, Haydar has released about a dozen new songs along with several videos. In November 2018, she distributed an EP Barbarican, that contained five songs, including "Barbarian." Released in June 2018, the video for "Barbarian" illustrates how skillfully Haydar combines astute lyrics with a multisensory style. Throughout the video, Haydar engages with the playful tactics like mimicry and rearticulation to embrace and celebrate the negative stereotypes that are often applied to colonized bodies. This creative approach is not used simply to prove that women

FIGURE 8. Still from Mona Haydar's "Barbarian" music video. Haydar (sitting on the right) lounges with two other women in a pose reminiscent of Orientalist paintings.

should be treated as equal human beings. Rather, Haydar and the other women in the video illustrate that their culture, style, and existence should be valued on their own terms. Muslims don't need to prove their humanity or to abandon their religious values to fit into American culture. Instead, "Barbarian" celebrates the superiority of these cultural and religious traditions that are regularly denigrated. The visual elements of the video and Haydar's lyrics flip the script and embrace labels like "savage," "exotic," and "barbarian" while at the same time pointing to the flaws in the dominant white European and American cultures.

The video opens with a shot of a colorful plate of fruit surrounded by folded legs, covered in vibrant materials. The video then presents quick clips that show women pouring tea and applying henna tattoos. After that, it shows Haydar with two other women (see figure 8). In that scene, Haydar makes her opening statement: "If they are civilized, then I'd rather stay savage."[60] The music then begins, with several cuts between different scenes that feature a colorful and multisensory expression of what Haydar means by the repeated phrase, "we them barbarians." The video illustrates the beauty of non-Western cultures, as we see women wearing their own cultural attire, eating food with their hands, sitting outside in a beautiful garden, playing the oud, dancing, clapping, and performing a *zaghrouta* (a high-pitched, tongue-rolling sound that is an indication of celebration among Arab women).

Haydar encouraged the women to wear their own cultural clothing and to do whatever actions were most natural. "Showcasing women from various cultures in cultural garb that they felt comfortable in and represented who they are—that was an act of resistance or subversion," she told me. "That was the idea that we are representing *ourselves* in ways that *we* feel comfortable and happy."[61] The result is a video that celebrates the beauty and color of a variety of cultural traditions that have been labeled and classified by Western culture. The layered elements of the music video enable Haydar to complicate the dominant Western gaze that often exoticizes and sexualizes similar images of Muslim women. While Haydar acknowledges that the Western Orientalist gaze is an "incredible imagination," she intentionally created this video to subvert the Western male gaze and Orientalist framings. She accomplishes this by first allowing the women to create their own visual style in their attire and actions. She also intentionally does not include men in the video. Similar to the gestures in "Hijabi (Wrap my Hijab)," the women either challenge the male gaze by staring directly at the camera with blank expressions or reject the gaze by performing for each other's pleasure.

Through the visual style of the "Barbarian" video and its sharp lyrics, Haydar is able to offer a decolonial critique that both celebrates the inherent value of Muslim lives and points to the deep rot of social injustice and oppression within Western culture. The entire video is framed as an effort to decolonize the minds of viewers, as Haydar and the other video participants reject the empty promises of Western culture and consumption in favor of embracing the "barbarian" lifestyle. Resembling statements like "Black is beautiful" or "the blacker the berry, the sweeter the juice," Haydar's video for "Barbarian" is an act of disarticulating the negative ideas that are applied to Muslim bodies and rearticulating these lives as valuable and beautiful.[62] Haydar both celebrates the cultural styles that have been denigrated and uses her lyrics to point to the ways that Western cultures are far from civilized.

Related to the decolonial tactic of mimicry that Homi Bhabha discusses, Haydar and the other women in the video embrace the visual styles that are often seen as exotic or backward to illustrate their beauty.[63] Haydar was inspired to write the song while taking a graduate course on ancient Greece and Rome and learning about the origins of the word "barbarian"—which is derived from the Greek *bárbaros*, a word used by early Greeks as the pejorative term for "foreigner" or "noncitizen." "I wanted to take back that word and say this is a word that has been used against us to deem us as noncitizens of empire," Haydar told me. "I wanted to say, we *are* those barbarians, we do not seek citizenship into the violence of empire, and we *are* beautiful despite what empire says or believes about us."[64] Throughout the video, the lyrics and the visuals reinforce the beauty of non-Western styles. As Haydar and a chorus of women repeat "beautiful barbarians," the video cuts to scenes of women wearing a variety of colorful fabrics and cultural styles.

The lyrics both celebrate the unprecedented beauty and value of non-Western cultures and assert that the women have strength that comes from their cultural backgrounds. Instead of accepting the Orientalist stereotype of the passive and hypersexualized Muslim woman oppressed by the veil and the licentious sheikh, the video presents the view that culture and beauty empower the women. The lyrics reinforce this strength: "We them barbarians / Beautiful and scaring them / Earth shakin' rattling / Be wild out loud again" and "Feminine

invading them / Beautiful Barbarians." The women do activities that are portrayed by Western culture as inferior and backward. Contrary to Western standards of eating food with silverware while sitting at a table, the women recline in
an outdoor space and eat with their hands, while wearing traditional attire from
Arab and South Asian cultures.

Rather than the perfect, plastic beauty of a magazine spread that promotes
white Western beauty standards, the video showcases a variety of body shapes,
skin colors, hair textures, facial features, and clothing styles. Instead of the sterile,
collagen-injected, and techno-modern imagery of Western cultural spaces, the
women in "Barbarian" are in natural settings, and they wear colorful clothing that
ties them to cultural traditions of their ancestors. The vibrancy of the outdoor
scenes is contrasted with several scenes featuring Haydar and a few other women
in a room with a bubblegum-pink color scheme. This room is notably plastic and
fake, reinforcing the saccharine and empty promises of Western consumer culture. While the women are still beautiful in this space, these scenes stand in
contrast to the natural beauty and substantial values of non-Western culture.

In the description of this video, Haydar explains that Western beauty standards continue to dominate and colonize our minds and comments: "We resist
white supremacy, 'western' superiority and colonized ways of thinking and being
by LOVING ourselves, generously, beautifully and joyfully in spite of any active
or subliminal efforts to make us feel unworthy of love and life."[65] Similar to the
cultural work of celebrating the idea that "Black is beautiful," this video disarticu-
lates the connection between cultural traditions and concepts of dirtiness, backwardness, and ugliness. Instead, the video decolonizes the mind-set of viewers, as
Haydar raps about being "fresh," "eloquent," "humble and elegant," and "joyful."

Furthermore, Haydar's lyrics use humor and irony to point out the hypocrisies in Western countries that claim to be civilized and progressive but perpetuate imperialist violence around the world. Throughout the song, Haydar plays
with irony and ambivalences as she points to what Angel Hinzo and Lynn Schofield Clark describe as "the instability of the relations between symbols and
meanings" in their discussion of Indigenous activism and trickster humor.[66]
Haydar often uses an if-then formulation that points to the incongruities
between how she is labeled and what these labels mean. For instance, the opening line says, "If they're civilized, I'd rather stay savage." Additionally, she raps, "If
I'm a savage, then you're a fraud." These lines assert that the label "civilized" no
longer has the original positive connotation when people seen as civilized are
oppressing anyone deemed to be a savage. A line in Haydar's video description
specifically points to this hypocrisy, "If drones dropping bombs and a war economy are civilized then we are proudly not that."[67] Haydar also addresses the endless wars over oil and drugs in the Middle East and Afghanistan in her lyrics:
"Barbarian? That's how you really feel? / Like you didn't start war over oil fields? /
Opium, poppy seed. / Money moves, Cardi B." Again, the idea is to question

who is the real "savage" or "barbarian" when the U.S. government invades countries over resources. As Haydar raps about these hypocrisies, the other women in
the video don't attempt to prove that they are civilized humans. Instead, they
simply exist and force viewers to acknowledge them as "beautiful barbarians."
The digital music video enables this layering of messages as well as the humor
and playfulness of Haydar's critiques.

MUSLIM FUTURISM

Prior to the release of Haydar's first video, "Hijabi (Wrap my Hijab)," one of the
most talked about videos among young Muslim Americans online was "Somewhere in America #MIPSTERZ." This two-and-a-half-minute video, featuring
Muslim women rocking fashion styles in various urban settings, garnered a wide
range of feedback from the Muslim American community. Some people argued
that the video was a vacuous display of fashion and women skateboarding,[68]
while those who participated in the video discussed how it allowed them to creatively display their identity.[69] When this video was released in 2013, the portrayal of Muslims in American culture was still limited to stereotypical terrorist
roles or Orientalist tropes. It was extremely rare to see a fully formed Muslim
character in TV shows or movies, let alone a Muslim character who wasn't
focused only on their faith. In the years since the Mipsterz emerged onto the
scene in 2013, there has been a relative plethora of cultural portrayals of Muslims:
from Kamala Khan as the first major Muslim female superhero in *Ms. Marvel* to
the personal struggles of a twenty-something Muslim man in Hulu's *Ramy*, Ibti-
haj Muhammad competing as the first American hijabi in the Olympics, and
countless Muslim comedians using humor in their specials to confront hatred.

Nearly six years after so much attention was brought to skateboarding Muslim hipsters, the Mipsterz started work in 2019 on ALHAMDU, a multimedia
project featuring video, music, fashion, photography, and other visual art. While
"Somewhere in America #MIPSTERZ" was released as a carefree fashion video
without much forethought, two of the creative directors of the video, Sara Alfageeh and Abbas Rattani, told me that "ALHAMDU" was developed specifically
"to create the visuals of Muslim Futurism."[70] This collaborative project is crowd-
funded and features professional actors and models along with emerging artists
and young Muslims eager to participate. Financial supporters of the project were
given pins, posters, and tote bags that feature graphic images of Muslim futurism. "ALHAMDU" came to fruition in April and May 2021 with the release of a
four-and-a-half-minute video[71] and a series of Instagram Stories and posts. Similar to the hip-hop music videos of Haydar, the Mipsterz embrace the hybridity
and flexibility of digital media spaces to celebrate the value of their interstitial
identities while also envisioning a future that breaks free from the oppression
and confines of identity labels. The Mipsterz use digital media tools to build

something new: a multimedia expression that rejects the empty promises of Western consumerism and builds on the foundational values of Islam and non-Western traditions.

One clear example of this hybridity and layering in "ALHAMDU" is the main song that plays throughout the music video. As I discussed above, the sampling and layering of different elements in hip-hop music often reflect the hybridity or in-betweenness of marginalized communities. In this case, the song intentionally layers elements of various cultures on top of each other, along with new and classic music styles. As Alfageeh and Rattani explained to me, "The music is best described as an alternative, third-culture hip-hop sonic experience."[72] The song, produced for the Mipsterz by Yusuf Siddiquee, samples a classic Egyptian wedding song along with recordings of Arab percussion instruments. The rappers Haseeb the Few and Ahmed El-Naggar add lyrics about their experiences as Americans from immigrant backgrounds. Finally, the Arabic word *alhamdulillah* (meaning "praise be to God") is exclaimed after each line in the lyrics like "This that new America. / We comin' to your area. / This that new utopia. / Nobody even heard of y'all." The sampling and layering in the song reflect the experiences of being caught between cultures. As Alfageeh and Rattani explained, "Much like its creators, the song samples previous generations and remixes it with the poetics of now."[73] The artists can layer different aspects of their background and include references to culture and history. As Ken McLeod discusses in an article on futurism in music, hip-hop music and the use "of sampling and multi-tracking also allows for a type of aural time travel through the simultaneous representation and experience of past and present."[74] The song in "ALHAMDU" celebrates the beauty of past cultural traditions while weaving these traditions into contemporary styles and experiences in an effort to build a vibrant future.

This focus on creating a joyful and bright future is also reflected in the visuals behind "ALHAMDU," with the title calling to mind *alhamdulillah*. When the video was launched on Instagram, the creators proclaim that this project is "a joyous, vibrant vision of liberation. A future where our dignity, flourishing, and imaginations as Muslims are actualized."[75] The fashion styles and visuals in the video emphasize how this eclectic group of Muslims brings color and creative energy to drab locations like the California desert, an urban street, or a subway station. The models in the video showcase exaggerated styles, as the statement for the Kickstarter campaign describes: "street fashion meets your grandma's closet, old world thobes and flowing hijabs, loud turbans and kufis, clashing patterns, obnoxious colors."[76] As in Haydar's "Barbarian," in "ALHAMDU" the participants present prolific Orientalist stereotypes to flip the script. The fashions feature Arab and Islamic styles like thobes (long robes), wide-legged harem pants, bangles, kufis, prayer beads, a bright pink niqab face veil, turbans, long tunics, and fezzes.

The overall aesthetic of the video is bright and colorful, almost to the point of being, as the Kickstarter description implies, gaudy, loud, and "obnoxious." The

FIGURE 9. Still from "ALHAMDU | MUSLIM FUTURISM," a MIPSTERZ project. Directed by Abbas Rattani. Art Direction by Sara Alfageeh and Sumer Zuberi. Photography by Diane Valera. Copyright MIPSTERZ 2020.

scenes in the desert most effectively convey this bright future, as the models bring dots of color to the drab landscape (see figure 9). The camera cuts quickly between scenes of models wearing multiple layers of clothing, necklaces, multiple bracelets, large earrings, flowing scarves, knit hats, and colored sunglasses. The cuts between scenes are so fast that the viewer can't focus on a single person but rather is immersed in a multisensory flood of bright colors, layered styles, and upbeat vibes. In some of the urban scenes the camera lingers for longer periods on certain models as they pose for and stare into the camera or, in other scenes, on participants who laugh and dance with each other.

The visuals in "ALHAMDU" reinforce the layering effect of the music, as the participants skillfully weave together colorful contemporary fashion with religious attire and traditional cultural styles. Just as the women in Haydar's "Barbarian" video express who they are in whatever way they see fit, the participants in "ALHAMDU" are unapologetic as they bring together different aspects of their identities. The goal of this multimedia project, according to Alfageeh and Rattani, its creative directors, was not to counter dominant stereotypes or critique oppressive systems. As Muslim creators expand the representations of Muslims that are available in American culture, Alfageeh and Rattani explained to me, "we're well beyond producing hand-holding PSAs promising that your Muslim neighbor isn't a terrorist."[77] Instead, the participants use fashion and visual styles to express their culture and religious identity. "We wanted to be colorful, unapologetic, loud, and stick out of any environment," Alfageeh and Rattani said. "ALHAMDU" and other work of the Mipsterz express a desire for Muslim Americans to exist as they are without having to apologize or always be resisting oppressive systems. "At some point, we must exist in spite of our oppression," Alfageeh and Rattani told me. "Our existence and our voice (and artwork by extension) then become resistance, defiance, and ultimately survival." "ALHAMDU" is an effort to create something for the enjoyment of fellow Mipsterz or anyone else who is a misfit in mainstream spaces.

The incorporation of futuristic themes in "ALHAMDU" also enables these Muslim creators to imagine a future when they will be able to share their own stories freed from the restrictions of categories. Alfageeh and Rattani discuss how the dominant American culture often wants to fit Muslims into set categories of either the model minority or the dangerous terrorist. Muslim Americans are pressured to play the role of the harmless and loyal American citizen who is always on the watch for sleeper cells of terrorists. The Mipsterz builds on the established work of Afrofuturism to develop what Alfageeh and Rattani call "Muslim Futurism." They explained to me that they define this term as "a cultural and artistic aesthetic that reimagines an American Muslim future free from the confines of orientalism and the language of the majority culture."[78] The incorporation of futurism in "ALHAMDU" allowed the Muslim creators to build on their histories and cultural traditions while creating a future that, as Alfageeh and Rattani state, will be "joyous and colorful."

As noted above, the concept of Muslim futurism builds on Afrofuturism. This is a cultural movement in music, film, art, and literature that incorporates Black diasporic history, futuristic technologies, and space exploration. According to Adam de Paor-Evans, "Afrofuturism is a contextual counter-position to mainstream western culture that reevaluates and reappropriates art and technology, within a frame that draws upon various concepts from the past in order to project a representation of the future."[79] By centering on past cultural traditions and looking toward the future, this cultural approach envisions a future free from oppressive structures. Marlo David explains that Afrofuturism moves beyond the current focus on identity politics: "Afrofuturist thought posits a reconciliation between an imagined disembodied, identity-free future and the embodied identity-specific past and present, which can provide a critical link through which post-soul artists can express a radical black subjectivity."[80] It's not that Black subjectivity won't matter in the future, or that the Islamic values and cultural traditions in "ALHAMDU" are irrelevant. Instead, the embrace of futuristic tropes, science fiction themes, and outer space imagery is a way for individuals to transcend the limitations of identity categories.

In the case of the Mipsterz and "ALHAMDU," these creative projects allow Muslim American participants to simply exist as they are and create a beautiful project for each other's enjoyment. The "ALHAMDU" video is interspersed with Arabic quotes that point to this joyous future, such as "What is coming is better than what has gone by" and "Time doesn't change, time reveals." The Instagram posts that promoted the launch of "ALHAMDU" during Ramadan 2021 emphasized the futurism theme by using outer space filters and graphics such as stars, planets, spaceships, and the moon. Along with the more lighthearted use of graphics and emojis, the Instagram content profiled some of the participants in the project and shared their vision of a joyous Muslim future. Adiva Daniar said, "I think a lot of times people try to put you in a box. . . . Being part of a Muslim future means reclaiming our identities and not having to hide."[81] Similarly, Reshma Hussam envisions a Muslim future as "a world in which one may be— and be celebrated and not judged for being—unapologetically yourself."[82] With the ideals of a future where identities don't force people into certain boxes, this is a utopian future of peace and justice. Nesima Aberra describes a Muslim future "as one where we can challenge the oppressive systems within and outside our communities, where we take care of each other and find joy and love and safety for all."[83] "ALHAMDU" resists the endless pressure for Muslims to prove their humanity or perform as the perfect Muslim American. Instead, this visual portrayal of a colorful and joyful future, full of misfits who playfully layer various styles, destabilizes the dominance of identity categories around religion, culture, race, gender, and sexuality—among other things.

A COLORFUL FUTURE FOR UNRULY MISFITS

Although separated by several decades, it is easy to see connections between the early feminist activist hip-hop music of the 1980s and 1990s and the contemporary digital music videos of Muslim American artists like Haydar and the Mipsterz. Through humor, playfulness, and layering, activist artists have long found hip-hop music to be a fruitful space in which to call out social injustices while celebrating the value of marginalized experiences. These music videos are expressions of pride and unity, with their anthemic lyrics like "ladies first," "keep swaggin' my hijabis," "beautiful barbarians," and "*alhamdulillah*, this that new America." The videos go beyond a beautiful expression of pride to address social oppression perpetuated by patriarchal, racist, and imperialist systems. At times, these issues involve faith leaders' covering up misogyny and sexual abuse through religious justifications or Western governments' perpetuating colonialism and imperialism through claims about the inferiority of Muslims and other non-Western groups. Creative work from Haydar and the Mipsterz demonstrates how the sampling and layering of hip-hop music, along with the playfulness and humor of multisensory videos, can be used to effectively call out social inequalities and oppression.

Furthermore, the ideals of an Afrofuturist world, free from the oppression of categories and labels, live on in the work of these Muslim artists, who use the layering and playfulness of digital music videos and hip-hop music to express their colorful and complex experiences. Rather than responding to stereotypes that dehumanize and devalue Muslim lives, these young creatives use the multisensory elements of music videos to simply show Muslims existing in their full complexities. A video like "Barbarian" or "ALHAMDU" flips the script and embraces elements of cultures that are so often denigrated. The women recline on an outdoor couch and eat food with their hands. Models showcase outfits with bright fabrics, gaudy jewelry, and colored sunglasses layered with traditional attire that has been worn in Middle Eastern and North African countries for centuries. These music videos, along with the wider digital media milieu in which they circulate, allow young Muslim Americans to rearticulate their inherent value as they imagine a future free from the constraints of identity categories. Rather than fight an almost impossible battle against enduring Orientalist stereotypes, Muslim creatives use digital media and music videos to simply exist on their own terms and show pride and unity in the complexities of the Muslim American experience.

CONCLUSION

In courses that I teach on digital media and religion, the students often look perplexed when we discuss some of the early studies of people creating virtual church communities that they never connect with in real life or performing as a completely distinct avatar in their Second Life Buddhist meditation circle. This sense of entering a new world and taking on a different persona in the online space is extremely foreign to most college students. People in the United States who were born in the 1990s and 2000s grew up with mobile devices, digital platforms, and social media as part of their everyday life. This generation is marked by never having to think deeply about that act of dialing up, logging in, and entering digital space. Digital media make up a layer of their lives and are a large part of the way they make friends, express themselves, seek spiritual inspiration, gather news and information, and participate in political action. The blurring of boundaries between digital media, mobile devices, online spaces, and physical spaces is natural for most young people.

At the same time, this hybridity and in-betweenness are also present in the blending of race, ethnicity, and religions of many young people. According to a Pew Research Center study, the generation of Americans born between 1997 and 2012 is the most racially diverse ever, with 52 percent white, 25 percent Hispanic, 14 percent Black, 6 percent Asian, and 4 percent other.[1] While there has been an increase in the proportion of Hispanic and Asian young Americans since the Millennial generation, notably the post-Millennials "are more likely to be U.S. born of at least one foreign-born parent (22%) compared with Millennials in 2002 (15%)."[2] Post-Millennials come from a variety of racial and ethnic backgrounds; are more likely to have a parent who immigrated to the United States; and if they are white, are inevitably going to have friends, classmates, and colleagues from diverse backgrounds. And a majority of both Gen-Zers (62 percent) and Millennials (61 percent) think that racial and ethnic diversity are good for society.[3] As the creative leaders behind the Mipsterz discussed, young Muslim Americans often reflect this "third culture" experience of having immigrant parents who bring their own cultural traditions, while being raised in the United States with its different values and capitalistic culture.[4] This interstitial identity is clearly present in American cultural representations on TV shows like *Ramy* and *Master of None* and in the *Ms. Marvel* comic books.

Compared to other generations, these younger ones are also the most religiously diverse, and their members are more likely to identify as unaffiliated with a religious denomination. A PRRI poll in 2017 found that adults ages 18–29 belong to a wide range of religious groups, including white Evangelical Protestant (8 percent); white mainline Protestant (8 percent); white Catholic (6 percent); Mormon (2 percent); Black Protestant (7 percent); Hispanic Protestant (6 percent); Hispanic Catholic (9 percent); other Christian (7 percent); Jewish (1 percent); and other religions, including Islam, Buddhism, and Hinduism (4 percent).[5] These numbers show a more equal distribution among the religious identities than among older generations, with no single religion having more than 10 percent of the population. Notably, the largest group (38 percent) of adults in this age group (18–29) reported being unaffiliated, which is a far larger share than for people ages 30–49 (26 percent), 50–64 (18 percent), and 65 and older (12 percent).[6]

Another relevant data point that illustrates the trend of increasing religious diversity is that Millennials and Gen-Zers make up a much larger proportion of the people affiliated with non-Christian religions. For instance, Americans born between 1981 and 1996 constitute 40 percent of the people in the United States who identify themselves as Buddhist, 50 percent of the Hindus, and 51 percent of the Muslims.[7] These numbers are far above those for Americans in this age group as a share of Catholics (22 percent), Evangelical Protestants (23 percent), Black Protestants (26 percent), or mainline Protestants (20 percent).[8] These data seem to indicate two trends: the population of members of Christian churches in the United States is growing older as young people become unaffiliated, and younger Americans have increasingly diverse religious and ethnic backgrounds. Young Americans are more likely to be exposed to religious diversity in society, school, and the culture at large. Finally, younger generations are living in a culture that is increasingly "religiously remixed," as Tara Isabella Burton terms these trends of blending rituals and beliefs from a variety of religious traditions, spiritualties, and wellness cultures. As people become less likely to belong to a specific religious institution, they develop personal and fluid spiritualities. As Burton writes, "The more individualized our religious identities become, the more willing we are to mix and match ideas and practices outside our primary religious affiliation."[9]

In addition to embracing racial, ethnic, and religious diversity, the two younger generations are also more likely than their elders to have positive views of a range of sexualities and gender expressions. For instance, 35 percent of Gen-Zers and 25 percent of Millennials personally know someone who prefers to go by a gender-neutral pronoun.[10] These statistics reflect my observations on college campuses, where students are comfortable talking about gender as a social construct in the classroom, express a spectrum of sexualities in social groups and online profiles, and experiment with gender-bending or gender-neutral fashion choices. The revolutionary queer theories of the 1990s are now almost second nature to a lot of young people. Obviously, there is pushback from the right and a resistance to learning about critical theory in terms of gender, sexuality, and race, but the train has left the station when children's books teach about gender performance and the social construction of race. Finally, surveys indicate that Gen-Zers and Millennials are more progressive than older Americans on a variety of social issues.[11] And these beliefs are supported by action, when young people are at the forefront of organized calls for change regarding racial justice, queer rights, climate change, reproductive justice, and immigration reform.

When we keep all of these factors in mind—the ubiquity of mobile devices and social media, the increases in racial and ethnic diversity, the acceptance of gender and sexual fluidity, and the support for progressive causes—it is not surprising that the young people profiled in this book would be engaging in the creative work discussed here to reimagine their faith traditions. Building on the hybridity of their backgrounds and their own comfort with queerness and breaking binaries, the flexibility of digital media and the playfulness of these creative online spaces enable young people who have been marginalized in religious institutions to envision their faith in new ways. I don't want to presume that the majority of young people are doing this work: there are obviously many people who remain content with the status quo or seek to disrupt it from a neoconservative perspective. However, for those young people who are already on the margins because of their in-between identity (in terms of race, ethnicity, immigration status, sexuality, or gender expression, for example), the hybrid and malleable aspects of digital media (such as hashtags, images, podcasts, and videos) provide a natural space for them to exist unapologetically.

Furthermore, since these young people are already comfortable working from the margins and engaging with these creative tactics of resistance, they are able to connect with other people doing this work. The examples in this book illustrate the overlaps between purity culture in Evangelical Christianity and modesty culture in Islam, as both religions promote the view that the pure and pious icon is a white, virginal, thin, and attractive woman. The critical work on racism and colonialism in the Truth's Table podcast, Blair Imani's Instagram posts, and Mona Haydar's music videos also illustrate the ways that a belief in the supremacy of white European culture supports the institution of slavery, mass genocide of Indigenous people, colonization, forced conversion to Christianity, and imperialism in Muslim-majority countries. Digital media serve as spaces outside of traditional religious institutions to both facilitate these critiques and raise awareness of how misogyny, anti-Blackness, homophobia, and colonialism are present in and transcend Christian and Muslim communities.

In this conclusion, I analyze what these examples of intersectional activism among young religious misfits can show about digital media's potential not only for facilitating intersectional feminist activism but also for developing supportive communities for people deemed unruly in traditional religious spaces. Young people are becoming more and more aware of how the individual oppression that they face relates to white, cisgendered, heteronormative, patriarchal structures whose reach goes beyond religious institutions. These dominant forces infiltrate religious communities and reinforce women's subordinate position, the belief in the disordered nature of female and queer sexuality, and the inferior status of both Black Muslims and Black Christians.

Throughout the conclusion, I examine some of the overlapping themes in the various cases discussed in this book, along with other examples. A lot of these projects resemble traditional forms of activism through which individuals engage with the flexible and creative aspects of digital media spaces to take down those in power, while also calling out injustices and hypocrisies in religious institutions. The work against sexual abuse and harassment in religious communities is one clear example of how digital activism has tangible consequences. Similarly, calls for racial justice in faith communities have also been effective at creating real change. Many activists realize that if these movements are to be successful, people need to look at intersecting forms of oppression and larger structures beyond certain religious communities. For instance, sexual abuse of children is no longer seen as simply a problem within the Catholic Church. Rather, there are larger problems of abuse and power imbalances that often fester within multiple religious communities. Discussions and connections on digital media enable the development of larger, collaborative initiatives.

Notably, this study of the creative projects of these unruly souls demonstrates that traditional activist work to challenge people in power and work toward justice is just the beginning. Although a lot of attention has been paid to the ways that digital media are shaping political work, such as how hashtags and memes are used for organizing and spreading information, less political effects of digital media projects often go unaddressed. The various cases in this book illustrate the ways that the open, malleable, playful, and intimate aspects of digital media help cultivate healing spaces, especially for people recovering from religious trauma. Additionally, new spiritual communities are forming that welcome those misfits who have been cast out of rigid religious spaces, centering on the intrinsic value of these unruly souls. Ultimately, these aspects of the digital moment enable not only crucial political work for equal justice but also the forming of supportive faith communities built on the foundation of marginalized spiritualities.

ACTIVIST WORK FOR JUSTICE AND EQUALITY

One of the primary ways that digital media have been essential to feminist activism within religions has been in providing creative spaces where these marginalized voices are able to speak out about oppressive systems and injustices. While young people may be prevented from using traditional modes of expression in religious institutions because of their gender, sexuality, class, or race, a hashtag on Twitter or Instagram (despite all of its limitations) provides a way for individuals to contribute to a larger conversation. Each individual statement may not be much, but the magnitude of the situation is clear when thousands of people share experiences of abuse and harassment under hashtags like #ChurchToo, #SilenceIsNotSpiritual, #MosqueMeToo, and #EmptyThePews. Digital media enable both this networking through hashtags and the feelings of connection with others who have experienced similar trauma. Furthermore, the playful use of humor and irony in the language of Tweets and comments succinctly displays the hypocrisy of religious leaders and institutions.

These activist projects to root out misogyny and white supremacy within religious institutions go deeper than holding people in positions of power to account for their misdeeds. Rather, the activists articulate the ways that religious leaders have misinterpreted the scriptures and are defiling faith communities by ignoring the foundational teachings of justice and equality within Islam and Christianity. As Haydar told me, "I think religion at its best is challenging mainstream ideas like patriarchy, misogyny, anti-Blackness, racism and unfettered capitalism."[12] She explained that religious figures like Jesus, Mohammad, and Black Elk did not just support the status quo. Rather, they "stood up to their own problematic industrial complexes of their day." Real religious leaders should be fighting for equality and justice for those on the margins of society. Similarly, in the *Truth's Table* episode about Black death and mourning, "Strange Fruit," the hosts discuss how American Evangelical Christianity ignores white supremacy to the point that whiteness becomes an idol to worship instead of a sin for which to repent. As Christina Edmondson explains in the episode, "People really eternally die when they have decided that the sin of racism is actually not a sin but rather the cornerstone of their theology."[13] These are prophetic voices, calling on religious leaders to account for how they have misconstrued the foundational messages of revolutionary justice within both Islam and Christianity.

Not only have these leaders misinterpreted the radical messages of faith communities, but they also use religious teachings around modesty or purity as justification for sexual harassment and abuse. The purity culture in Evangelical Christianity and the promotion of modest fashion in Islam are not simply ways to protect women from unwanted sexual attention or to keep them safe from assault. Instead, they reflect the larger forces of white supremacy, homophobia, and misogyny that transcend Islam or Evangelical Christianity. As Emily Joy Allison observes, Evangelical churches would like to see the abuses brought to light by #ChurchToo as an individual problem that can be addressed through better training and background checks. Instead, Allison argues that the theologies around purity culture "actually play into building a culture of abuse" by reinforcing the superiority of white, straight, cisgendered men.[14] Additionally, Haydar sees clear parallels between the sexual abuse in Islamic communities that she raps about in "Dog" and the misogyny of Christian purity culture. Haydar told me that she earned a master's degree in Christian ethics in part to understand how white supremacy and imperialism are infused into religious spaces and promote these ideologies of modesty and purity: "That is why I studied Christian ethics—because I think that if we heal the problematic parts of empire at a foundational point, then we can really transform the world."[15]

People who have been victimized by religious leaders and institutions participate in similar online campaigns—sharing Haydar's "Dog" video, participating in online discussions of purity culture, or sharing stories of abuse under tags like #MosqueMeToo, #ChurchToo, and #SilenceIsNotSpiritual. In all these cases, activists use similar strategies of circulating stories of abuse to shame powerful men, pointing out the hypocrisies of religious leaders and highlighting the ways that religious teachings have been corrupted and are used to justify sinfulness and evil. Allison describes the creation of the #ChurchToo movement in late 2017 as "grassroots" and "organic."[16] In the midst of conversations around #MeToo, Allison took to Twitter to share her own story of how a youth pastor had coaxed her into starting an unhealthy and abusive relationship with him. Allison and her friend Hannah Paasch created #ChurchToo, and it took off as others shared stories of abuse and harassment in Christian communities. #ChurchToo and related hashtags around purity culture and sexuality can be a space for people to share personal stories and support each other through trauma.

The hashtags have had tangible consequences, as the circulating stories call out and publicly shame abusive leaders. Several religious leaders have been forced to resign over allegations of sexual misconduct, including Bill Hybels, one of the founders of the suburban megachurch Willow Creek Community Church in Illinois; Frank Page, the president of the Southern Baptist Convention's Executive Committee; and Andy Savage, the pastor of a megachurch in Memphis, Tennessee.[17] Circulating stories about these abusers through social media may not always lead to legal prosecution, but Allison notes that there are other forms of justice, such as exposing these individuals and getting them removed from their religious posts. "It's not what the survivors deserve," Allison explained to me. "It's not [done] as swiftly as we would like, but it is something. Even if we can't change the criminal justice system with a hashtag, we can change how society looks at this."[18]

Alongside these efforts to publicly shame and remove abusive religious leaders is a tamer project centered on the #SilenceIsNotSpiritual statement that was released in December 2017, which called on church organizations and leaders to take more tangible actions to stop gender-based violence. Signed by several thousand people, the statement said, "We call our pastors, our elders, and our parishioners who have been silent to speak up and stand up for all who experience abuse. There is no institution with greater capacity to create protected spaces for healing and restoration for survivors, as well as confession, repentance and rehabilitation for perpetrators."[19] This statement was an effort to get church leaders to stop ignoring and silencing women when they come forward with stories of sexual abuse, harassment, or domestic violence. Not only are pastors often unaware of how to give pastoral care to women dealing with gender-based violence, but they also may push women to stay in violent relationships out of a belief that wives must submit to their husbands.[20] These hashtag movements reveal the ways that deep-seated patriarchy and misogyny perpetuate the idea that women need to submit to male authority even in a violent and abusive relationship. Religious teachings should not be misinterpreted to justify violence and abuse against women.

Within Islam, related but distinct projects have also arisen to tackle misogyny and gender-based violence. Inspired by the story of a young Pakistani woman named Sabica Khan who was sexually harassed during the hajj to Mecca, the feminist activist Mona Eltahawy shared her own experiences of sexual assault while on the hajj and launched #MosqueMeToo in 2018. The online discussion around this hashtag allowed other Muslims to share experiences of being assaulted or harassed in Islamic holy sites. Eltahawy explains in an article the deep shame and conflicted feelings of being groped while on pilgrimage: "That such a violation was happening to me as we performed the fifth pillar of our religion at Islam's holiest site traumatized and shamed me, even though I had obviously done nothing to be ashamed of."[21] Eltahawy's experiences illustrate similar trends within Islam and Christianity, as religious teachings are used to hide the sinful actions of men in power while at the same time making women and girls feel deep shame and responsibility for these terrible acts. Eltahawy advocates for tangible changes in the Muslim community, such as more sermons on the sin of gender-based violence and the need to respect women, more training on how to handle assaults in holy sites, and having more female guards and personnel at the sites.

A figure like Eltahawy leans into her unruliness by using forceful tactics to break the silence on abusive systems. The #MosqueMeToo hashtag not only addresses particular issues within Islam but also connects them to wider issues of misogyny and gender-based violence. Like similar movements in Christianity, the #MeToo movement within Islam also brought to light sexual misdeeds of prominent leaders—in this case, Nouman Ali Khan and Tariq Ramadan. Alongside these takedowns of powerful figures, more organizations and resources have emerged to address sexual abuse within Muslim communities. For example, the prominent Canadian Muslim scholar Ingrid Mattson founded the Hurma Project to provide resources to end violence and abuse in Islamic spaces.

Facing Abuse in Community Environments (FACE) was created to share resources and take direct action against religious leaders who are abusing their power. There is no institutional structure in American Islam for reporting misconduct, but FACE provides an online form where people can report abuse or financial misconduct by Muslim leaders or organizations. Just as Allison and others in the #ChurchToo movement use the collective power of social media and digital tools, organizations like FACE bring to light abuses in Muslim communities and hold these leaders accountable for their actions. FACE also posts infographics on its Instagram page to share information about how to report abuse, resources for dealing with gender-based violence, and upcoming workshops and events.[22] For instance, FACE hosted an interfaith *iftar* (a fast-breaking meal) during Ramadan 2020. This work would be difficult to accomplish without the ability of hashtags and social media to share information with a wider audience and break people's feelings of isolation. When a victim sees similar stories being shared under hashtags like #ChurchToo or #MosqueMeToo or through organizations like FACE, the hope is that they will feel less alone and less ashamed about the abuse they experienced in religious communities.

HEALING FROM RELIGIOUS TRAUMA

The cases examined in this book illustrate that the work to call out injustices in religious institutions and to hold religious leaders to account for their sinful indiscretions is only one part of addressing deeper concerns. The harm caused is often particularly serious because it is a spiritual hurt, inflicted on the soul. Purity culture teaches that women and queer individuals are inherently impure; modest fashion promotes thin, light-skinned, and attractive women as more pious than other women; Christianity portrays Jesus as a blue-eyed white man; and Western culture shows Muslim women as backward and exotic. All of these examples reflect a Western project of creating a hierarchy that places white, straight, cisgendered, Christian men at the apex of holiness and thus closest to divinity. People who don't fit into these categories are placed lower in the hierarchy of power and thus further away from the divine and holiness. Consequently, abusive behavior is often justified when it happens to those lower in this hierarchy, and such behavior reinforces their sense of inferiority. As Allison told me, a deeper harm is inflicted when a terrible thing happens and then religious leaders claim, "God's fine with this. There's no problem with what has happened to you in the eyes of God."[23]

The activist projects in this book, I assert, have a more substantial impact because of how they are centered on the inherent value of people who have been dismissed and denigrated as unruly souls. The playful nature of digital media and online social networks provides opportunities for activists to bring these religious misdeeds to light, but this online work also enables these young people to creatively and authentically articulate their intrinsic value in the eyes of God. Communities of these religious misfits are emerging online, as digital media facilitate these connections through hashtags, Instagram images, podcasts, music videos, and private Facebook groups. Digital media are becoming healing spaces for people recovering from religious trauma, and the media help develop new spiritual communities centered on the inherent value of these unruly souls.

In almost all of my conversations with these young activists, they discussed the importance of providing healing spaces for people harmed by traumatic religious teachings. Not only do these individuals feel marginalized in religious communities because of their intersectional identities, but they also often feel like outsiders in nonreligious contexts because they grew up in niche religious communities. For example, a queer person may leave an Evangelical Christian church and find a queer community of friends, but they may have a hard time finding support for dealing with feelings of shame and trauma that relate to religion. Digital platforms like #ChurchToo on Twitter, the *Queerology* podcast, Imani's Instagram page, or the Mipsterz website may provide caring and supportive spaces for people whose experiences intersect with religious faith. Many activists emphasize the importance of breaking free from isolation and developing supportive communities of others who understand the experiences of being marginalized and victimized. As Allison told me about #ChurchToo and the Twitter threads against purity culture, there is a power in saying "me too" and connecting over a "really niche experience that other people don't understand."[24]

Similarly, Haydar told me that one of her goals with "Dog" was to connect with viewers and overcome the shame associated with religious abuse. She wrote and recorded "Dog" before the spread of the #MeToo movement, but she hopes that it makes viewers feel less shame. "If I talk about it in a song, then I hope anyone can come forward with their stories too," Haydar said. "This is something that they can tell their friends about or talk about in a safe space. I did the work of speaking about it publicly before there was a public discourse about it to lighten the load so that people wouldn't feel alone."[25] Digital media provide supportive spaces where people can see that their experiences are not only valid but also not rare.

People experiencing the shame of religious trauma are also seeking support and connection with others who find that they don't fit into traditional religious spaces. As Matthias Roberts observes, one of the main goals for creating *Queerology* was to signal to listeners that they are not alone in being queer and interested in questions of faith. "I have so many of my listeners who tell me 'I don't have access to *anyone* who is having these conversations,'" Roberts told me. For people living in rural areas with few or no queer support structures, he explained that it is essential "to be able to have access to these kinds of stimulating conversations and for them to be able to work on their own identities and play with those in an unthreatening environment."[26] *Queerology* and other digital platforms help people stop feeling isolated, and listeners are able to dig deeper into questions of queerness and faith.

In addition to addressing religious shame associated with sexuality, digital media spaces cultivate supportive communities for people marginalized in religious spaces because of their race, skin color, and body shape. For Black women, experiencing the daily onslaught of misogynoir, new media platforms provide a sanctuary full of love and affirmation. The hosts of *Truth's Table* frequently discuss how they created the show to honor Black women—especially the beauty of their physical features and their inner spirituality. They hosted a series on "Embodied Blackness," in which they emphasized that Black women are beautifully made in God's image. Their skin color, hair texture, facial features, and body shape are all perfect, despite the white supremacist and colonialist standards of beauty. The ideas of decolonizing one's mind-set about beauty are also reflected in Haydar's song "Barbarian," when she repeats the mantra: "This nose, decolonize. / This hair, decolonize. / This skin, decolonize. / This body, decolonize. / This mind, decolonize."[27] Both Haydar's music videos and the *Truth's Table* episodes are ways to bring to light the problematic aspects of Western beauty standards while resuscitating the inherent beauty of Black and brown bodies.

Furthermore, the hosts of *Truth's Table* encourage listeners to join them at their metaphorical table, where they will support each other and provide the spiritual armor that is needed in the world. *Truth's Table* ran another series of episodes called "You Okay, Sis?," in which the hosts offered emotional support for their listeners. They also released an episode titled "Black Christian Woman's Survival Guide" that Ekemini Uwan calls a "love letter" to Black women serving in Christian churches.[28] It is essential to have these supportive communities whose members not only understand the trauma and pain of daily life but also cherish and affirm the beauty of Black women, inside and out. As Michelle Higgins states in an episode on Black suffering and trauma, "We have to have us because ain't nobody got us."[29] The podcast is a space of encouragement and love that is outside the confines of the white supremacist culture. The Black Christian author Austin Channing Brown writes about this need for ministries that celebrate the beauty and talents of Black people: "We must remind ourselves and one another that we are fearfully and wonderfully made, arming ourselves against the ultimate message of whiteness—that we are inferior."[30] Similar to the Mipsterz' multimedia work of Muslim futurism, *Truth's Table* also formulates a healing utopia, free from the confines of oppressive systems. If mainstream cultural spaces are not going to acknowledge the humanity of Black women or Muslims, then these creative digital projects will foreground the value of these lives.

In her online work as The Village Auntie, Angelica Lindsey-Ali takes on the role of an aunt who provides care and support for young women. She uses her Instagram page to create a supportive community where young women can learn from each other and share their own experiences with issues like sexuality, health, relationships, and faith. Lindsey-Ali uses a natural and comforting aesthetic style to foreground the intrinsic beauty and inherent value of women, especially Black Muslim women. She explains that this space is "for women, by women,"[31] and that this foregrounding of women's experiences is essential for cultivating a community whose members can talk about issues of sexuality and racial justice that are often silenced in Muslim communities.

In a similar manner, Leah Vernon (another Instagram figure) works to celebrate the beauty of bodies that have been denigrated while cultivating a supportive space for people struggling with body image, racism, misogyny, and abuse.
As a fat, Black Muslim woman, Vernon frequently posts about her struggles to
meet unrealistic standards of beauty and modesty. She is too fat, too dark, and
too Muslim to meet Western fashion standards for models, but she is also dismissed in the Muslim fashion industry for being fat and Black while also falling
short of the modesty standards of being soft, quiet, and demure. "We all grew up
super damaged because of images that we cannot attain," Vernon told me. "You
have an image that says this is how hijabis look like only! And anything outside
of that is wrong, bad, haram. If you don't tie your scarf like this, then no, you are
not accepted."[32] Vernon hopes that her Instagram page and comment threads
will form a community of other people who have been left out by these unattain-
able beauty standards because of their skin color, class, body shape, religion, or
ability. "It's creating a forum, and people are also sharing their own stories, and
sharing stories is healing," Vernon explained.

The individuals starting these projects are less concerned with promoting
their own story or even developing a brand than they are with using their creative
talents to develop healing communities. Another common thread in these projects is the ways that their creators use humor and playfulness to both strike down
their oppressors and heal their own wounds. Roberts explains that humor can be
a way to ease tensions while still making an argument. "Humor really is this subversive means of making a point," he told me. "You get that laugh, that chuckle. It
brings people together around these supertense issues. But also laughter relieves
trauma."[33] Haydar similarly talks about how she's found it easier to attract more
"flies with honey," as the saying goes, by using the uplifting aspects of music to
tackle difficult topics like sexual violence, public harassment, and colonialism.
Haydar cleverly eviscerates her oppressors through humor, irony, and sarcasm in
her songs, and her music videos are healing spaces for other women harmed by
these oppressors. For example, she uses humor in the music video for "Dog" to
address the difficult topic of religious abuse without retraumatizing victims. Haydar explained her intention to me by saying "I wanted to talk about it in a way that
could help make people feel seen while also celebrating our resilience."[34]

EMERGING FAITH TRADITIONS OF UNRULY SOULS

As this digital activism of unruly souls shifts away from the call-out and takedown of powerful religious figures and institutions, there are growing movements of young people seeking to build up something new. Although some
activists are perfectly happy to leave behind faith entirely, others engage with the
malleable and cooperative aspects of digital media to develop new faith traditions and spiritual communities, centered on equal justice and the value of mar-

ginalized voices. New movements are springing up that originate in online communities, such as Exvangelicals or Mipsterz, and are built around activism related to issues like gender-based violence, queer rights, or racial justice. These online projects easily merge and blur into offline life. Again, these movements reflect the ways that younger generations exist in these in-between spaces and seamlessly blend various religious traditions and rituals.[35]

The history of the Mipsterz illustrates how a short fashion video released in 2013 launched a larger movement of young, hip, eclectic, urban Muslims who seek to use their creativity to envision a beautiful future for people of their faith. The movement could have started and ended with this lighthearted video, but instead the Mipsterz has grown into a larger community. Young Muslims connect online through social media sites and an email listserv, support each other's work by purchasing books and artwork, indicate membership in the group through the use of fun Mipsterz accessories, and come together for offline events. Prior to the COVID-19 pandemic shutdowns in 2020, the Mipsterz organized a traveling variety show called "Good Fun Muslim Friends Club" to highlight the talents and resources of the community. The show features conversations about current issues, musical performances, comedy, and interactive artwork. The group has also hosted events that spotlight all the creative talent in the community, such as members involved in music, artwork, comics, literature, and spoken word. These events not only give artists a chance to share their work, but they also bring together Muslims and other young people who want to build something new—a creative future that is "joyous and colorful," to use the words of Mipsterz directors Sara Alfageeh and Abbas Rattani. They told me, "We can start creating that future by embodying and fighting for those ideals today and make them tangible through our art now."[36]

Podcasts have also constituted a significant site for community building among younger generations, whose members are more likely than previous generations to seek meaning outside of religious institutions. The most successful podcasts maintain strong communities of listeners through active social media accounts that allow listeners to interact with the hosts and each other. Podcast listening itself is a very solo activity, but listeners are easily able to respond to what they hear through various platforms. *The Liturgists* podcast went even further and developed a community of listeners from the prepandemic gatherings that resembled Christian church services, creating private online "hang out rooms" where people can discuss their struggles with faith and traumatic experiences in religious institutions. On *The Liturgists'* website, the hosts explain that the goal of the podcast is to create a supportive space for people who feel like outsiders in traditional religious spaces. At the same time, this support should extend beyond the podcast. According to the hosts, "It's one thing to hear a podcast and felt heard, but we care deeply about creating opportunities for connection, dialogue, and ultimately community. To facilitate that, The Liturgists operate and maintain platforms for community formation."[37] Because of the pandemic, the offline gatherings have been transformed into "The Sunday Thing," a weekly gathering on a video conferencing platform, in which the podcast hosts discuss a set topic and members dialogue with each other in digital breakout rooms. *The Liturgists* illustrates how digital media platforms like podcasts, hashtags, and videos can initiate connections among religious misfits that can then extend into more sustained community building and political action.

Furthermore, the hosts of *Truth's Table* develop a community feel by encouraging listeners to "pull up a seat at the table" and join in a larger dialogue about faith. The hosts even recognize that their Black Christian female listeners often incorporate listening to *Truth's Table* into their Saturday rituals of cleaning house and cooking. In prepandemic days, the hosts occasionally recorded live shows with an audience or spoke at public events. These events serve to connect listeners with each other into a community, and the hosts used livestreaming to host a day of prayer and praise for Juneteenth 2020. While this event did not take place in person, it was a way for listeners to come together in live time to pray; listen to sermons from various pastors, as well as speeches from scholars and activists; and dialogue about their faith. The hosts center *Truth's Table* on the value of Black women, and this event allowed the community of listeners to build a new expression of Christianity on the foundation of the holiness and knowledge of Black women.

Similarly, Roberts hopes that *Queerology* expands the understanding of Christianity to focus on the values and contributions of queer people. He always tries to get the conversations on his show to move beyond what he calls the "initial question," which involves how people reconcile queerness with religion. Once people realize that God created all people to be beautiful and gave them a range of sexualities and gender expressions, deeper questions arise about how to live a life of faith that is centered on queerness. This project is similar to the womanist tradition of constructing a faith that honors the value of Black women. Shows like *Queerology* and *Truth's Table* examine what faith looks like when people focus on marginalized perspectives. Roberts told me, "I think with *Queerology* and that question of living a life beyond just that initial question, it invites a level of imagination for people to be able to see like, oh I can now imagine what my life could look like, where maybe imagination didn't exist before."[38] In particular, young people can listen to interviews with people who are already in process of building these new faith expressions. Roberts refers to the work of the Catholic theologian James Allison, who asserts that the younger generations are the first to proudly and publicly live their faith as queer people. "We are the first to model what it actually looks like, to be queer people of faith," Roberts explained to me. "This is an exploration of building something new. . . . There's this generative creativity in the midst of—we actually get to decide what this looks like, we get to decide these models."

An emphasis on queerness and the value of queer lives may offer a path forward for young religious misfits who are seeking to build faith communities that work for justice. As Elizabeth Edman argues in *Queer Virtue*, queer folks are far from the morally inferior, intrinsically disordered people that religious institutions like to criticize. Instead, she sees queer people as more closely connected to the divine and as embodying virtuous acts of breaking down binaries and barriers. This dismantling of dichotomies is central to Christianity, Edman argues, as Jesus was a figure who "ruptured simplistic dualism all the time: life and death, human and divine, sacred and profane."[39] Roberts discussed the influence of Edman's work with me, saying that "if we define queerness as the breaking of boundaries, then if we conceptualize the divine as that which transcends boundaries, there's an intersection there."[40] Queerness places individuals in this interstitial and marginal position, where they are more easily able to tap into the realm of the divine or transcendent.

Furthermore, Edman argues that these experiences of marginality and hybridity have encouraged queer individuals to be more compassionate and to seek justice for others who are marginalized because of their gender, race, class, immigration status, and so on. These are the misfits that Jesus hung around with in the gospels. These are the issues of injustice and inequality that the Prophet Muhammad strived to overcome. Edman asserts that queer folks know the experiences of being marginalized and powerless and often are inherently pulled toward helping other people on the margins and in liminal positions.[41] At its origins, Christianity is about rupturing binaries and challenging institutions that make claims about who has power and value in a society. Similarly, the Qur'an promotes equal justice for all people, and the Prophet Muhammad taught, as Muhsin Hendricks writes, "that the vulnerable and discriminated against should be protected."[42] Early Islamic communities illustrated this concern for the oppressed, as resources were redistributed to women, children, and the poor. Moreover, Hendricks explains that the Qur'an emphasizes justice and equality while it clearly "offers no justification for male authority over ostensibly weaker actors in society."[43] Institutional structures that perpetuate the unequal distribution of power and resources must be dismantled to serve the marginalized.

A digital media space like a podcast, Twitter discussion, Instagram meme, or online forum can help reveal some of the intersections between queerness and a quest for justice within different religious traditions. For instance, the first Queer Youth of Faith Day was held on June 30, 2020, by a new organization called Beloved Arise. This day is unique for celebrating the specific intersections of queerness, youth, and a variety of faith traditions. Following the practice of other digital media events, organizers encouraged participants to share stories and images on social media through a hashtag—in this case, #QYFday. The main event was a livestreamed gathering with various speakers, including the first transgender minister in the Evangelical Lutheran Church in America, a queer Muslim youth, the director of Jewish Queer Youth, and a representative from a Buddhist organization. The event also featured an artist creating a live painting, a trivia contest about queer history, and the announcement of the winners of an essay competition. Because of COVID-19 restrictions, participants (who used a variety of rainbow-colored backgrounds) all joined the event via video. Many of them reflected on the beauty that queer youth bring to faith communities and the ways that queerness and spirituality inform each other.

In a special episode of *Queerology*, Roberts interviewed four youths from different faith traditions for the event. Talin, an Armenian Christian, commented that her bisexuality and faith "are both parts of me that coexist and work together to inform who I am."[44] Related to what Edman wrote in *Queer Virtue*, these young people see queerness not as a flaw but as a moral asset that helps them live a faith-driven life. Amera, a transgender Bengali American Muslim, expressed similar feelings of how her queerness and faith are deeply entwined, particularly in the work for justice and equality. She has come to realize the ways that marginalized groups often intersect. "The struggles that people of minority faiths face, and that queer people face, and that people of color and Black folks face in this country are all tied up together in a collective liberation," she observed. "I've learned a lot in challenging this very affluent theology that I was taught and replacing it with a much more gritty, liberation theology, like a theology of the people."[45] Because of her experience as a member of a marginalized religious group and as a transgender youth, Amera related more to the liberation struggles of Black, Indigenous, Latino, and queer people than she did to the affluent and aspirational culture she observed in other South Asian members of the professional class. As she stated on the podcast, "our connection to God, our connection to divinity, is tied up with our connection to justice." The emphasis on justice in Islam and her interstitial experiences as a queer youth motivate Amera to participate in social causes beyond those related to her own experiences.

While not all of the activists discussed in this book identify as queer, they are doing similar work to challenge injustices and rupture binaries by celebrating the value of their marginalized experiences—including the work on Twitter to embrace a range of sexualities instead of the oppressive purity myth, the visual images that display the beauty of various body shapes and fashion styles, the dialogue on podcasts built on the spirituality of Black women, and the creative play in hip-hop music videos to envision a future free from oppression. These digital projects call out injustices and challenge binaries, but they also serve as inspiration for constructing faith communities built on the value of unruly souls. As Roberts notes, young people are starting to move away from just responsive activism to developing new faith communities. "As we move out of this more reactive space, this space where we are reacting against these faith spaces where we are coming from, . . . [we are moving] into a more creative, generative space to actually be like, here's something new. Here is what a queer spirituality looks like, here's what a queer Christianity looks like," Roberts explained to me.[46] Ultimately, the most innovative aspects of all the projects profiled in this book are not related to the fact that they are calling out these injustices. Significantly, this digital activism on behalf of marginalized groups is being used to cultivate supportive communities and envision religion that breaks down binaries and brings to the center people on the margins.

These new faith communities celebrate unruly souls, not simply by including these people but by making them the focus of spirituality. Communities such as The Liturgists or Exvangelicals address the spiritual questions and concerns of people who are dismissed and denigrated in Evangelical Christian churches. The hosts of *Truth's Table* use their podcast, social media platforms, and events to develop a sanctuary for Black Christian women to receive God's love. Finally, critiques within Islam about modesty teachings, homophobia, sexual abuse, and anti-Black racism motivate structural reform through organizations such as FACE (with its work against gender-based violence) and the Muslim Anti-Racism Collaborative (with its projects for racial justice). Additionally, Mipsterz is a creative community that celebrates the in-betweenness of Muslim youth, who may struggle to find a home in traditional Muslim communities or in mainstream American cultural spaces.

THE UNAFFILIATED, IMPURE, UNRULY, QUEER, AND HYBRID GENERATION

The younger generations of activists in the United States are more accustomed than previous generations to blurring boundaries, breaking down binaries, resisting categories, and embracing hybridity. Compared with older generations, the Millennials and Gen-Zers are the far more diverse in terms of race, ethnicity, and religion. Surveys indicate their openness to various expressions of sexuality and gender.[47] Furthermore, they are more supportive of progressive causes, as shown by the popularity among these generations of democratic socialist politicians like Bernie Sanders and Alexandria Ocasio-Cortez and by the essential role of young activists in movements for racial justice, climate policy changes, immigration reform, Indigenous rights, and reproductive freedom. Digital media add a layer to the lives of young people, as they embrace the creative elements of these digital tools as ways to express their identities, develop community connections, and participate in larger work for justice.

While younger Americans are less affiliated with religious institutions, this book has shown how young people turn to digital media to explore deeper questions of spirituality and faith and create communities with others seeking meaning. Concerns about various forms of oppression and injustice are often silenced in traditional religious spaces, and digital media enable coordinated efforts to speak from these marginalized perspectives. These examples also illustrate how issues like racism, misogyny, and homophobia transcend single religions. Through online efforts such as #ChurchToo and #MosqueMeToo, young activists begin to see the ways that power imbalances enable abuse. Besides using digital media tools to challenge people in positions of power, these activists develop supportive spaces both online and offline for those recovering from religious trauma. Just as early feminists used theology projects to celebrate the divine feminine, these activists use the creativity of digital spaces like Twitter hashtags, Instagram images, podcasts, and music videos to reformulate faith centered on the value of Blackness, queerness, and femininity. This is not a generation uninterested in questions of faith and spirituality. Rather, it is a generation of religious misfits— young people who embrace the interstitial, playful, and flexible aspects of digital media to develop supportive faith communities built on the foundation of queerness, hybridity, and unruliness.

ACKNOWLEDGMENTS

At times, writing can be a lonely pursuit, but writing a book during a global pandemic is particularly isolating. I am very grateful to have had support from so many people near and far to make this process less solitary. First and foremost, I must thank all the writers, activists, and creators who took time to speak with me about their incredible work: Emily Joy Allison, Linda Kay Klein, Keisha McKenzie, Matthias Roberts, Zainab bint Younus, Leah Vernon, Mona Haydar, Abbas Rattani, and Sara Alfageeh. This book would be nothing without your reflective comments and your extensive work to demonstrate the value of all souls.

Thank you to Nicole Solano and the staff at Rutgers University Press for your guidance and editorial advice throughout this process. I am grateful for your interest in and encouragement of this project from the beginning. My appreciation also goes to the anonymous reviewers, who provided helpful and astute feedback.

I am very grateful to have found a supportive academic home at Boston College (BC). Thank you to Dean Greg Kalscheur, Provost David Quigley, and the other members of the administration for the opportunity for a semester's sabbatical to complete the book, as well as other institutional support for my research. I am greatly appreciative of colleagues in the Communication Department, who provided research advice and feedback on my work, as well as a friendly and encouraging atmosphere. Thank you to Matt Sienkiewicz, Lisa Cuklanz, Ali Erol, Mike Serazio, Ashley Duggan, Lindsay Hogan, Celeste Wells, Tony Tran, Renée Pastel, Rita Rosenthal, Ernesto Livon-Grosman, Mo Jang, Brett Ingram, Don Fishman, Marcus Breen, Ann Marie Barry, Kristin Hartnett, and Christine Caswell. Thanks especially to Leslie Douglas for always making sure that the administrative matters run smoothly. Completing this book in the middle of a global pandemic would have been impossible without the child care provided by the BC Children's Center. I am grateful to Karen Cristello, Taylor Crowley, and Annmarie Lee for providing a nurturing environment for my daughter.

Thank you to my wider academic community in religion and media, especially those who supported me during my graduate studies at the University of Colorado: Stewart Hoover, Nabil Echchaibi, Deborah Whitehead, Nathan Schneider, Lynn Schofield Clark, Heidi Campbell, Jeffrey Mahan, Samira Rajabi, Susanne Stadlbauer, Rachel Lara van der Merwe, Ashley Campbell, Art Bamford, Ryan Bartlett, Seung Soo Kim, Giulia Evolvi, Ruth Tsuria, Tim Hutchings, Johanna Sumiala, Mia Lövheim, Andrea Stanton, Rosemary Pennington, Corrina Laughlin, Rianne Subijanto, Ji Yoon Ryu, and Shannon O'Sullivan. Thank you especially to Gino Canella for providing encouragement as we go through the Boston academic job experience together.

I'm grateful to my friends who have provided support, from neighbors in Boston to Dominican University friends in Chicago and friends in Colorado, Oregon, and Alaska: Claire McCormick, Angela Maly, Danielle Lancellotti, Michele Lepietre, Tony Dreyfus, Cindy Dittbrenner, Chris Barry, Eileen Cahill Newman, Grant Newman, Erika Corona Owens, Jessie Vazquez, Stefanie Piatkiewicz, Jessica Mackinnon, MaDonna Thelen, John Jenks, Sarah Jones, Bridget Antil, Courtney Adams, Kaela Geschke, Chelsea Gulling, and Oz Hazel. I'm also grateful to my family, especially my parents, Don and Rae-Marie Peterson; and my in-laws, Jack and Angie Keane.

Completing this book in a pandemic would have been nearly impossible without the never-ending support of my partner, Jesse Keane, and the never-ending energy of my daughter, Frances. I can't imagine going through the pandemic experience without you both. In the spring of 2020 when I was faced with the prospect of writing this book while inside a small apartment with a three-year-old and no separate office with a door that locked, I was doubtful that the project would ever be completed. I am so thankful to have an incredible partner, who not only kept the kiddo from always barging through the door to see Mommy, but who also provided emotional encouragement, diverting distractions, delicious meals, and insightful feedback on my writing and research. To Frances, I am amazed at your love of life and your willingness to jump headfirst into new adventures. It is an honor to be your mother and watch you learn and grow.

Finally, in writing this book, I was greatly moved by the tragedy and grief that surrounded all of us. In particular, I want to acknowledge the deaths of two people who served as personal mentors and showed me a path to unruliness. To Sister Joan O'Shea and all the Dominican Sisters who modeled what it means for women in the Catholic Church to be unruly souls with their quest for justice and equality, and to Father Chuck Peterson, a towering but sensitive figure, who demonstrated how to be a priest whose heart ached for the concerns of the people: your models of how to live out a faith that cares for those on the margins greatly influenced my writing in this book.

NOTES

INTRODUCTION

1. Mona Haydar, "Dog (ft. Jackie Cruz)," YouTube, July 17, 2017, video, 4:12, https://youtu.be/idMJIEFH_ns.

2. Hannah Paasch (@hannahpaasch), "#kissshamebye normalized the idea that the girls," Twitter, July 18, 2016.

3. Keisha McKenzie (@mackenzian), "Combination of theologically justified racism," Twitter, July 18, 2016.

4. Although this book is focused on feminist activism, not all of the participants in this work identify as women. In discussing the cases, mention is often made to women or female identity, but the activists behind these projects are cognizant that this work also incorporates those who are genderqueer or transgender, as well as male allies.

5. Sarah Banet-Weiser, *Empowered: Popular Feminism and Popular Misogyny* (Durham, NC: Duke University Press, 2018).

6. Evgeny Morozov, "Foreign Policy: Brave New World of Slacktivism," *NPR*, May 19, 2009, https://www.npr.org/templates/story/story.php?storyId=104302141.

7. Michelle Higgins, Christina Edmondson, and Ekemini Uwan, "Embodied Blackness: Objectification," *Truth's Table*, April 14, 2017, podcast audio, 50:02, https://soundcloud.com/truthstable/embodied-blackness-objectification.

8. Alice E. Marwick, *Status Update: Celebrity, Publicity, and Branding in the Social Media Age* (New Haven, CT: Yale University Press, 2013), 5.

9. Nick Couldry, *Why Voice Matters: Culture and Politics after Neoliberalism* (London: SAGE, 2010).

10. Jodi Dean, *Democracy and Other Neoliberal Fantasies: Communicative Capitalism and Left Politics* (Durham, NC: Duke University Press, 2009), 22.

11. Ibid., 24.

12. Ibid., 40.

13. Henry Jenkins, Mizuko Ito, danah boyd, *Participatory Culture in a Networked Era: A Conversation on Youth, Learning, Commerce, and Politics* (Cambridge, UK: Polity, 2016).

14. Christian Fuchs, *Social Media: A Critical Introduction*, 2nd ed. (London: SAGE, 2017), 73.

15. Sarah Banet-Weiser, *Authentic™: The Politics of Ambivalence in a Brand Culture* (New York: New York University Press, 2013).

16. W. Lance Bennett and Alexandra Segerberg, "The Logic of Connective Action: Digital Media and the Personalization of Contentious Politics," *Information, Communication and Society* 15, no. 5 (2012): 748–749.

17. Ibid., 744.

18. Zizi Papacharissi, *Affective Publics: Sentiment, Technology, and Politics* (New York: Oxford University Press, 2014), 8.

19. Zizi Papacharissi, "Affective Publics and Structures of Storytelling: Sentiment, Events and Mediality," *Information, Communication and Society* 19, no. 3 (2016): 310.

20. Ibid., 321.

21. Peter Dahlgren, *Media and Political Engagement: Citizens, Communication, and Democracy.* (Cambridge: Cambridge University Press, 2009), 116.

22. Ibid., 167.

23. Lynn Schofield Clark, "Participants on the Margins: #BlackLivesMatter and the Role That Shared Artifacts of Engagement Played among Minoritized Political Newcomers on Snapchat, Facebook, and Twitter," *International Journal of Communication* 10 (2016): 237.

24. Zeynep Tufekci, *Twitter and Tear Gas: The Power and Fragility of Networked Protest* (New Haven, CT: Yale University Press), 112.

25. Ibid., xxvi.

26. Michela Ardizzoni, *Matrix Activism: Global Practices of Resistance* (New York: Routledge, 2017), 1–2.

27. Rosemary Clark-Parsons, "'I SEE YOU, I BELIEVE YOU, I STAND WITH YOU': #MeToo and the Performance of Networked Feminist Visibility," *Feminist Media Studies* 21, no. 3 (2019): 369.

28. Sarah J. Jackson, Moya Bailey, and Brooke Foucault Welles, *#HashtagActivism: Networks of Race and Gender Justice* (Cambridge, MA: MIT Press, 2020), xxxviii.

29. Stuart Hall, "What Is This 'Black' in Black Popular Culture?" *Social Justice* 20, nos. 1–2 (1993): 107.

30. Birgit Meyer, "Introduction: From Imagined Communities to Aesthetic Formations: Religious Mediations, Sensational Forms, and Styles of Binding," in *Aesthetic Formations: Media, Religion, and the Senses*, ed. Birgit Meyer (New York: Palgrave Macmillan, 2009), 11.

31. Mia Lövheim, "Media and Religion through the Lens of Feminist and Gender Theory," in *Media, Religion and Gender: Key Issues and New Challenges*, ed. Mia Lövheim (London: Routledge, 2013), 24.

32. Anna Piela, "I Am Just Doing My Bit to Promote Modesty: Niqabis' Self-Portraits on Photo-Sharing Websites," *Feminist Media Studies* 13, no. 5 (2013): 788.

33. Rosemary Pennington, "Making Space in Social Media: #MuslimWomensDay in Twitter," *Journal of Communication Inquiry* 42, no. 3 (July 2018): 200.

34. Steven Fekete and Jessica Knippel, "The Devil You Know: An Exploration of Virtual Religious Deconstruction Communities," *Journal of Religion, Media, and Digital Culture* 9, no. 2 (2020): 176.

35. Andrew F. Herrmann, "Purity, Nationalism, and Whiteness: The Fracturing of Fundamentalist Evangelicalism," *International Review of Qualitative Research* 13, no. 4 (July 2020): 423.

36. Joshua Harris, *I Kissed Dating Goodbye: A New Attitude toward Romance and Relationships* (Sisters, OR: Multnomah Books, 1997).

37. Mona Haydar, "Barbarian," YouTube, June 15, 2018, video, 3:45, https://youtu.be/lfDQ5REWCuo.

38. Whitney Phillips and Ryan M. Milner, *The Ambivalent Internet: Mischief, Oddity, and Antagonism Online* (Cambridge: Polity Press, 2017), 14.

39. Kimberlé Williams Crenshaw, "Demarginalizing the Intersection of Race and Sex: A Black Feminist Critique of Antidiscrimination Doctrine, Feminist Theory and Antiracist Politics," *University of Chicago Legal Forum* 1989, no. 1 (1989): 140.

40. Combahee River Collective in Second Wave, "A Black Feminist Statement," in *The Second Wave: A Reader in Feminist Theory*, ed. Linda Nicholson (New York: Routledge, 1997), 64.

41. Frances M. Beal, "Double Jeopardy: To Be Black and Female," *Meridians* 8, no. 2 (2008): 174.

42. Gloria Anzaldúa, *Borderlands/La Frontera: The New Mestiza* (San Francisco, CA: Aunt Lute Book Company, 1987).

43. Lisa A. Flores, "Creating Discursive Space through a Rhetoric of Difference: Chicana Feminists Craft a Homeland," *Quarterly Journal of Speech* 82, no. 2 (1996): 143.

44. Ibid., 146.

45. Sarah Florini, *Beyond Hashtags: Racial Politics and Black Digital Networks* (New York: New York University Press, 2019), 18.

46. Homi K. Bhabha, *The Location of Culture* (London: Routledge, 1994), 126.

47. Angel M. Hinzo and Lynn Schofield Clark, "Digital Survivance and Trickster Humor: Exploring Visual and Digital Indigenous Epistemologies in the #NoDAPL Movement," *Information, Communication and Society* 22, no. 6 (2019): 802.

48. José Esteban Muñoz, *Disidentifications: Queers of Color and the Performance of Politics* (Minneapolis: University of Minnesota Press, 1999), 12.

49. Ibid., 31.

50. bell hooks, *Black Looks: Race and Representation* (Boston: South End Press, 1992), 126.

51. Sara Ahmed, *The Cultural Politics of Emotion*, 2nd ed. (New York: Routledge, 2014), 224.

52. Stuart Hall, "Signification, Representation, Ideology: Althusser and the Post-Structuralist Debate," *Critical Studies in Mass Communication* 2, no. 2 (1985): 91–114.

53. Lawrence Grossberg, "On Postmodernism and Articulation: An Interview with Stuart Hall," in *Stuart Hall: Critical Dialogues in Cultural Studies*, ed. David Morley and Kuan-Hsing Chen (London: Routledge, 1996), 142.

54. Yarimar Bonilla and Jonathan Rosa, "#Ferguson: Digital Protest, Hashtag Ethnography, and the Racial Politics of Social Media in the United States," *American Ethnologist* 42, no. 1 (2015): 9.

55. Ibid.

56. Sarah Pink, "Visual Ethnography and the Internet: Visuality, Virtuality and the Spatial Turn," in *Advances in Visual Methodology*, ed. Sarah Pink (London: SAGE, 2012), 119.

57. John Postill and Sarah Pink, "Social Media Ethnography: The Digital Researcher in a Messy Web," *Media International Australia*, 145, no. 1 (November 2012): 124.

58. Katherine Borland, "'That's Not What I Said': Interpretive Conflict in Oral Narrative Research," in *Women's Words: The Feminist Practice of Oral History*, ed. Sherna Berger Gluck and Daphne Patai (New York: Routledge, 1991), 64.

59. Annette Markham and Elizabeth Buchanan, "Ethical Decision-Making and Internet Research: Recommendations from the AoIR Ethics Working Committee (Version 2.0)," AOIR, 2012, http://www.aoir.org/reports/ethics2.pdf, 6.

60. Gayatri Chakravorty Spivak, "Can the Subaltern Speak?," in *Marxism and the Interpretation of Culture*, ed. Cary Nelson and Lawrence Grossberg (Urbana: University of Illinois Press, 1988), 271–313.

61. bell hooks, *Talking Back: Thinking Feminist, Thinking Black* (New York: Routledge, 2015), 43.

62. Patricia Zavella, "Feminist Insider Dilemmas: Constructing Ethnic Identity with Chicana Informants," in *Feminist Dilemmas in Fieldwork*, ed. Diane Wolf (Boulder, CO: Westview Press, 1996), 140–141.

1. DISMANTLING THE HIERARCHY OF SOULS

1. Rosemary Radford Ruether, "Sexism and Misogyny in the Christian Tradition: Liberating Alternatives," *Buddhist-Christian Studies* 34 (2014): 85.

2. Rita M. Gross, *Feminism and Religion: An Introduction* (Boston: Beacon Press, 1996), 114.

3. Amanda Barbee, "Naked and Ashamed: Women and Evangelical Purity Culture," *Other Journal*, no. 23 (March 3, 2014), https://theotherjournal.com/2014/03/03/naked-and-ashamed-women-and-evangelical-purity-culture/.

4. Ryan P. Burge, *The Nones: Where They Came From, Who They Are, and Where They Are Going* (Minneapolis, MN: Fortress Press, 2021), 15.

5. Deborah Jian Lee, *Rescuing Jesus: How People of Color, Women, and Queer Christians Are Reclaiming Evangelicalism* (Boston: Beacon Press, 2015), 44.

6. Anthea Butler, *White Evangelical Racism: The Politics of Morality in America* (Chapel Hill: University of North Carolina Press, 2021), 67.

7. Kelly Brown Douglas, *Stand Your Ground: Black Bodies and the Justice of God* (Maryknoll, NY: Orbis, 2015), 16.

8. Jeannine Hill Fletcher, *The Sin of White Supremacy: Christianity, Racism, and Religious Diversity in America* (Maryknoll, NY: Orbis, 2017), 5.

9. Ibid., 36.

10. Ibid., 80.

11. Douglas, *Stand Your Ground*, 30.

12. Ibid.

13. Ibid., 31.

14. Stephanie Y. Mitchem, *Introducing Womanist Theology* (Maryknoll, NY: Orbis Books, 2002), 26.

15. Ibid., 27.

16. Katie Geneva Cannon, *Katie's Canon: Womanism and the Soul of the Black Community* (New York: Continuum, 1998), 42.

17. Butler, *White Evangelical Racism*, 11.

18. Ibid., 66–69; Lee, *Rescuing Jesus*, 66–68; Burge, *The Nones*, 51.

19. Austin Channing Brown, *I'm Still Here: Black Dignity in a World Made for Whiteness* (New York: Convergent, 2018), 23.

20. James Cone, "Theology's Great Sin: Silence in the Face of White Supremacy," *Black Theology* 2, no. 2 (2004): 141.

21. Butler, *White Evangelical Racism*, 104.

22. Mahmood Mamdani, "Good Muslim, Bad Muslim: A Political Perspective on Culture and Terrorism," *American Anthropologist* 104, no. 3 (2002): 771.

23. Butler, *White Evangelical Racism*, 107.

24. Saher Selod and David G. Embrick, "Racialization and Muslims: Situating the Muslim Experience in Race Scholarship," *Sociology Compass* 7, no. 8 (2013): 652.

25. Cheryl I. Harris, "Whiteness as Property," in *Critical Race Theory: The Key Writings That Formed the Movement*, ed. Kimberlé Crenshaw, Neil Gotanda, Gary Peller, and Kendall Thomas (New York: New Press, 1995), 277.

26. Amaney Jamal, "The Racialization of Muslim Americans," in *Muslims in Western Politics*, ed. Abdulkader H. Sinno (Bloomington: Indiana University Press, 2009), 205.

27. Junaid Rana, *Terrifying Muslims: Race and Labor in the South Asian Diaspora* (Durham, NC: Duke University Press, 2011), 32.

28. Selod and Embrick, "Racialization and Muslims," 646.

29. Khyati Joshi, "The Racialization of Hinduism, Islam, and Sikhism," *Equality and Excellence in Education* 39, no. 3 (2006): 213.

30. Lila Abu-Lughod, "Do Muslim Women Really Need Saving? Anthropological Reflections on Cultural Relativism and Its Others," *American Anthropologist* 104, no. 3 (September 2002): 783–790.

31. miriam cooke, "The Muslimwoman," *Contemporary Islam* 1, no. 2 (2007): 139–154.

32. Alia Al-Saji, "The Racialization of Muslim Veils: A Philosophical Analysis," *Philosophy and Social Criticism* 36, no. 8 (2010): 877.

33. Malek Alloula, *The Colonial Harem* (Minneapolis: University of Minnesota Press, 1986).

34. Dina Siddiqi, "Sexuality as Liberation? The Work of Salvation Narratives in Neoliberal Times," *Alal O Dulal*, March 2014, http://alalodulal.org/2014/03/13/sexuality-as-liberation/.

35. Mona Eltahawy, "#MosqueMeToo: What Happened When I Was Sexually Assaulted during the Hajj," *Washington Post*, February 15, 2018, https://www.washingtonpost.com/news /global-opinions/wp/2018/02/15/mosquemetoo-what-happened-when-i-was-sexually -assaulted-during-the-hajj/.

36. See Amaney Jamal and Nadine Naber, *Race and Arab Americans before and after 9/11: From Invisible Citizens to Visible Subjects* (Syracuse, NY: Syracuse University Press, 2008); Khaled A. Beydoun, *American Islamophobia: Understanding the Roots and Rise of Fear* (Oakland: University of California Press, 2018); Louise A. Cainkar, *Homeland Insecurity: The Arab American and Muslim American Experience after 9/11* (New York: Russell Sage Foundation, 2009).

37. Namira Islam, "Soft Islamophobia," *Religions* 9, no. 10 (2018): 5.

38. Juliette Galonnier, "The Racialization of Muslims in France and the United States: Some Insights from White Converts to Islam," *Social Compass* 62, no.4 (2015): 570–583.

39. Pew Research Center, "U.S. Muslims Concerned About Their Place in Society, but Continue to Believe in the American Dream," Pew Research Center, July 26, 2017, https://www .pewforum.org/2017/07/26/findings-from-pew-research-centers-2017-survey-of-us-muslims/.

40. Su'ad Abdul Khabeer, *Muslim Cool: Race, Religion, and Hip Hop in the United States* (New York: New York University Press, 2016), 14.

41. Ibid.

42. Ibid.

43. Ibid., 15.

44. Emmanuel Mauleón, "Black Twice: Policing Black Muslim Identities," *UCLA Law Review* 65, no. 5 (June 2018): 1332.

45. Jamillah Karim, *American Muslim Women: Negotiating Race, Class, and Gender within the Ummah* (New York: New York University Press, 2009), 10.

46. Pamela J. Prickett, *Believing in South Central: Everyday Islam in the City of Angels* (Chicago: University of Chicago Press, 2021), 106.

47. Khabeer, *Muslim Cool*, 15.

48. Prickett, *Believing in South Central*, 103–104.

49. Margari Hill, Daniel Kowalski, Meral Kocak, Hakeem Muhammad, Sherouk Ahmed, and Namira Islam, "Study of Intra-Muslim Ethnic Relations: Muslim American Views on Race Relations," Muslim Anti-Racism Collaborative, June 4, 2015, https://www.muslimarc.org /interethnic/, 20.

50. Leila Ahmed, *Women and Gender in Islam: Historical Roots of a Modern Debate* (New Haven, CT: Yale University Press, 1992).

51. Amina Wadud, *Qur'an and Woman: Rereading the Sacred Text from a Woman's Perspective* (New York: Oxford University Press, 1999).

52. Carol P. Christ, "Why Women Need the Goddess," *HERESIES* 2, no. 1 (Spring 1978): 8–13.

53. Mary Daly, *The Church and the Second Sex* (Boston: Beacon Press, 1985).

54. Mary Daly, *Beyond God the Father: Toward a Philosophy of Women's Liberation* (Boston: Beacon Press, 1973).

55. Gross, *Feminism and Religion*, 42.

56. Pamela D. H. Cochran, *Evangelical Feminism: A History* (New York: New York University Press, 2005), 8.

57. Letha Scanzoni and Nancy Hardesty, *All We're Meant to Be: A Biblical Approach to Women's Liberation* (Grand Rapids, MI: William B. Eerdmans Publishing Company, 1992), 16.

58. Eliza Griswold, "The Radically Inclusive Christianity of Rachel Held Evans," *New Yorker*, May 6, 2019, https://www.newyorker.com/news/postscript/the-radically-inclusive-christianity -of-rachel-held-evans.

59. See, for example, Sarah Stankorb, "Inside the Scam of the 'Purity' Movement," *Cosmopolitan*, February 5, 2019, https://www.cosmopolitan.com/politics/a26026217/sexual-abstinence-joshua-harris-purity-movement-scam/; Ruth Graham, "Hello *Goodbye*," *Slate*, August 26, 2016, https://slate.com/human-interest/2016/08/i-kissed-dating-goodbye-author-is-maybe-kind-of-sorry.html; Christine Emba, "The Dramatic Implosion of 'I Kissed Dating Goodbye' Is a Lesson—and a Warning," *Washington Post*, November 14, 2018, https://www.washingtonpost.com/opinions/the-dramatic-implosion-of-i-kissed-dating-goodbye-is-a-lesson--and-a-warning/2018/11/14/eeecd65c-e850-11e8-bbdb-72fdbf9d4fed_story.html.

60. See Emma Green, "Rachel Held Evans, Hero to Christian Misfits," *Atlantic*, May 6, 2019, https://www.theatlantic.com/politics/archive/2019/05/rachel-held-evans-death-progressive-christianity/588784/; Elizabeth Dias and Sam Roberts, "Rachel Held Evans, Voice of the Wandering Evangelical, Dies at 37," *New York Times*, May 4, 2019, https://www.nytimes.com/2019/05/04/us/rachel-held-evans.html.

61. See Bradley Onishi, "The Rise of #Exvangelical," *Religion and Politics*, April 9, 2019, https://religionandpolitics.org/2019/04/09/the-rise-of-exvangelical/; Blake Chastain, *#Exvangelical* podcast, https://www.exvangelicalpodcast.com/; "Exvangelical Private Group," *Facebook*, https://www.facebook.com/groups/exvangelical/ (accessed July 25, 2019); "#Exvangelical," *Twitter*, accessed July 25, 2019, https://twitter.com/hashtag/exvangelical?lang=en.

62. See Megan Marz, "Personal Stories of the Exodus from Christianity," *Washington Post*, January 16, 2020, https://www.washingtonpost.com/outlook/personal-stories-of-the-exodus-from-christianity/2020/01/16/7594a8f8-1472-11ea-a659-7d69641c6ff7_story.html.

63. "Deconstructing My Religion," CBS News, December 1, 2018, video, 26:55, https://www.cbs.com/shows/cbs-news-specials/video/jBSOpwEP1_gFcxYqGIU_oPjxUqETIpGN/deconstructing-my-religion/.

64. Nina Burleigh, "Evangelical Christians Helped Elect Donald Trump, but Their Time as a Major Political Force Is Coming to an End," *Newsweek*, December 13, 2018, https://www.newsweek.com/2018/12/21/evangelicals-republicans-trump-millenials-1255745.html.

65. See Rachel Held Evans, *Searching for Sunday: Loving, Leaving, and Finding the Church* (Nashville, TN: Nelson Books, 2015), and *A Year of Biblical Womanhood: How a Liberated Woman Found Herself Sitting on Her Roof, Covering Her Head, and Calling Her Husband "Master"* (Nashville, TN: Nelson Books, 2012).

66. See Mihee Kim-Kort, *Outside the Lines: How Embracing Queerness Will Transform Your Faith* (Minneapolis, MN: Fortress Press, 2018); Lee, *Rescuing Jesus*; Elizabeth M. Edman, *Queer Virtue: What LGBTQ People Know about Life and Love and How It Can Revitalize Christianity* (Boston: Beacon Press, 2016).

67. See Brown, *I'm Still Here*; Lenny Duncan, *Dear Church: A Love Letter from a Black Preacher to the Whitest Denomination in the U.S.* (Minneapolis, MN: Fortress Press, 2019).

68. Brown, *I'm Still Here*, 168.

69. Lee, *Rescuing Jesus*, 177.

70. Muslim ARC, "About," 2018, https://www.muslimarc.org/about.

71. Islam, "Soft Islamophobia," 4.

72. Su'ad Abdul Khabeer, Arshad Ali, Evelyn Alsultany, Sohail Daulatzai, Lara Deeb, Carol Fadda, Zareena Grewal, Juliane Hammer, Nadine Naber, and Junaid Rana, "Islamophobia Is Racism: Resource for Teaching and Learning about Anti-Muslim Racism in the United States," 2018, https://islamophobiaisracism.wordpress.com/.

73. Beydoun, *American Islamophobia*.

74. Islam, "Soft Islamophobia," 4.

75. Sylvia Chan-Malik, *Being Muslim: A Cultural History of Women of Color in American Islam* (New York: New York University Press, 2018), 26.

76. Linda Kay Klein, *Pure: Inside the Evangelical Movement That Shamed a Generation of Young Women and How I Broke Free* (New York: Touchstone, 2018), 62.

77. Sarah Banet-Weiser, *Empowered: Popular Feminism and Popular Misogyny* (Durham, NC: Duke University Press, 2018), 15.

2. #KISSSHAMEBYE

1. Matthias Roberts (@matthiasroberts), "I kissed straighting goodbye," Twitter, July 25, 2019.

2. Joshua Harris, *I Kissed Dating Goodbye: A New Attitude toward Romance and Relationships* (Sisters, OR: Multnomah Books, 1997).

3. Gina Masullo Chen, Paromita Pain, and Jinglun Zhang, "#NastyWomen: Reclaiming the Twitterverse from Misogyny," in *Mediating Misogyny: Gender, Technology, and Harassment*, ed. Jacqueline Ryan Vickery and Tracy Everbach (New York: Palgrave Macmillan, 2018), 371–388.

4. Liz Sills, "Hashtag Comedy: From Muslim Rage to #Muslimrage," *ReOrient* 2, no. 2 (2017): 160–174.

5. Sarah Florini, "Tweets, Tweeps, and Signifyin': Communication and Cultural Performance on 'Black Twitter,'" *Television and New Media* 15, no. 3 (March 2014): 223–237.

6. Stephen Arterburn, Fred Stoeker, and Mike Yorkey, *Every Young Man's Battle: Strategies for Victory in the Real World of Sexual Temptation* (Colorado Springs: WaterBrook Press, 2002).

7. Amanda Barbee, "Naked and Ashamed: Women and Evangelical Purity Culture," *Other Journal*, 23 (March 3, 2014), https://theotherjournal.com/2014/03/03/naked-and-ashamed -women-and-evangelical-purity-culture/.

8. Ibid.

9. Sarah Stankorb, "Inside the Scam of the 'Purity' Movement," *Cosmopolitan*, February 5, 2019, https://www.cosmopolitan.com/politics/a26026217/sexual-abstinence-joshua-harris -purity-movement-scam/.

10. Linda Kay Klein, *Pure: Inside the Evangelical Movement That Shamed a Generation of Young Women and How I Broke Free* (New York: Touchstone, 2018), 23.

11. Ibid.

12. Stankorb, "Inside the Scam of the 'Purity' Movement."

13. Ruth Graham, "Hello *Goodbye*," *Slate*, August 26, 2016, https://slate.com/human-interest /2016/08/i-kissed-dating-goodbye-author-is-maybe-kind-of-sorry.html.

14. Christine Emba, "The Dramatic Implosion of 'I Kissed Dating Goodbye' Is a Lesson— and a Warning," *Washington Post*, November 14, 2018, https://www.washingtonpost.com /opinions/the-dramatic-implosion-of-i-kissed-dating-goodbye-is-a-lesson--and-a-warning /2018/11/14/eeecd65c-e850-11e8-bbdb-72fdbf9d4fed_story.html.

15. See Jessica Valenti, *The Purity Myth: How America's Obsession with Virginity Is Hurting Young Women* (Berkeley, CA: Seal Press, 2009); Klein, *Pure*; Dianna Anderson, *Damaged Goods: New Perspectives on Christian Purity* (New York: Jericho Books, 2015).

16. Valenti, *The Purity Myth*, 142–143.

17. Sandi Villarreal, "Their Generation Was Shamed by Purity Culture. Here's What They're Building in Its Place," *Sojourners*, March 7, 2019, https://sojo.net/interactive/their-generation -was-shamed-purity-culture-heres-what-theyre-building-its-place.

18. Amy DeRogatis, *Saving Sex: Sexuality and Salvation in American Evangelicalism* (Oxford: Oxford University Press, 2015), 13.

19. Ibid., 30.

20. Ibid., 14.

21. Klein, *Pure*, 3.

22. Ibid., 14.

23. DeRogatis, *Saving Sex*, 40.

24. Linda Kay Klein, "Am I Impure?" *The Liturgists*, January 23, 2020, podcast audio, 47:14, https://theliturgists.com/podcast/2020/1/23/am-i-impure.

25. Valenti, *The Purity Myth*, 10.

26. Ruth Everhart, *The #MeToo Reckoning: Facing the Church's Complicity in Sexual Abuse and Misconduct* (Downers Grove, IL: InterVarsity Press, 2020), 52.

27. Ibid., 125.

28. Stankorb, "Inside the Scam of the 'Purity' Movement."

29. Barbee, "Naked and Ashamed."

30. Ibid.

31. Emily Joy Allison, "Emily Joy: About," 2016, http://emilyjoypoetry.com/about.

32. Klein, "Am I Impure?"

33. Valenti, *The Purity Myth*, 30.

34. DeRogatis, *Saving Sex*, 130.

35. Klein, "Am I Impure?"

36. Ibid.

37. Keisha McKenzie, interview with author, November 22, 2019.

38. Ibid.

39. Linda Kay Klein, interview with author, October 24, 2019.

40. McKenzie, interview with author.

41. Klein, interview with author.

42. Ibid.

43. Emily Joy Allison, interview with author, October 26, 2019.

44. Ibid.

45. *No Shame Movement*, "About," accessed November 20, 2021, https://noshamemovement .tumblr.com/about

46. *Thank God for Sex*, "About Us," accessed October 30, 2021, http://www.thankgodforsex .org/about.html.

47. Lyz Lenz, "Recovering from *I Kissed Dating Goodbye*: A Roundtable," *The Toast*, June 8, 2016, https://the-toast.net/2016/06/08/recovering-from-i-kissed-dating-goodbye-a-roundtable/.

48. Allison, interview with author.

49. Klein, interview with author.

50. Ibid.

51. Yarimar Bonilla and Jonathan Rosa, "#Ferguson: Digital Protest, Hashtag Ethnography, and the Racial Politics of Social Media in the United States," *American Ethnologist* 42, no. 1 (2015): 9.

52. Rosemary Pennington, "Making Space in Social Media: #MuslimWomensDay in Twitter," *Journal of Communication Inquiry* 42, no. 3 (July 2018): 199–217.

53. Rosemary Clark-Parsons, "'I SEE YOU, I BELIEVE YOU, I STAND WITH YOU': #MeToo and the Performance of Networked Feminist Visibility," *Feminist Media Studies* 21, no. 3 (2019): 369.

54. Ibid., 363.

55. José Esteban Muñoz, *Disidentifications: Queers of Color and the Performance of Politics* (Minneapolis: University of Minnesota Press, 1999), 4.

56. Ibid.

57. Ibid., 11–12.

58. Klein, interview with author.

59. Allison, interview with author.

60. Klein, interview with author.

61. Break Free Together (@breakfreetogether), Instagram, https://www.instagram.com /breakfreetogether/.

62. Allison, interview with author.

63. Sarah J. Jackson, Moya Bailey, and Brooke Foucault Welles, #HashtagActivism: Networks of Race and Gender Justice (Cambridge, MA: MIT Press, 2020), 26.

64. Allison, interview with author.

65. Hannah Paasch (@riverpaasch), "My body & reputation belonged to everyone but me #KissShameBye," Twitter, July 18, 2016.

66. Samantha Field (@samanthapfield), "A3: but b/c women are so infantilized in #IKDG," Twitter, August 3, 2016.

67. Verdell Wright (@VdotW), "Main lessons: my body is mine and it's okay to use it," Twitter, July 18, 2016.

68. Samantha Field (@samanthapfield), "A3: my libido is higher than my partner's," Twitter, August 3, 2016.

69. Lola Prescott (@seelolago), "when you frame a NATURAL HUMAN EMOTION," Twitter, August 3, 2016.

70. No Shame Movement (@noshamemov), "A2: #IKDG framed sex as something that 'happened,'" Twitter, August 3, 2016.

71. Break Free Together (@breakfreetogether), "#BreakFreeTogether," Instagram photo, November 1, 2018, https://www.instagram.com/p/Bpp0EGRhGNN/.

72. TMW (@breakfreetogether), "#BreakFreeTogether," Instagram photo, September 16, 2018, https://www.instagram.com/p/BnziEtJgzIX/.

73. No Shame Movement (@noshamemov), "PLEASE REMEMBER: you have value, regardless of what you do," Twitter, August 3, 2016.

74. Sarah (@breakfreetogether), "#BreakFreeTogether," Instagram photo, October 4, 2018, https://www.instagram.com/p/BohSuDhgrSm/

75. Allison, interview with author.

76. Samantha Field (@samanthapfield), "A2: my first 'official' courtship we followed," Twitter, August 3, 2016.

77. Klein, interview with author.

78. Keisha McKenzie (@mackenzian), "There's a way in which purity culture isolates us," Twitter, July 18, 2016.

79. Keisha McKenzie (@mackenzian), "One of the biggest ways to #KissShameBye," Twitter, July 18, 2016.

80. Verdell Wright (@VdotW), "We created the tag #kissshamebye," Twitter, July 18, 2016.

81. Keisha McKenzie (@mackenzian), "If tonight's conversation stirred up old," Twitter, July 18, 2016.

82. Samantha Field, "It's Not OK and We're Not Alright," Life after "I Kissed Dating Goodbye," August 26, 2016, https://web.archive.org/web/20161006004741/http://www.lifeafterikdg .com/not-ok-not-alright/.

83. Emily Joy Allison, #ChurchToo: How Purity Culture Upholds Abuse and How to Find Healing (Minneapolis, MN: Broadleaf Books, 2021).

84. Emily Joy Allison, "Emily Joy on Purity Culture," Queerology, September 24, 2019, podcast audio, 39:24, https://matthiasroberts.com/queerology/e089-emily-joy/.

85. Ibid.

86. Vyxsin Drake, "I'm Not the Result They Were Looking For," Life after "I Kissed Dating Goodbye," October 8, 2016, https://web.archive.org/web/20171227080235/http://www .lifeafterikdg.com/im-not-result-looking.

87. Keisha McKenzie (@mackenzian), "A3: Non-heterosexual people are entirely absent," Twitter, July 18, 2016.

88. No Shame Movement (@noshamemov), "Right. Black women especially stay pressured to conform," Twitter, July 18, 2016.

89. Verdell Wright (@VdotW), "Purity culture is rooted in Victorian ideals," Twitter, July 18, 2018.

90. Lyz Lenz, "Recovering from *I Kissed Dating Goodbye:* A Roundtable," *The Toast,* June 8, 2016, https://the-toast.net/2016/06/08/recovering-from-i-kissed-dating-goodbye-a-roundtable/.

91. Ibid.

92. Jameelah Jones, "When a Black Girl Pursues Purity," *Life after "I Kissed Dating Goodbye,"* April 14, 2017, https://web.archive.org/web/20171227075940/http://www.lifeafterikdg.com /black-girl-pursues-purity/.

93. Ibid.

3. BOLD AND BEAUTIFUL

1. Géraldine Mossière, "Modesty and Style in Islamic Attire: Refashioning Muslim Garments in a Western context," *Contemporary Islam* 6 (2012): 117.

2. Reina Lewis, *Muslim Fashion: Contemporary Style Cultures* (Durham, NC: Duke University Press, 2015), 18.

3. Elizabeth Bucar, *Pious Fashion: How Muslim Women Dress* (Cambridge, MA: Harvard University Press, 2017), 2.

4. Ibid., 18.

5. Annelies Moors and Emma Tarlo, *Islamic Fashion and Anti-Fashion: New Perspectives from Europe and North America* (London: Bloomsbury, 2013), 20.

6. Susan B. Kaiser, *Fashion and Cultural Studies* (London: Berg, 2012), 37.

7. Leah Vernon, "The Deletion of the Perfect Instagram Hijabi," *MuslimGirl,* March 7, 2018, http://muslimgirl.com/47646/the-deletion-of-the-perfect-instagram-hijabi/.

8. Amena Khan (@amenakhan), "Vitamin sea Pink coffee And family," Instagram photo, January 9, 2021, https://www.instagram.com/p/CJ1wCaonMwl/

9. Reina Lewis, "Modest Body Politics: The Commercial and Ideological Intersect of Fat, Black, and Muslim in the Modest Fashion Market and Media," *Fashion Theory* 23, no. 2 (2019): 257.

10. Tim Highfield and Tama Leaver, "Instagrammatics and Digital Methods: Studying Visual Social Media, from Selfies and GIFs to Memes and Emoji," *Communication Research and Practice* 2, no. 1 (2016): 48.

11. Tama Leaver, Tim Highfield and Crystal Abidin, *Instagram: Visual Social Media Cultures* (Cambridge: Polity, 2020), 39.

12. Ibid., 43.

13. Ibid., 49.

14. Ibid., 59.

15. Brooke Erin Duffy and Emily Hund, "Gendered Visibility on Social Media: Navigating Instagram's Authenticity Bind," *International Journal of Communication* 13 (2019): 4984.

16. Emily Hund, "Measured Beauty: Exploring the Aesthetics of Instagram's Fashion Influencers," *#SMSociety17: Proceedings of the 8th International Conference on Social Media & Society* (New York: Association for Computing Machinery, 2017): 2.

17. Ibid., 1.

18. Crystal Abidin, "'Aren't These Just Young, Rich Women Doing Vain Things Online?': Influencer Selfies as Subversive Frivolity," *Social Media + Society* 2, no. 2 (April–June 2016): 3.

19. Duffy and Hund, "Gendered Visibility on Social Media," 4984–4985.

20. Hund, "Measured Beauty," 4.

21. Vernon, "The Deletion of the Perfect," *MuslimGirl*.

22. Leah Vernon, interview with author, July 11, 2019.

23. Leah Vernon, "Resume," *Beauty and the Muse*, accessed November 21, 2021, http://www.beautyandthemuse.net/resume-1.

24. Leah Vernon, *Unashamed: Musings of a Fat, Black Muslim* (Boston: Beacon, 2019).

25. Vernon, interview with author.

26. Leah Vernon [@lvernon2000], "A friend and I talked about our experiences as big women," Instagram photo, January 31, 2019, https://www.instagram.com/p/BtT-zwInpgW/.

27. Leah Vernon [@lvernon2000], "'These are fat mommies sitting with their bags of potato chips in front of the television,'" Instagram photo, February 19, 2019, https://www.instagram.com/p/BuElAdtncUk/.

28. Leah Vernon, [@lvernon2000], "Being comfortable, confident in my curvy body, makes insecure people feel very uncomfortable," Instagram photo, January 19, 2019, https://www.instagram.com/p/Bs1FoO1gVOw/.

29. Leah Vernon, [@lvernon2000], "I'm not losing weight in order for you to love me," Instagram photo, May 29, 2021, https://www.instagram.com/p/CPeHhfRpgW1/.

30. Vernon, interview with author.

31. bell hooks, *Black Looks: Race and Representation* (Boston: South End Press, 1992), 126.

32. Sara Ahmed, *The Cultural Politics of Emotion*, 2nd ed. (New York: Routledge, 2014), 224.

33. Leah Vernon [@lvernon2000], "I never set out to be political," Instagram photo, March 20, 2019, https://www.instagram.com/p/BvPvQwUn4MR/.

34. Leah Vernon [@lvernon2000], "Had to block a total of ten people last night who tried it," Instagram photo, March 3, 2019, https://www.instagram.com/p/Buj3cwKHIPl/.

35. Leah Vernon [@lvernon2000], "I recorded a set of IG stories on how to be a white and/or white passing ally," Instagram photo, January 21, 2019, https://www.instagram.com/p/Bs6I78-gMPx/.

36. Leah Vernon [@lvernon2000], "@thecut featured a vid of me dancing on their page for #muslimwomensday," Instagram photo, March 27, 2019, https://www.instagram.com/p/Bvh4TALHnjO/.

37. Leah Vernon [@lvernon2000], "As I am still quite shaken up from yesterday's events," Instagram photo, March 16, 2019, https://www.instagram.com/p/BvFYuW-Hr-Z/.

38. Leah Vernon [@lvernon2000], "After 9/11, I would go to the mosque for Jumah and wonder if someone would come shoot me," Instagram photo, March 15, 2019, https://www.instagram.com/p/BvCp3EAnXAl/.

39. Leah Vernon [@lvernon2000], "I couldn't even post yesterday because I was over it," Instagram photo, January 23, 2019, https://www.instagram.com/p/Bs_TB_6AGeE/.

40. Leah Vernon [@lvernon2000], "On Monday, I'll be headed to Westminster College in Salt Lake City for the week," Instagram photo, March 22, 2019, https://www.instagram.com/p/BvU4MhpHm8Y/.

41. Blair Imani, "About," *Blair Imani*, accessed November 1, 2021, http://blairimani.com/about.

42. Blair Imani, [@blairimani], "It's #LearnOClock This week: OUTDATED PHRASES," Instagram photo, September 6, 2020, https://www.instagram.com/p/CEogqAMnOWe/.

43. Blair Imani, [@blairimani], "I decided to get in on the #Cottagecore moments," Instagram photo, September 19, 2020, https://www.instagram.com/p/CFVgAvinAmC/.

44. Blair Imani, [@blairimani], "THANK YOU FOR 250K FOLLOWERS, LOVELIES!," Instagram photo, August 22, 2020, https://www.instagram.com/p/CEMoYL_H-tf/.

45. Blair Imani, [@blairimani], "YOU should be the absolute last person sh*t talking yourself," Instagram photo, August 19, 2020, https://www.instagram.com/p/CEDyPF8n-6v/.

46. Homi K. Bhabha, *The Location of Culture* (London: Routledge, 1994), 126.

47. Omar Mouallem, "5 Women Quashing Preconceptions about Islam on Social Media," *Wired*, December 3, 2015, http://www.wired.com/2015/12/muslim-women-twitter/.

48. See Zainab bint Younus, "Veiled Snapshots: Muslim Women Who Are Begging to Be Saved," *BuzzFeed*, June 1, 2015, http://www.buzzfeed.com/zainabbintyounus/veiled-snap shots-muslim-women-who-are-begging-to-1lokj; "Covering One's Face Does Not Render One Silent or Stupid," *HuffPost*, December 6, 2017, http://www.huffingtonpost.com/zainab -bint-younus/overing-ones-face-does-not-render-one-silent-or-stupid_b_7539964.html ?utm_hp_ref=tw; and "For Me, Niqab Is a Feminist Statement," *Medium*, June 4, 2015, https:// medium.com/aj-story-behind-the-story/for-me-niqab-is-a-feminist-statement-13ca2fc2fe9a# .m7dvi936t.

49. Zainab bint Younus, interview with author, November 3, 2020.

50. Ibid.

51. Zainab bint Younus, [@bintyounus], "I believe in curating joy," Instagram photo, October 4, 2020, https://www.instagram.com/p/CF6gdlQAvH4/.

52. Bint Younus, interview with author.

53. Zainab bint Younus, [@bintyounus], "{Verily, with hardship comes ease!}," Instagram photo, November 3, 2020, https://www.instagram.com/p/CHJF9G6jNz-/.

54. Zainab bint Younus, [@bintyounus], "Curate faith, and beauty, and joy, in your home and your heart," Instagram photo, September 18, 2020, https://www.instagram.com/p /CFSxZhtD1Zm/.

55. See, for example, Zainab bint Younus, [@bintyounus], "I know I already did a #booksta gram post for The Girl in the Tangerine Scarf," Instagram photo, October 21, 2020, https:// www.instagram.com/p/CGnWo24D8zN/.

56. Zainab bint Younus, [@bintyounus], "I can't believe I haven't officially reviewed the Dae vabad Chronicles yet," Instagram photo, November 4, 2020, https://www.instagram.com/p /CHLtwMPDWJv/.

57. Angelica Lindsey-Ali, [@villageauntie], "In traditional African societies, there was always at least one woman," Instagram photo, November 14, 2019, https://www.instagram.com/p /B43IPMxg9tL/.

58. Angelica Lindsey-Ali, [@villageauntie], "In some West African countries like Maurita nia," Instagram photo, June 9, 2020, https://www.instagram.com/p/CBOde_5jjE-/.

59. Angelica Lindsey-Ali, [@villageauntie], "Who is TVA?," Instagram Stories, June 18, 2020, https://www.instagram.com/stories/highlights/18103315954011379/.

60. Angelica Lindsey-Ali, [@villageauntie], "who is TVA?," Instagram Stories, August 27, 2020, https://www.instagram.com/stories/highlights/18103315954011379/.

61. See Angelica Lindsey-Ali, [@villageauntie], "My Village is global, inclusive, interfaith," Instagram photo, March 13, 2020, https://www.instagram.com/p/B9r3-CIgKSM/; and "A group of Black male Christian clergy heard about a workshop," Instagram photo, April 16, 2020, https://www.instagram.com/p/B_DI_-MAXNG/.

62. Angelica Lindsey-Ali, [@villageauntie], "My work is grounded in my faith," Instagram photo, February 18, 2020, https://www.instagram.com/p/B8uctFdA6OK/.

63. Quoted in Leila Ettachfini, "This Muslim Sex Educator Believes God Wants Us to Orgasm," *Vice*, February 4, 2020, https://www.vice.com/en/article/k7e7z3/the-muslim-sex -educator-who-believes-god-wants-us-to-orgasm.

64. Angelica Lindsey-Ali, [@villageauntie], "Period," Instagram photo, February 11, 2020, https://www.instagram.com/p/B8bd2QQASpO/.

65. Vernon, interview with author.

4. A SEAT AT THE TABLE

1. Matthias Roberts, "On Justice," *Queerology*, June 2, 2020, podcast audio, 56:24, https://queerology.libsyn.com/on-justice.

2. Blake Chastain, "Austin Channing Brown (Re-Release)," *Exvangelical*, June 26, 2020, podcast audio, 55:07, https://www.exvangelicalpodcast.com/austin-channing-brown-re-release/.

3. Andrew J. Bottomley, "Podcasting: A Decade in the Life of a 'New' Audio Medium: Introduction," *Journal of Radio and Audio Media* 22, no. 2 (2015): 165.

4. Richard Berry, "A Golden Age of Podcasting? Evaluating *Serial* in the Context of Podcast Histories," *Journal of Radio and Audio Media* 22, no. 2 (2015): 171.

5. Ben Hammersley, "Audible Revolution," *Guardian*, February 11, 2004, https://www.theguardian.com/media/2004/feb/12/broadcasting.digitalmedia.

6. Bottomley, "Podcasting," 166.

7. Martin Spinelli and Lance Dann, *Podcasting: The Audio Media Revolution* (New York: Bloomsbury, 2019), 7.

8. Ibid., 8.

9. Steven Fekete and Jessica Knippel, "The Devil You Know: An Exploration of Virtual Religious Deconstruction Communities," *Journal of Religion, Media, and Digital Culture* 9, no. 2 (2020): 167.

10. Ibid., 177.

11. Spinelli and Dann, *Podcasting*, 7.

12. Richard Berry, "Part of the Establishment: Reflecting on 10 Years of Podcasting as an Audio Medium," *Convergence* 22, no. 6 (December 2016): 664.

13. Ibid., 666.

14. Ibid.

15. Spinelli and Dann, *Podcasting*, 77.

16. Sarah Florini, "The Podcast 'Chitlin' Circuit': Black Podcasters, Alternative Media, and Audio Enclaves," *Journal of Radio and Audio Media* 22, no. 2 (2015): 212.

17. Blake Chastain, "About," *Exvangelical*, 2020, https://web.archive.org/web/20200525163522/https://exvangelicalpodcast.com/about/.

18. Ibid.

19. Matthias Roberts, "Hi, I'm Matthias!," *Matthias Roberts*, 2021, https://matthiasroberts.com/about/.

20. Matthias Roberts, interview with author, August 27, 2020.

21. Ibid.

22. Spinelli and Dann, *Podcasting*, 69.

23. Berry, "Part of the Establishment," 666.

24. Florini, "The Podcast 'Chitlin' Circuit,'" 212.

25. Michael Gungor, "A Brief History of the Liturgists," *The Liturgists*, 2020. https://web.archive.org/web/20200609031937/https://theliturgists.com/about-us.

26. Ibid.

27. Lisa A. Flores, "Creating Discursive Space through a Rhetoric of Difference: Chicana Feminists Craft a Homeland," *Quarterly Journal of Speech*, 82, no. 2 (1996): 143.

28. bell hooks, *Talking Back: Thinking Feminist, Thinking Black* (New York: Routledge, 2015), 6.

29. Ibid., 8.

30. Ibid., 9.

31. Patricia-Anne Johnson, "Womanist Theology as Counter-Narrative," in *Gender, Ethnicity, and Religion: Views from the Other Side*, ed. Rosemary Radford Ruether (Minneapolis, MN: Fortress Press, 2002), 197–214.

32. Stephanie Y. Mitchem, *Introducing Womanist Theology* (Maryknoll, NY: Orbis Books, 2002), 49.

33. Katie Geneva Cannon, *Katie's Canon: Womanism and the Soul of the Black Community* (New York: Continuum, 1998), 33.

34. Michelle Higgins, Christina Edmondson, and Ekemini Uwan, "Receipts," *Truth's Table*, February 17, 2017, podcast audio, 18:14, https://soundcloud.com/truthstable/truths-table-receipts.

35. Michelle Higgins, Christina Edmondson, and Ekemini Uwan, "Pass the Table: To Our Listeners with Love," *Truth's Table*, April 14, 2018, podcast audio, 52:29, https://soundcloud.com/truthstable/pass-the-table-to-our-listeners-with-love.

36. Michelle Higgins, Christina Edmondson, and Ekemini Uwan, "Pass the Tea: Live at LDR," *Truth's Table*, September 9, 2017, podcast audio, 34:05, https://soundcloud.com/truthstable/pass-the-tea-live-at-ldr.

37. Pretty_Brown_Woman, comment on Truth's Table, January 6, 2020, iTunes Store.

38. Patrice Gopo, February 18, 2018, comment on Truth's Table, February 18, 2018, iTunes Store.

39. Brookeashley89, comment on Truth's Table, October 16, 2017, iTunes Store.

40. ChrisR28, comment on Truth's Table, June 12, 2019, iTunes Store.

41. Soma Iani, comment on Truth's Table, April 7, 2018, iTunes Store.

42. Florini, "The Podcast 'Chitlin' Circuit,'" 210.

43. Ibid.

44. Jasy Flower, comment on Truth's Table, April 15, 2017, iTunes Store.

45. Michelle Higgins, Christina Edmondson, and Ekemini Uwan, "How to Listen to Truth's Table," *Truth's Table*, June 1, 2019, podcast audio, 51:06, https://soundcloud.com/truthstable/how-to-listen-to-truths-table.

46. Higgins, Edmondson, and Uwan, "Pass the Table."

47. DrivnNAbug, comment on Truth's Table, August 16, 2019, iTunes Store.

48. Pathfinder04, comment on Truth's Table, April 11, 2017, iTunes Store.

49. Florini, "The Podcast 'Chitlin' Circuit,'" 215.

50. This term for the intersectional experiences of anti-Black racism and misogyny was coined by Moya Bailey (*Misogynoir Transformed: Black Women's Digital Resistance* [New York: New York University Press, 2021]).

51. Michelle Higgins, Christina Edmondson, and Ekemini Uwan, "You Okay, Sis? Murder Bees, Disease, Oh My!," *Truth's Table*, May 16, 2020, podcast audio, 55:18, https://soundcloud.com/truthstable/tt-recutbeesv3fin.

52. Cannon, *Katie's Canon*, 56.

53. Michelle Higgins, Christina Edmondson, and Ekemini Uwan, "Resistance Series: Historical and Contemporary Resistance," *Truth's Table*, March 7, 2017, podcast audio, 45:07, https://soundcloud.com/truthstable/resistance-series-historical-and-contemporary-resistance

54. Gabby_Bonner1993, comment on Truth's Table, April 1, 2017, iTunes Store.

55. Alice Walker, *In Search of Our Mothers' Gardens: Womanist Prose* (New York: Harcourt, 1983).

56. Cannon, *Katie's Canon*, 128.

57. Linda E. Thomas, "Womanist Theology, Epistemology, and a New Anthropological Paradigm," *Cross Currents* 48, no. 4 (Winter 1998–1999): 489.

58. Michelle Higgins, Christina Edmondson, and Ekemini Uwan, "Embodied Blackness: Crowns of Glory," *Truth's Table*, March 18, 2017, podcast audio, 31:36, https://soundcloud.com/truthstable/embodied-blackness-crowns-of-glory

59. Ibid.

60. Michelle Higgins, Christina Edmondson, and Ekemini Uwan, "Embodied Blackness: Colorism," *Truth's Table*, August 11, 2017, podcast audio, 1:03:07, https://soundcloud.com /truthstable/embodied-blackness-colorism.

61. LaCerro, comment on Truth's Table, June 28, 2017, iTunes Store.

62. Jennifer_ESTL, comment on Truth's Table, July 12, 2017, iTunes Store.

63. TrishaJoy32, comment on Truth's Table, October 6, 2017, iTunes Store.

64. @Alexis_Stanford, comment on Truth's Table, April 2, 2017, iTunes Store.

65. Michelle Higgins, Christina Edmondson, and Ekemini Uwan, "Resistance Series: Resistance in the Bible," *Truth's Table*, March 7, 2017, podcast audio, 32:58, https://soundcloud.com /truthstable/resistance-series-resistance-in-the-bible

66. Michelle Higgins, Christina Edmondson, and Ekemini Uwan, "Operation 'Sunken Place' Rescue," *Truth's Table*, May 27, 2017, podcast audio, 35:37, https://soundcloud.com/truthstable /operation-sunken-place-rescue.

67. Michelle Higgins, Christina Edmondson, and Ekemini Uwan, "Gender Apartheid," *Truth's Table*, March 25, 2017, podcast audio, 38:00, https://soundcloud.com/truthstable /gender-apartheid.

68. Michelle Higgins, Christina Edmondson, and Ekemini Uwan, "Embodied Blackness: Blackness as Being," *Truth's Table*, June 16, 2019, podcast audio, 47:04, https://soundcloud .com/truthstable/embodied-blackness-blackness-as-being

69. Michelle Higgins, Christina Edmondson, and Ekemini Uwan, "Reparations NOW: Ecclesiastical Reparations with Rev. Duke Kwon," *Truth's Table*, February 2, 2018, podcast audio, 48:38, https://soundcloud.com/truthstable/reparations-now-ecclesiastical-reparations -with-rev-duke-kwon.

70. Ibid.

71. Michelle Higgins, Christina Edmondson, and Ekemini Uwan, "Strange Fruit," *Truth's Table*, June 30, 2017, podcast audio, 50:54, https://soundcloud.com/truthstable/strange -fruit.

72. Ibid.

73. Ibid.

74. Truth's Table [@truthstable], "HAPPY JUNETEENTH!," Instagram photo, June 19, 2020, https://www.instagram.com/p/CBnWKj7hzqn/.

5. "WE THEM BARBARIANS"

1. *Hip Hop: The Songs That Shook America*, season 1, episode 6, "Ladies First: 1989," aired November 17, 2019, on AMC.

2. Robin Roberts, "'Ladies First': Queen Latifah's Afrocentric Feminist Music Video," *African American Review* 28, no. 2 (1994): 249.

3. Mona Haydar, interview with author, July 23, 2020.

4. Ibid.

5. #MIPSTERZ, "ALHAMDU," Kickstarter, last updated May 5, 2021, https://www .kickstarter.com/projects/mipsterz/alhamdu/description.

6. Haydar, interview with author.

7. Tricia Rose, *Black Noise: Rap Music and Black Culture in Contemporary America* (Hanover, NH: Wesleyan University Press, 1994), 3.

8. Ibid., 19.

9. Nancy Guevara, "Women Writin' Rappin' Breakin,'" in *Droppin' Science: Critical Essays on Rap Music and Hip Hop Culture*, ed. William Eric Perkins (Philadelphia, PA: Temple University Press, 1996), 55.

10. S. Craig Watkins, *Hip Hop Matters: Politics, Pop Culture, and the Struggle for the Soul of a Movement* (Boston: Beacon Press, 2005), 164.

11. Daniel White Hodge, "AmeriKKKa's Most Wanted: Hip Hop Culture and Hip Hop Theology as Challenges to Oppression," *Journal of Popular Music Education* 2, nos. 1–2 (2018): 15.

12. Ibid., 16.

13. Mary Celeste Kearney, *Girls Make Media* (New York: Routledge, 2006), 57.

14. Ibid., 45.

15. William Eric Perkins, "The Rap Attack: An Introduction," in *Droppin' Science: Critical Essays on Rap Music and Hip Hop Culture*, ed. William Eric Perkins (Philadelphia, PA: Temple University Press, 1996), 28.

16. Ibid., 34.

17. Rose, *Black Noise*, 154.

18. Ibid., 150.

19. Ibid., 146.

20. Ibid., 150.

21. Yolanda Pierce, "Black Women and the Sacred: With 'Lemonade,' Beyoncé Takes Us to Church," *Religion Dispatches*, May 3, 2016, https://religiondispatches.org/black-women-and -the-sacred-beyonce-takes-us-to-church/.

22. Ibid.

23. Tamara Henry, "Reimagining Religious Education for Young, Black, Christian Women: Womanist Resistance in the Form of Hip-Hop," *Religions* 9, no. 409 (December 2018): 8.

24. Kearney, *Girls Make Media*, 13.

25. bell hooks, *Talking Back: Thinking Feminist, Thinking Black* (New York: Routledge, 2015).

26. Kearney, *Girls Make Media*, 161.

27. Ibid., 157.

28. Ibid.

29. Mona Haydar, "Barbarian," YouTube, June 15, 2018, video, 3:45, https://youtu.be /lfDQ5REWCuo

30. Haydar, interview with author.

31. Mona Haydar, "Hijabi (Wrap my Hijab)," YouTube, March 27, 2017, video, 3:19. https:// youtu.be/XOX9O_kVPeo.

32. Haydar, interview with author.

33. Haydar, "Hijabi (Wrap my Hijab)," YouTube.

34. Rose, *Black Noise*, 8–9.

35. Haydar, interview with author.

36. Ibid.

37. Rose, *Black Noise*, 164.

38. Ibid., 8–9, 10.

39. Ibid., 11.

40. Ibid.

41. Haydar, interview with author.

42. 나즈리 (@iamsoulstyle), "ISTG this song is dope.. beat so lit too," Twitter, April 7, 2017.

43. Parichay Barpanda (@baymac04), "So even if you hate it—I still wrap my hijab," Twitter, April 10, 2017.

44. Callie (@neylano), "I love this video. Hijabi by Mona Haydar," Twitter, April 24, 2017.

45. Alaa (@alaamagedali), "this is beyond perfection," Twitter, March 31, 2017.

46. ini xeem lah (@meexroon), "OMG this is my anthem now," Twitter, March 28, 2017.

47. Haydar, interview with author.

48. Watkins, *Hip Hop Matters*, 15.

49. R. Roberts, "'Ladies First,'" 246.

50. Watkins, *Hip Hop Matters*, 213.

51. Mona Haydar, "Dog (ft. Jackie Cruz)," YouTube, July 17, 2017, video, 4:12, https://youtu .be/idMJIEFH_ns.

52. Ibid.

53. Rose, *Black Noise*, 100.

54. Ibid., 163.

55. Ibid., 155.

56. Ibid., 163.

57. Haydar, "Dog," YouTube.

58. Haydar, interview with author.

59. Ibid.

60. Haydar, "Barbarian," YouTube.

61. Haydar, interview with author.

62. Stuart Hall, "Signification, Representation, Ideology: Althusser and the Post-Structuralist Debate," *Critical Studies in Mass Communication* 2, no. 2 (1985): 91–114.

63. Homi K. Bhabha, *The Location of Culture* (London: Routledge, 1994), 126.

64. Haydar, interview with author.

65. Haydar, "Barbarian," YouTube.

66. Angel M. Hinzo and Lynn Schofield Clark, "Digital Survivance and Trickster Humor: Exploring Visual and Digital Indigenous Epistemologies in the #NoDAPL Movement," *Information, Communication and Society* 22, no. 6 (2019): 802.

67. Haydar, "Barbarian," YouTube.

68. See, for example, Sana Saeed, "Somewhere in America, Muslim Women Are 'Cool,'" *Islamic Monthly*, December 2, 2013, www.theislamicmonthly.com/somewhere-in-america -muslim-women-are-cool; Dr. Suad, "All I Know to Be Is a Solider [*sic*], for My Culture," *Tumblr*, December 1, 2013, http://drsuad.tumblr.com/post/68745089632/somewhere-in-america -somewhere-in-america-there.

69. Layla Shaikley, "The Surprising Lessons of the 'Muslim Hipsters' Backlash," *Atlantic*, March 13, 2014, www.theatlantic.com/entertainment/archive/2014/03/the-surprising-lessons -of-the-muslim-hipsters-backlash/284298; Aminah Sheikh, "Why I Participated in the 'Somewhere in America' #Mipsterz Video," *Altmuslim*, December 4, 2013, http://www.patheos.com /blogs/altmuslim/2013/12/why-i-participated-in-the-somewhere-in-america-mipsterz-video.

70. Sara Alfageeh and Abbas Rattani, email interview with author, August 10, 2020.

71. MIPSTERZ, "ALHAMDU | MUSLIM FUTURISM," YouTube, May 11, 2021, video, 4:38, https://www.youtube.com/watch?v=IbhIHNjKoMY.

72. Alfageeh and Rattani, email interview with author.

73. Ibid.

74. Ken McLeod, "Space Oddities: Aliens, Futurism and Meaning in Popular Music," *Popular Music* 22, no. 3 (2003): 345.

75. MIPSTERZ (@MipsterzOfficial), "We submit to you a joyous, vibrant vision of liberation," Instagram video, May 11, 2021, https://www.instagram.com/p/COvPvZyjSVG/.

76. #MIPSTERZ, "ALHAMDU," Kickstarter.

77. Alfageeh and Rattani, email interview with author.

78. Ibid.

79. Adam de Paor-Evans, "The Futurism of Hip Hop: Space, Electro and Science Fiction in Rap," *Open Cultural Studies* 2, no. 1 (2018): 126.

80. Marlo David, "Afrofuturism and Post-Soul Possibility in Black Popular Music," *African American Review* 41, no. 4 (2007): 697.

81. MIPSTERZ (@MipsterzOfficial), "You may not acknowledge our past, but you will know our future," Instagram photo, April 17, 2021, https://www.instagram.com/p/CNxQc6 uLG7g/.

82. MIPSTERZ (@MipsterzOfficial), "#Alhamdulillah, we are out here and unapologetically ourselves," Instagram photo, April 30, 2021, https://www.instagram.com/p/COSu3d krOnt/.

83. MIPSTERZ (@MipsterzOfficial), "See y'all in a 1,000 years," Instagram photo, April 22, 2021, https://www.instagram.com/p/CN-IdW-LNi2/.

CONCLUSION

1. Richard Fry and Kim Parker, "Early Benchmarks Show 'Post-Millennials' on Track to Be Most Diverse, Best-Educated Generation Yet," Pew Research Center, November 15, 2018, https://www.pewsocialtrends.org/2018/11/15/early-benchmarks-show-post-millennials-on -track-to-be-most-diverse-best-educated-generation-yet/.

2. Ibid.

3. Kim Parker, Nikki Graf, and Ruth Igielnik, "Generation Z Looks a Lot Like Millennials on Key Social and Political Issues," Pew Research Center, January 17, 2019, https://www .pewsocialtrends.org/2019/01/17/generation-z-looks-a-lot-like-millennials-on-key-social -and-political-issues/.

4. Sara Alfageeh and Abbas Rattani, email interview with author, August 10, 2020.

5. Daniel Cox and Robert P. Jones, "America's Changing Religious Identity," PRRI, 2017, https://www.prri.org/research/american-religious-landscape-christian-religiously -unaffiliated/.

6. Ibid.

7. Pew Research Center, "Religious Landscape Study: Generational Cohort," Pew Research Center, September 2020, https://www.pewforum.org/religious-landscape-study/generational -cohort/.

8. Ibid.

9. Tara Isabella Burton, *Strange Rites: New Religions for a Godless World* (New York: Public-Affairs, 2020), 23.

10. Parker, Graf, and Igielnik, "Generation Z Looks a Lot Like Millennials on Key Social and Political Issues."

11. Ibid.

12. Mona Haydar, interview with author, July 23, 2020.

13. Michelle Higgins, Christina Edmondson and Ekemini Uwan, "Strange Fruit," *Truth's Table*, June 30, 2017, podcast audio, 50:54, https://soundcloud.com/truthstable/strange -fruit.

14. Emily Joy Allison, interview with author, October 26, 2019.

15. Haydar, interview with author.

16. Allison, interview with author.

17. Harry Bruinius, "Churches Struggle with Their #MeToo Moment," *Christian Science Monitor*, April 20, 2018, https://www.csmonitor.com/USA/Politics/2018/0420/Churches -struggle-with-their-MeToo-moment.

18. Allison, interview with author.

19. Quoted in Kate Shellnutt, "Women Speak Up in #SilenceIsNotSpiritual Campaign," *Christianity Today*, December 20, 2017, https://www.christianitytoday.com/ct/2017/december -web-only-women-speak-up-in-silenceisnotspiritual-campaign.html.

20. Eliza Griswold, "Silence Is Not Spiritual: The Evangelical #MeToo Movement," *New Yorker*, June 15, 2018, https://www.newyorker.com/news/on-religion/silence-is-not-spiritual-the-evangelical-metoo-movement.

21. Mona Eltahawy, "#MosqueMeToo: What Happened When I Was Sexually Assaulted during the Hajj," *Washington Post*, February 15, 2018, https://www.washingtonpost.com/news/global-opinions/wp/2018/02/15/mosquemetoo-what-happened-when-i-was-sexually-assaulted-during-the-hajj/.

22. FACE (@facingabuse), Instagram, https://www.instagram.com/facingabuse/.

23. Allison, interview with author.

24. Ibid.

25. Haydar, interview with author.

26. Matthias Roberts, interview with author, August 27, 2020.

27. Mona Haydar, "Barbarian," YouTube, June 15, 2018, video, 3:45, https://youtu.be/lfDQ5REWCuo

28. Michelle Higgins, Christina Edmondson, and Ekemini Uwan, "Black Christian Woman's Survival Guide," *Truth's Table*, April 28, 2017, podcast audio, 1:00:04, https://soundcloud.com/truthstable/black-christian-womans-survival-guide.

29. Higgins, Edmondson, and Uwan, "Strange Fruit."

30. Austin Channing Brown, *I'm Still Here: Black Dignity in a World Made for Whiteness* (New York: Convergent, 2018), 79–80.

31. Angelica Lindsey-Ali, [@villageauntie], "Who is TVA?," Instagram Stories, June 18, 2020, https://www.instagram.com/stories/highlights/18103315954011379/.

32. Leah Vernon, interview with author, July 11, 2019.

33. Roberts, interview with author.

34. Haydar, interview with author.

35. Burton, *Strange Rites.*

36. Alfageeh and Rattani, email interview with author.

37. *The Liturgists*, "We're Better Together," 2021, https://web.archive.org/web/20210605183006/

38. Roberts, interview with author.

39. Elizabeth M. Edman, *Queer Virtue: What LGBTQ People Know about Life and Love and How It Can Revitalize Christianity* (Boston: Beacon Press, 2016), 4.

40. Roberts, interview with author.

41. Edman, *Queer Virtue*, 137–138.

42. Muhsin Hendricks, "Islamic Texts: A Source for Acceptance of Queer Individuals into Mainstream Muslim Society," *Equal Rights Review* 5 (2010): 34.

43. Ibid.

44. Matthias Roberts, "#QYFDay," *Queerology*, June 30, 2020, podcast audio, 45:40, https://matthiasroberts.com/queerology/qyfday/.

45. Ibid.

46. Roberts, interview with author.

47. Parker, Graf, and Igielnik, "Generation Z Looks a Lot Like Millennials on Key Social and Political Issues."

BIBLIOGRAPHY

Abidin, Crystal. "'Aren't These Just Young, Rich Women Doing Vain Things Online?': Influencer Selfies as Subversive Frivolity." *Social Media + Society* 2, no. 2 (April–June 2016): 1–17.

Abu-Lughod, Lila. "Do Muslim Women Really Need Saving? Anthropological Reflections on Cultural Relativism and Its Others." *American Anthropologist* 104, no. 3 (September 2002): 783–790.

Ahmed, Leila. *Women and Gender in Islam: Historical Roots of a Modern Debate*. New Haven, CT: Yale University Press, 1992.

Ahmed, Sara. *The Cultural Politics of Emotion*. 2nd ed. New York: Routledge, 2014.

Allison, Emily Joy. *#ChurchToo: How Purity Culture Upholds Abuse and How to Find Healing*. Minneapolis, MN: Broadleaf Books, 2021.

———. "Emily Joy: About." 2016. http://emilyjoypoetry.com/about.

———. "Emily Joy on Purity Culture." *Queerology*, September 24, 2019. Podcast audio, 39:24. https://matthiasroberts.com/queerology/e089-emily-joy/.

Alloula, Malek. *The Colonial Harem*. Minneapolis: University of Minnesota Press, 1986.

Al-Saji, Alia. "The Racialization of Muslim Veils: A Philosophical Analysis." *Philosophy and Social Criticism* 36, no. 8 (2010): 875–902.

Anderson, Dianna. *Damaged Goods: New Perspectives on Christian Purity*. New York: Jericho Books, 2015.

Anzaldúa, Gloria. *Borderlands/La Frontera: The New Mestiza*. San Francisco, CA: Aunt Lute, 1987.

Ardizzoni, Michela. *Matrix Activism: Global Practices of Resistance*. New York: Routledge, 2017.

Arterburn, Stephen, Fred Stoeker, and Mike Yorkey. *Every Young Man's Battle: Strategies for Victory in the Real World of Sexual Temptation*. Colorado Springs: WaterBrook Press, 2002.

Bailey, Moya. *Misogynoir Transformed: Black Women's Digital Resistance*. New York: New York University Press, 2021.

Banet-Weiser, Sarah. *Authentic™: The Politics of Ambivalence in a Brand Culture*. New York: New York University Press, 2013.

———. *Empowered: Popular Feminism and Popular Misogyny*. Durham, NC: Duke University Press, 2018.

Barbee, Amanda. "Naked and Ashamed: Women and Evangelical Purity Culture." *Other Journal*, no. 23 (March 3, 2014). https://theotherjournal.com/2014/03/03/naked-and-ashamed-women-and-evangelical-purity-culture/.

Beal, Frances M. "Double Jeopardy: To Be Black and Female." *Meridians* 8, no. 2 (2008): 166–176.

Bennett, W. Lance, and Alexandra Segerberg. "The Logic of Connective Action: Digital Media and the Personalization of Contentious Politics." *Information, Communication and Society* 15, no. 5 (2012): 739–768.

Berry, Richard. "A Golden Age of Podcasting? Evaluating *Serial* in the Context of Podcast Histories." *Journal of Radio and Audio Media* 22, no. 2 (2015): 170–178.

———. "Part of the Establishment: Reflecting on 10 Years of Podcasting as an Audio Medium." *Convergence* 22, no. 6 (December 2016): 661–671.

Beydoun, Khaled A. *American Islamophobia: Understanding the Roots and Rise of Fear.* Oakland: University of California Press, 2018.

Bhabha, Homi K. *The Location of Culture.* London: Routledge, 1994.

Bint Younus, Zainab. "Covering One's Face Does Not Render One Silent or Stupid." *HuffPost,* December 6, 2017. https://www.huffpost.com/entry/overing-ones-face-does-not-render -one-silent-or-stupid_b_7539964?utm_hp_ref=tw.

———. "For Me, Niqab Is a Feminist Statement." *Medium,* June 4, 2015. https://medium .com/aj-story-behind-the-story/for-me-niqab-is-a-feminist-statement-13ca2fc2fe9a# .m7dvi936t.

———. "Veiled Snapshots: Muslim Women Who Are Begging to Be Saved." *BuzzFeed,* June 1, 2015. http://www.buzzfeed.com/zainabbintyounus/veiled-snapshots-muslim-women-who -are-begging-to-1lokj.

Bint Younus, Zainab (@bintyounus). "Curate faith, and beauty, and joy, in your home and your heart." Instagram photo, September 18, 2020. https://www.instagram.com/p /CFSxZhtD1Zm/.

———. "I believe in curating joy." Instagram photo, October 4, 2020. https://www.instagram .com/p/CF6gdlQAvH4/.

———. "I can't believe I haven't officially reviewed the Daevabad Chronicles yet." Instagram photo, November 4, 2020. https://www.instagram.com/p/CHLtwMPDWJv/.

———. "I know I already did a #bookstagram post for The Girl in the Tangerine Scarf." Instagram photo, October 21, 2020. https://www.instagram.com/p/CGnWo24D8zN/.

———. "{Verily, with hardship comes ease!}." Instagram photo, November 3, 2020. https:// www.instagram.com/p/CHJF9G6jNz-/.

Bonilla, Yarimar, and Jonathan Rosa. "#Ferguson: Digital Protest, Hashtag Ethnography, and the Racial Politics of Social Media in the United States." *American Ethnologist* 42, no. 1 (2015): 4–17.

Borland, Katherine. "'That's Not What I Said': Interpretive Conflict in Oral Narrative Research." In *Women's Words: The Feminist Practice of Oral History,* edited by Sherna Berger Gluck and Daphne Patai, 63–76. New York: Routledge, 1991.

Bottomley, Andrew J. "Podcasting: A Decade in the Life of a 'New' Audio Medium: Introduction." *Journal of Radio and Audio Media* 22, no. 2 (2015): 164–169.

Brown, Austin Channing. *I'm Still Here: Black Dignity in a World Made for Whiteness.* New York: Convergent, 2018.

Break Free Together (@breakfreetogether). "#BreakFreeTogether." Instagram photo, November 1, 2018. https://www.instagram.com/p/Bpp0EGRhGNN/.

Bruinius, Harry. "Churches Struggle with Their #MeToo Moment." *Christian Science Monitor,* April 20, 2018. https://www.csmonitor.com/USA/Politics/2018/0420/Churches-struggle -with-their-MeToo-moment.

Bucar, Elizabeth. *Pious Fashion: How Muslim Women Dress.* Cambridge, MA: Harvard University Press, 2017.

Burge, Ryan P. *The Nones: Where They Came From, Who They Are, and Where They Are Going.* Minneapolis, MN: Fortress Press, 2021.

Burleigh, Nina. "Evangelical Christians Helped Elect Donald Trump, but Their Time as a Major Political Force Is Coming to an End." *Newsweek,* December 13, 2018. https://www .newsweek.com/2018/12/21/evangelicals-republicans-trump-millenials-1255745.html.

Burton, Tara Isabella. *Strange Rites: New Religions for a Godless World.* New York: PublicAffairs, 2020.

Butler, Anthea. *White Evangelical Racism: The Politics of Morality in America.* Chapel Hill: University of North Carolina Press, 2021.

Cainkar, Louise A. *Homeland Insecurity: The Arab American and Muslim American Experience after 9/11*. New York: Russell Sage Foundation, 2009.

Cannon, Katie Geneva. *Katie's Canon: Womanism and the Soul of the Black Community*. New York: Continuum, 1998.

Chan-Malik, Sylvia. *Being Muslim: A Cultural History of Women of Color in American Islam*. New York: New York University Press, 2018.

Chastain, Blake. "About." *Exvangelical*. 2020. https://web.archive.org/web/20200525163522 /https://exvangelicalpodcast.com/about/

———. "Austin Channing Brown (Re-Release)." *Exvangelical*. June 26, 2020. Podcast audio, 55:07. https://www.exvangelicalpodcast.com/austin-channing-brown-re-release/.

———. *#Exvangelical Podcast*. Accessed January 22, 2021. https://www.exvangelicalpodcast .com/

Chen, Gina Masullo, Paromita Pain, and Jinglun Zhang. "#NastyWomen: Reclaiming the Twitterverse from Misogyny." In *Mediating Misogyny: Gender, Technology, and Harassment*, edited by Jacqueline Ryan Vickery and Tracy Everbach, 371–388. New York: Palgrave Macmillan, 2018.

Christ, Carol P. "Why Women Need the Goddess." *HERESIES* 2, no. 1 (Spring 1978): 8–13.

Clark, Lynn Schofield. "Participants on the Margins: #BlackLivesMatter and the Role That Shared Artifacts of Engagement Played among Minoritized Political Newcomers on Snapchat, Facebook, and Twitter." *International Journal of Communication* 10 (2016): 235–253.

Clark-Parsons, Rosemary. "'I SEE YOU, I BELIEVE YOU, I STAND WITH YOU': #MeToo and the Performance of Networked Feminist Visibility." *Feminist Media Studies* 21, no. 3 (2019): 362–380.

Cochran, Pamela D. H. *Evangelical Feminism: A History*. New York: New York University Press, 2005.

Combahee River Collective in Second Wave. "A Black Feminist Statement." In *The Second Wave: A Reader in Feminist Theory*, edited by Linda Nicholson, 63–70. New York: Routledge, 1997.

Cone, James. "Theology's Great Sin: Silence in the Face of White Supremacy." *Black Theology* 2, no. 2 (2004): 139–152.

cooke, miriam. "The Muslimwoman." *Contemporary Islam* 1, no. 2 (2007): 139–154.

Couldry, Nick. *Why Voice Matters: Culture and Politics after Neoliberalism*. London: SAGE, 2010.

Cox, Daniel, and Robert P. Jones. "America's Changing Religious Identity." PRRI, 2017. https://www.prri.org/research/american-religious-landscape-christian-religiously -unaffiliated/.

Crenshaw, Kimberlé Williams. "Demarginalizing the Intersection of Race and Sex: A Black Feminist Critique of Antidiscrimination Doctrine, Feminist Theory and Antiracist Politics." *University of Chicago Legal Forum* 1989, no. 1 (1989): 139–167.

Dahlgren, Peter. *Media and Political Engagement: Citizens, Communication, and Democracy*. Cambridge: Cambridge University Press, 2009.

Daly, Mary *Beyond God the Father: Toward a Philosophy of Women's Liberation*. Boston: Beacon Press, 1973.

———. *The Church and the Second Sex*. Boston: Beacon Press, 1985.

David, Marlo. "Afrofuturism and Post-Soul Possibility in Black Popular Music." *African American Review* 41, no. 4 (2007): 695–707.

De Paor-Evans, Adam. "The Futurism of Hip Hop: Space, Electro and Science Fiction in Rap." *Open Cultural Studies* 2, no. 1 (2018): 122–135.

Dean, Jodi. *Democracy and Other Neoliberal Fantasies: Communicative Capitalism and Left Politics*. Durham, NC: Duke University Press, 2009.

"Deconstructing My Religion." CBS News, December 1, 2018. Video, 26:55. https://www.cbs
    .com/shows/cbs-news-specials/video/jBSOpwEP1_gFcxYqGIU_oPjxUqETIpGN
    /deconstructing-my-religion/.

DeRogatis, Amy. *Saving Sex: Sexuality and Salvation in American Evangelicalism*. Oxford:
    Oxford University Press, 2015.

Dias, Elizabeth, and Sam Roberts. "Rachel Held Evans, Voice of the Wandering Evangelical,
    Dies at 37." *New York Times*, May 4, 2019. https://www.nytimes.com/2019/05/04/us
    /rachel-held-evans.html.

Douglas, Kelly Brown. *Stand Your Ground: Black Bodies and the Justice of God*. Maryknoll, NY:
    Orbis, 2015.

Dr. Suad. "All I Know to Be Is a Solider [*sic*], for My Culture." *Tumblr*, December 1, 2013.
    http://drsuad.tumblr.com/post/68745089632/somewhere-in-america-somewhere-in
    -america-there.

Drake, Vyxsin. "I'm Not the Result They Were Looking For." *Life after "I Kissed Dating Good-
    bye,"* October 8, 2016. https://web.archive.org/web/20171227080235/http://www
    .lifeafterikdg.com/im-not-result-looking.

Duffy, Brooke Erin, and Emily Hund. "Gendered Visibility on Social Media: Navigating Insta-
    gram's Authenticity Bind." *International Journal of Communication* 13 (2019): 4983–5002.

Duncan, Lenny. *Dear Church: A Love Letter from a Black Preacher to the Whitest Denomination
    in the U.S.* Minneapolis, MN: Fortress Press, 2019.

Edman, Elizabeth M. *Queer Virtue: What LGBTQ People Know about Life and Love and How It
    Can Revitalize Christianity*. Boston: Beacon Press, 2016.

Eltahawy, Mona. "#MosqueMeToo: What Happened When I Was Sexually Assaulted during
    the Hajj." *Washington Post*, February 15, 2018. https://www.washingtonpost.com/news
    /global-opinions/wp/2018/02/15/mosquemetoo-what-happened-when-i-was-sexually
    -assaulted-during-the-hajj/.

Emba, Christine. "The Dramatic Implosion of 'I Kissed Dating Goodbye' Is a Lesson—and a
    Warning." *Washington Post*, November 14, 2018. https://www.washingtonpost.com
    /opinions/the-dramatic-implosion-of-i-kissed-dating-goodbye-is-a-lesson--and-a
    -warning/2018/11/14/eeecd65c-e850-11e8-bbdb-72fdbf9d4fed_story.html.

Ettachfini, Leila. "This Muslim Sex Educator Believes God Wants Us to Orgasm." *Vice*, Febru-
    ary 4, 2020. https://www.vice.com/en/article/k7e7z3/the-muslim-sex-educator-who
    -believes-god-wants-us-to-orgasm.

Evans, Rachel Held. *Searching for Sunday: Loving, Leaving, and Finding the Church*. Nashville,
    TN: Nelson Books, 2015.

———. *A Year of Biblical Womanhood: How a Liberated Woman Found Herself Sitting on Her
    Roof, Covering Her Head, and Calling Her Husband "Master."* Nashville, TN: Nelson Books,
    2012.

Everhart, Ruth. *The #MeToo Reckoning: Facing the Church's Complicity in Sexual Abuse and
    Misconduct*. Downers Grove, IL: InterVarsity Press, 2020.

FACE (@facingabuse). Instagram. https://www.instagram.com/facingabuse/.

Fekete, Steven, and Jessica Knippel. "The Devil You Know: An Exploration of Virtual Reli-
    gious Deconstruction Communities." *Journal of Religion, Media, and Digital Culture* 9,
    no. 2 (2020): 165–184.

Field, Samantha. "It's Not OK and We're Not Alright." *Life after "I Kissed Dating Goodbye,"*,
    August 26, 2016. https://web.archive.org/web/20161006004741/http://www.lifeafterikdg
    .com/not-ok-not-alright/.

Fletcher, Jeannine Hill. *The Sin of White Supremacy: Christianity, Racism, and Religious Diver-
    sity in America*. Maryknoll, NY: Orbis, 2017.

Flores, Lisa A. "Creating Discursive Space through a Rhetoric of Difference: Chicana Feminists Craft a Homeland." *Quarterly Journal of Speech* 82, no. 2 (1996): 142–156.

Florini, Sarah. *Beyond Hashtags: Racial Politics and Black Digital Networks.* New York: New York University Press, 2019.

———. "The Podcast 'Chitlin' Circuit'": Black Podcasters, Alternative Media, and Audio Enclaves." *Journal of Radio and Audio Media* 22, no. 2 (2015): 209–219.

———. "Tweets, Tweeps, and Signifyin': Communication and Cultural Performance on 'Black Twitter.'" *Television and New Media* 15, no. 3 (March 2014): 223–237.

Fry, Richard, and Kim Parker. "Early Benchmarks Show 'Post-Millennials' on Track to Be Most Diverse, Best-Educated Generation Yet." Pew Research Center, November 15, 2018. https://www.pewsocialtrends.org/2018/11/15/early-benchmarks-show-post-millennials -on-track-to-be-most-diverse-best-educated-generation-yet/.

Fuchs, Christian. *Social Media: A Critical Introduction.* 2nd ed. London: SAGE, 2017.

Galonnier, Juliette. "The Racialization of Muslims in France and the United States: Some Insights from White Converts to Islam." *Social Compass* 62, no. 4 (2015): 570–583.

Graham, Ruth. "Hello *Goodbye.*" *Slate,* August 26, 2016. https://slate.com/human-interest /2016/08/i-kissed-dating-goodbye-author-is-maybe-kind-of-sorry.html.

Green, Emma. "Rachel Held Evans, Hero to Christian Misfits." *Atlantic,* May 6, 2019. https:// www.theatlantic.com/politics/archive/2019/05/rachel-held-evans-death-progressive -christianity/588784/.

Griswold, Eliza. "The Radically Inclusive Christianity of Rachel Held Evans." *New Yorker,* May 6, 2019. https://www.newyorker.com/news/postscript/the-radically-inclusive-christianity -of-rachel-held-evans.

———. "Silence Is Not Spiritual: The Evangelical #MeToo Movement." *New Yorker,* June 15, 2018. https://www.newyorker.com/news/on-religion/silence-is-not-spiritual-the-evang elical-metoo-movement.

Gross, Rita M. *Feminism and Religion: An Introduction.* Boston: Beacon Press, 1996.

Grossberg, Lawrence. "On Postmodernism and Articulation: An Interview with Stuart Hall." In *Stuart Hall: Critical Dialogues in Cultural Studies,* edited by David Morley and Kuan-Hsing Chen, 131–150. London: Routledge, 1996.

Guevara, Nancy. "Women Writin' Rappin' Breakin.'" In *Droppin' Science: Critical Essays on Rap Music and Hip Hop Culture,* edited by William Eric Perkins, 49–62. Philadelphia, PA: Temple University Press, 1996.

Gungor, Michael. "A Brief History of The Liturgists." *The Liturgists.* 2020. https://web.archive .org/web/20200609031937/https://theliturgists.com/about-us.

Hall, Stuart. "Signification, Representation, Ideology: Althusser and the Post-Structuralist Debate." *Critical Studies in Mass Communication* 2, no. 2 (1985): 91–114.

———. "What Is This 'Black' in Black Popular Culture?" *Social Justice* 20, nos. 1–2 (1993): 104–115.

Hammersley, Ben. "Audible Revolution." *Guardian,* February 11, 2004. https://www.theguardian .com/media/2004/feb/12/broadcasting.digitalmedia.

Harris, Cheryl I. "Whiteness as Property." In *Critical Race Theory: The Key Writings That Formed the Movement,* edited by Kimberlé Crenshaw, Neil Gotanda, Gary Peller, and Kendall Thomas, 276–291. New York: New Press, 1995.

Harris, Joshua. *I Kissed Dating Goodbye: A New Attitude toward Romance and Relationships.* Sisters, OR: Multnomah Books, 1997.

Haydar, Mona. "Barbarian." YouTube, June 15, 2018. Video, 3:45. https://youtu.be/lfDQ5REWCu0.

———. "Dog (ft. Jackie Cruz)." YouTube, July 17, 2017. Video, 4:12. https://youtu.be /idMJIEFH_ns.

———. "Hijabi (Wrap my Hijab)." YouTube. March 27, 2017. Video, 3:19. https://youtu.be/XOX9O_kVPe0

Hendricks, Muhsin. "Islamic Texts: A Source for Acceptance of Queer Individuals into Mainstream Muslim Society." *Equal Rights Review* 5 (2010): 31–51.

Henry, Tamara. "Reimagining Religious Education for Young, Black, Christian Women: Womanist Resistance in the Form of Hip-Hop." *Religions* 9, no. 409 (December 2018): 1–11.

Herrmann, Andrew F. "Purity, Nationalism, and Whiteness: The Fracturing of Fundamentalist Evangelicalism." *International Review of Qualitative Research* 13, no. 4 (July 2020): 414–432.

Higgins, Michelle, Christina Edmondson, and Ekemini Uwan. "Black Christian Woman's Survival Guide." *Truth's Table*, April 28, 2017. Podcast audio, 1:00:04. https://soundcloud.com/truthstable/black-christian-womans-survival-guide.

———. "Embodied Blackness: Blackness as Being." *Truth's Table*, June 16, 2019. Podcast audio, 47:04. https://soundcloud.com/truthstable/embodied-blackness-blackness-as-being.

———. "Embodied Blackness: Colorism." *Truth's Table*, August 11, 2017. Podcast audio, 1:03:07. https://soundcloud.com/truthstable/embodied-blackness-colorism.

———. "Embodied Blackness: Crowns of Glory." *Truth's Table*, March 18, 2017. Podcast audio, 31:36. https://soundcloud.com/truthstable/embodied-blackness-crowns-of-glory.

———. "Embodied Blackness: Objectification." *Truth's Table*, April 14, 2017. Podcast audio, 50:02. https://soundcloud.com/truthstable/embodied-blackness-objectification.

———. "Gender Apartheid." *Truth's Table*, March 25, 2017. Podcast audio, 38:00. https://soundcloud.com/truthstable/gender-apartheid.

———. "How to Listen to Truth's Table." *Truth's Table*, June 1, 2019. Podcast audio, 51:06. https://soundcloud.com/truthstable/how-to-listen-to-truths-table.

———. "Operation 'Sunken Place' Rescue." *Truth's Table*, May 27, 2017. Podcast audio, 35:37. https://soundcloud.com/truthstable/operation-sunken-place-rescue.

———. "Pass the Table: To Our Listeners with Love." *Truth's Table*, April 14, 2018. Podcast audio, 52:29. https://soundcloud.com/truthstable/pass-the-table-to-our-listeners-with-love.

———. "Pass the Tea: Live at LDR." *Truth's Table*, September 9, 2017. Podcast audio, 34:05. https://soundcloud.com/truthstable/pass-the-tea-live-at-ldr.

———. "Receipts." *Truth's Table*, February 17, 2017. Podcast audio, 18:14. https://soundcloud.com/truthstable/truths-table-receipts.

———. "Reparations NOW: Ecclesiastical Reparations with Rev. Duke Kwon." *Truth's Table*, February 2, 2018. Podcast audio, 48:38. https://soundcloud.com/truthstable/reparations-now-ecclesiastical-reparations-with-rev-duke-kwon.

———. "Resistance Series: Historical and Contemporary Resistance." *Truth's Table*, March 7, 2017. Podcast audio, 45:07. https://soundcloud.com/truthstable/resistance-series-historical-and-contemporary-resistance.

———. "Resistance Series: Resistance in the Bible." *Truth's Table*, March 7, 2017. Podcast audio, 32:58. https://soundcloud.com/truthstable/resistance-series-resistance-in-the-bible.

———. "Strange Fruit." *Truth's Table*, June 30, 2017. Podcast audio, 50:54. https://soundcloud.com/truthstable/strange-fruit.

———. "You Okay, Sis? Murder Bees, Disease, Oh My!" *Truth's Table*, May 16, 2020. Podcast audio, 55:18. https://soundcloud.com/truthstable/tt-recutbeesv3fin.

Highfield, Tim, and Tama Leaver. "Instagrammatics and Digital Methods: Studying Visual Social Media, from Selfies and GIFs to Memes and Emoji." *Communication Research and Practice* 2, no. 1 (2016): 47–62.

Hill, Margari, Daniel Kowalski, Meral Kocak, Hakeem Muhammad, Sherouk Ahmed, and Namira Islam. "Study of Intra-Muslim Ethnic Relations: Muslim American Views on Race Relations." Muslim Anti-Racism Collaborative. June 4, 2015. https://www.muslimarc.org/interethnic/.

Hinzo, Angel M., and Lynn Schofield Clark. "Digital Survivance and Trickster Humor: Exploring Visual and Digital Indigenous Epistemologies in the #NoDAPL Movement." *Information, Communication and Society* 22, no. 6 (2019): 791–807.

Hip Hop: The Songs That Shook America. Season 1, episode 6, "Ladies First: 1989." Aired November 17, 2019, on AMC.

Hodge, Daniel White. "AmeriKKKa's Most Wanted: Hip Hop Culture and Hip Hop Theology as Challenges to Oppression." *Journal of Popular Music Education* 2, nos. 1–2 (2018): 13–28.

hooks, bell. *Black Looks: Race and Representation.* Boston: South End Press, 1992.

———. *Talking Back: Thinking Feminist, Thinking Black.* New York: Routledge, 2015.

Hund, Emily. "Measured Beauty: Exploring the Aesthetics of Instagram's Fashion Influencers." *#SMSociety17: Proceedings of the 8th International Conference on Social Media & Society* (New York: Association for Computing Machinery, 2017): 1–5.

Imani, Blair. "About." *Blair Imani.* Accessed November 1, 2021. http://blairimani.com/about.

———. (@blairimani). "I decided to get in on the #Cottagecore moments." Instagram photo, September 19, 2020. https://www.instagram.com/p/CFVgAvinAmC/.

———. "It's #LearnOClock This week: OUTDATED PHRASES." Instagram photo, September 6, 2020. https://www.instagram.com/p/CEogqAMnOWe/.

———. "THANK YOU FOR 250K FOLLOWERS, LOVELIES!" Instagram photo, August 22, 2020. https://www.instagram.com/p/CEM0YL_H-tf/.

———. "YOU should be the absolute last person sh*t talking yourself." Instagram photo, August 19, 2020. https://www.instagram.com/p/CEDyPF8n-6v/.

Islam, Namira. "Soft Islamophobia." *Religions* 9, no. 10 (2018): 1–16.

Jackson, Sarah J., Moya Bailey, and Brooke Foucault Welles. *#HashtagActivism: Networks of Race and Gender Justice.* Cambridge, MA: MIT Press, 2020.

Jamal, Amaney. "The Racialization of Muslim Americans." In *Muslims in Western Politics,* edited by Abdulkader H. Sinno, 200–215. Bloomington: Indiana University Press, 2009.

Jamal, Amaney, and Nadine Naber. *Race and Arab Americans before and after 9/11: From Invisible Citizens to Visible Subjects.* Syracuse, NY: Syracuse University Press, 2008.

Jenkins, Henry, Mizuko Ito, and danah boyd. *Participatory Culture in a Networked Era: A Conversation on Youth, Learning, Commerce, and Politics.* Cambridge, UK: Polity, 2016.

Johnson, Patricia-Anne. "Womanist Theology as Counter-Narrative." In *Gender, Ethnicity, and Religion: Views from the Other Side,* edited by Rosemary Radford Ruether, 197–214. Minneapolis, MN: Fortress Press, 2002.

Jones, Jameelah. "When a Black Girl Pursues Purity." *Life after "I Kissed Dating Goodbye,"* April 14, 2017. https://web.archive.org/web/20171227075940/http://www.lifeafterikdg.com/black-girl-pursues-purity/.

Joshi, Khyati. "The Racialization of Hinduism, Islam, and Sikhism." *Equality and Excellence in Education* 39, no. 3 (2006): 211–226.

Kaiser, Susan B. *Fashion and Cultural Studies.* London: Berg, 2012.

Karim, Jamillah. *American Muslim Women: Negotiating Race, Class, and Gender within the Ummah.* New York: New York University Press, 2009.

Kearney, Mary Celeste. *Girls Make Media.* New York: Routledge, 2006.

Khabeer, Su'ad Abdul. *Muslim Cool: Race, Religion, and Hip Hop in the United States.* New York: New York University Press, 2016.

Khabeer, Su'ad Abdul, Arshad Ali, Evelyn Alsultany, Sohail Daulatzai, Lara Deeb, Carol Fadda, Zareena Grewal, Juliane Hammer, Nadine Naber, and Junaid Rana. "Islamophobia Is Racism: Resource for Teaching and Learning about Anti-Muslim Racism in the United States." 2018. https://islamophobiaisracism.wordpress.com.

Khan, Amena (@amenakhan). "Vitamin sea Pink coffee And family." Instagram photo, January 9, 2021. https://www.instagram.com/p/CJ1wCaonMwl/

Kim-Kort, Mihee. *Outside the Lines: How Embracing Queerness Will Transform Your Faith.* Minneapolis, MN: Fortress Press, 2018.

Klein, Linda Kay. "Am I Impure?" *The Liturgists*, January 23, 2020. Podcast audio, 47:14. https://theliturgists.com/podcast/2020/1/23/am-i-impure.

———. *Pure: Inside the Evangelical Movement That Shamed a Generation of Young Women and How I Broke Free.* New York: Touchstone, 2018.

Leaver, Tama, Tim Highfield, and Crystal Abidin. *Instagram: Visual Social Media Cultures.* Cambridge: Polity, 2020.

Lee, Deborah Jian. *Rescuing Jesus: How People of Color, Women, and Queer Christians Are Reclaiming Evangelicalism.* Boston: Beacon Press, 2015.

Lenz, Lyz. "Recovering from *I Kissed Dating Goodbye:* A Roundtable." *The Toast*, June 8, 2016. https://the-toast.net/2016/06/08/recovering-from-i-kissed-dating-goodbye-a-roundtable/.

Lewis, Reina. "Modest Body Politics: The Commercial and Ideological Intersect of Fat, Black, and Muslim in the Modest Fashion Market and Media." *Fashion Theory* 23, no. 2 (2019): 243–273.

———. *Muslim Fashion: Contemporary Style Cultures.* Durham, NC: Duke University Press, 2015.

Lindsey-Ali, Angelica (@villageauntie). "A group of Black male Christian clergy heard about a workshop." Instagram photo, April 16, 2020. https://www.instagram.com/p/B_DI_-MAXNG/.

———. "In some West African countries like Mauritania." Instagram photo, June 9, 2020. https://www.instagram.com/p/CBOde_5jjE-/.

———. "In traditional African societies, there was always at least one woman." Instagram photo, November 14, 2019. https://www.instagram.com/p/B43IPMxg9tL/.

———. "My Village is global, inclusive, interfaith." Instagram photo, March 13, 2020. https://www.instagram.com/p/B9r3-CIgKSM/.

———. "My work is grounded in my faith." Instagram photo, February 18, 2020. https://www.instagram.com/p/B8uctFdA6OK/.

———. "Period." Instagram photo, February 11, 2020. https://www.instagram.com/p/B8bd2QQASpO/.

———. "Who is TVA?" Instagram Stories, June 18, 2020. https://www.instagram.com/stories/highlights/18103315954011379/.

———. "Who is TVA?" Instagram Stories, August 27, 2020. https://www.instagram.com/stories/highlights/18103315954011379/.

The Liturgists. "We're Better Together." 2021. https://web.archive.org/web/20210605183006/https://theliturgists.com/community

Lövheim, Mia. "Media and Religion through the Lens of Feminist and Gender Theory." In *Media, Religion and Gender: Key Issues and New Challenges*, edited by Mia Lövheim, 15–32. London: Routledge, 2013.

Mamdani, Mahmood. "Good Muslim, Bad Muslim: A Political Perspective on Culture and Terrorism." *American Anthropologist* 104, no. 3 (2002): 766–775.

Markham, Annette, and Elizabeth Buchanan, "Ethical Decision-Making and Internet Research: Recommendations from the AoIR Ethics Working Committee (Version 2.0)." AOIR, 2012. http://www.aoir.org/reports/ethics2.pdf.

Marwick, Alice E. *Status Update: Celebrity, Publicity, and Branding in the Social Media Age.* New Haven, CT: Yale University Press, 2013.

Marz, Megan. "Personal Stories of the Exodus from Christianity." *Washington Post*, January 16, 2020. https://www.washingtonpost.com/outlook/personal-stories-of-the-exodus-from -christianity/2020/01/16/7594a8f8-1472-11ea-a659-7d69641c6ff7_story.html.

Mauleón, Emmanuel. "Black Twice: Policing Black Muslim Identities." *UCLA Law Review* 65, no. 5 (June 2018): 1326–1390.

McLeod, Ken. "Space Oddities: Aliens, Futurism and Meaning in Popular Music." *Popular Music* 22, no. 3 (2003): 337–355.

Meyer, Birgit. "Introduction: From Imagined Communities to Aesthetic Formations: Religious Mediations, Sensational Forms, and Styles of Binding." In *Aesthetic Formations: Media, Religion, and the Senses*, edited by Birgit Meyer, 1–28. New York: Palgrave Macmillan, 2009.

MIPSTERZ. "ALHAMDU." Kickstarter, last updated May 5, 2021. https://www.kickstarter .com/projects/mipsterz/alhamdu/description.

———. "ALHAMDU | MUSLIM FUTURISM." YouTube, May 11, 2021. Video, 4:38. https://www.youtube.com/watch?v=IbhIHNjKoMY.

MIPSTERZ (@MipsterzOfficial). "#Alhamdulillah, we are out here and unapologetically ourselves." Instagram photo, April 30, 2021. https://www.instagram.com/p/COSu3dkr Ont/.

———. "See y'all in a 1,000 years." Instagram photo, April 22, 2021. https://www.instagram .com/p/CN-IdW-LNi2/.

———. "We submit to you a joyous, vibrant vision of liberation." Instagram video, May 11, 2021. https://www.instagram.com/p/COvPvZyjSVG/.

———. "You may not acknowledge our past, but you will know our future." Instagram photo, April 17, 2021. https://www.instagram.com/p/CNxQc6uLG7g/.

Mitchem, Stephanie Y. *Introducing Womanist Theology*. Maryknoll, NY: Orbis Books, 2002.

Moors, Annelies, and Emma Tarlo. *Islamic Fashion and Anti-Fashion: New Perspectives from Europe and North America*. London: Bloomsbury, 2013.

Morozov, Evgeny. "Foreign Policy: Brave New World of Slacktivism." *NPR*, May 19, 2009. https://www.npr.org/templates/story/story.php?storyId=104302141

Mossière, Géraldine. "Modesty and Style in Islamic Attire: Refashioning Muslim Garments in a Western Context." *Contemporary Islam* 6 (2012): 115–134.

Mouallem, Omar. "5 Women Quashing Preconceptions about Islam on Social Media." *Wired*, December 3, 2015. http://www.wired.com/2015/12/muslim-women-twitter/.

Muñoz, José Esteban. *Disidentifications: Queers of Color and the Performance of Politics*. Minneapolis: University of Minnesota Press, 1999.

Muslim ARC. "About." 2018. https://www.muslimarc.org/about.

No Shame Movement. "About." Accessed November 20, 2021. https://noshamemovement .tumblr.com/about.

Onishi, Bradley. "The Rise of #Exvangelical." *Religion and Politics*, April 9, 2019. https:// religionandpolitics.org/2019/04/09/the-rise-of-exvangelical/.

Papacharissi, Zizi. "Affective Publics and Structures of Storytelling: Sentiment, Events and Mediality." *Information, Communication and Society* 19, no. 3 (2016): 307–324.

———. *Affective Publics: Sentiment, Technology, and Politics*. New York: Oxford University Press, 2014.

Parker, Kim, Nikki Graf, and Ruth Igielnik. "Generation Z Looks a Lot Like Millennials on Key Social and Political Issues." Pew Research Center, January 17, 2019. https://www.pewsocialtrends.org/2019/01/17/generation-z-looks-a-lot-like-millennials-on-key-social-and-political-issues/.

Pennington, Rosemary. "Making Space in Social Media: #MuslimWomensDay in Twitter." *Journal of Communication Inquiry* 42, no. 3 (July 2018): 199–217.

Perkins, William Eric. "The Rap Attack: An Introduction." In *Droppin' Science: Critical Essays on Rap Music and Hip Hop Culture*, edited by William Eric Perkins, 1–45. Philadelphia, PA: Temple University Press, 1996.

Pew Research Center. "Religious Landscape Study: Generational Cohort." Pew Research Center, September 2020. https://www.pewforum.org/religious-landscape-study/generational-cohort/.

———. "U.S. Muslims Concerned About Their Place in Society, but Continue to Believe in the American Dream." Pew Research Center, July 26, 2017, https://www.pewforum.org/2017/07/26/findings-from-pew-research-centers-2017-survey-of-us-muslims/.

Phillips, Whitney, and Ryan M. Milner. *The Ambivalent Internet: Mischief, Oddity, and Antagonism Online*. Cambridge: Polity Press, 2017.

Piela, Anna. "I Am Just Doing My Bit to Promote Modesty: Niqabis' Self-Portraits on Photo-Sharing Websites." *Feminist Media Studies* 13, no. 5 (2013): 781–790.

Pierce, Yolanda. "Black Women and the Sacred: With 'Lemonade,' Beyoncé Takes Us to Church." *Religion Dispatches*, May 3, 2016. https://religiondispatches.org/black-women-and-the-sacred-beyonce-takes-us-to-church/.

Pink, Sarah. "Visual Ethnography and the Internet: Visuality, Virtuality and the Spatial Turn." In *Advances in Visual Methodology*, edited by Sarah Pink, 113–130. London: SAGE, 2012.

Postill, John, and Sarah Pink. "Social Media Ethnography: The Digital Researcher in a Messy Web." *Media International Australia* 145, no. 1 (November 2012): 123–134.

Prickett, Pamela J. *Believing in South Central: Everyday Islam in the City of Angels*. Chicago: University of Chicago Press, 2021.

Rana, Junaid. *Terrifying Muslims: Race and Labor in the South Asian Diaspora*. Durham, NC: Duke University Press, 2011.

Roberts, Matthias. "Hi, I'm Matthias!" *Matthias Roberts*, 2021. https://matthiasroberts.com/about/.

———. "On Justice." *Queerology*, June 2, 2020. Podcast audio, 56:24. https://queerology.libsyn.com/on-justice.

———. "#QYFDay." *Queerology*. June 30, 2020. Podcast audio, 45:40. https://matthiasroberts.com/queerology/qyfday/.

Roberts, Robin. "'Ladies First': Queen Latifah's Afrocentric Feminist Music Video." *African American Review* 28, no. 2 (1994): 245–257.

Rose, Tricia. *Black Noise: Rap Music and Black Culture in Contemporary America*. Middletown, CT: Wesleyan University Press, 1994.

Ruether, Rosemary Radford. "Sexism and Misogyny in the Christian Tradition: Liberating Alternatives." *Buddhist-Christian Studies* 34 (2014): 83–94.

Saeed, Sana. "Somewhere in America, Muslim Women Are 'Cool.'" *Islamic Monthly*, December 2, 2013. www.theislamicmonthly.com/somewhere-in-america-muslim-women-are-cool.

Sarah (@breakfreetogether). "#BreakFreeTogether." Instagram photo, October 4, 2018. https://www.instagram.com/p/BohSuDhgrSm/

Scanzoni, Letha, and Nancy Hardesty. *All We're Meant to Be: A Biblical Approach to Women's Liberation*. Grand Rapids, MI: William B. Eerdmans Publishing Company, 1992.

Selod, Saher, and David G. Embrick. "Racialization and Muslims: Situating the Muslim Experience in Race Scholarship." *Sociology Compass* 7, no. 8 (2013): 644–655.

Shaikley, Layla. "The Surprising Lessons of the 'Muslim Hipsters' Backlash." *Atlantic*, March 13, 2014. www.theatlantic.com/entertainment/archive/2014/03/the-surprising-lessons-of-the-muslim-hipsters-backlash/284298.

Sheikh, Aminah. "Why I Participated in the 'Somewhere in America' #Mipsterz Video." *Altmuslim*, December 4, 2013. http://www.patheos.com/blogs/altmuslim/2013/12/why-i-participated-in-the-somewhere-in-america-mipsterz-video.

Shellnutt, Kate. "Women Speak Up in #SilenceIsNotSpiritual Campaign." *Christianity Today*, December 20, 2017. https://www.christianitytoday.com/ct/2017/december-web-only/women-speak-up-in-silenceisnotspiritual-campaign.html.

Siddiqi, Dina. "Sexuality as Liberation? The Work of Salvation Narratives in Neoliberal Times." *Alal O Dulal*, March 2014. http://alalodulal.org/2014/03/13/sexuality-as-liberation/.

Sills, Liz. "Hashtag Comedy: From Muslim Rage to #Muslimrage." *ReOrient* 2, no. 2 (2017): 160–174.

Spinelli, Martin, and Lance Dann. *Podcasting: The Audio Media Revolution*. New York: Bloomsbury, 2019.

Spivak, Gayatri Chakravorty. "Can the Subaltern Speak?" In *Marxism and the Interpretation of Culture*, edited by Cary Nelson and Lawrence Grossberg, 271–313. Urbana: University of Illinois Press, 1988.

Stankorb, Sarah. "Inside the Scam of the 'Purity' Movement." *Cosmopolitan*, February 5, 2019. https://www.cosmopolitan.com/politics/a26026217/sexual-abstinence-joshua-harris-purity-movement-scam/.

Thank God for Sex. "About Us." Accessed October 30, 2021. http://www.thankgodforsex.org/about.html.

Thomas, Linda E. "Womanist Theology, Epistemology, and a New Anthropological Paradigm." *Cross Currents* 48, no. 4 (Winter 1998–1999): 488–499.

Truth's Table (@truthstable). "HAPPY JUNETEENTH!." Instagram photo, June 19, 2020. https://www.instagram.com/p/CBnWKj7hzqn/.

TMW (@breakfreetogether). "#BreakFreeTogether." Instagram photo, September 16, 2018. https://www.instagram.com/p/BnziEtJgzIX/.

Tufekci, Zeynep. *Twitter and Tear Gas: The Power and Fragility of Networked Protest*. New Haven, CT: Yale University Press.

Valenti, Jessica. *The Purity Myth: How America's Obsession with Virginity Is Hurting Young Women*. Berkeley, CA: Seal Press, 2009.

Vernon, Leah. "The Deletion of the Perfect Instagram Hijabi." *MuslimGirl*, March 7, 2018. http://muslimgirl.com/47646/the-deletion-of-the-perfect-instagram-hijabi/.

———. "Resume." *Beauty and the Muse*. Accessed November 20, 2021. http://www.beautyandthemuse.net/resume-1.

———. *Unashamed: Musings of a Fat, Black Muslim*. Boston: Beacon, 2019.

Vernon, Leah (@lvernon2000). "@thecut featured a vid of me dancing on their page for #muslimwomensday." Instagram photo, March 27, 2019. https://www.instagram.com/p/Bvh4TALHnjO/.

———. "A friend and I talked about our experiences as big women." Instagram photo, January 31, 2019. https://www.instagram.com/p/BtT-zwInpgW/.

———. "After 9/11, I would go to the mosque for Jumah and wonder if someone would come shoot me." Instagram photo, March 15, 2019. https://www.instagram.com/p/BvCp3EAnXAl/.

———. "As I am still quite shaken up from yesterday's events." Instagram photo, March 16, 2019. https://www.instagram.com/p/BvFYuW-Hr-Z/.

———. "Being comfortable, confident in my curvy body, makes insecure people feel very uncomfortable." Instagram photo, January 19, 2019. https://www.instagram.com/p/Bs1FoO1gVOw/.

———. "Had to block a total of ten people last night who tried it." Instagram photo, March 3, 2019. https://www.instagram.com/p/Buj3cwKHIPl/.

———. "I couldn't even post yesterday because I was over it." Instagram photo, January 23, 2019. https://www.instagram.com/p/Bs_TB_6AGeE/.

———. "I never set out to be political." Instagram photo, March 20, 2019. https://www.instagram.com/p/BvPvQwUn4MR/.

———. "I recorded a set of IG stories on how to be a white and/or white passing ally." Instagram photo, January 21, 2019. https://www.instagram.com/p/Bs6I78-gMPx/.

———. "I'm not losing weight in order for you to love me." Instagram photo, May 29, 2021. https://www.instagram.com/p/CPeHhfRpgW1/.

———. "On Monday, I'll be headed to Westminster College in Salt Lake City for the week." Instagram photo, March 22, 2019. https://www.instagram.com/p/BvU4MhpHm8Y/.

———. "'These are fat mommies sitting with their bags of potato chips in front of the television.'" Instagram photo, February 19, 2019. https://www.instagram.com/p/BuElAdtncUk/.

Villarreal, Sandi. "Their Generation Was Shamed by Purity Culture. Here's What They're Building in Its Place." *Sojourners*, March 7, 2019. https://sojo.net/interactive/their-generation-was-shamed-purity-culture-heres-what-theyre-building-its-place.

Wadud, Amina. *Qur'an and Woman: Rereading the Sacred Text from a Woman's Perspective.* New York: Oxford University Press, 1999.

Walker, Alice. *In Search of Our Mothers' Gardens: Womanist Prose.* New York: Harcourt, 1983.

Watkins, S. Craig. *Hip Hop Matters: Politics, Pop Culture, and the Struggle for the Soul of a Movement.* Boston: Beacon Press, 2005.

Zavella, Patricia, "Feminist Insider Dilemmas: Constructing Ethnic Identity with Chicana Informants." In *Feminist Dilemmas in Fieldwork,* edited by Diane Wolf, 138–159 Boulder, CO: Westview Press, 1996.

INDEX

ABOUT THE AUTHOR

KRISTIN M. PETERSON is an assistant professor in the Communication Department at Boston College and teaches courses related to the intersections of media and religion. She earned her PhD in media studies from the University of Colorado Boulder, where she was also a research fellow in the Center for Media, Religion, and Culture. Her research focuses on religious expression in digital media, and she has published articles and book chapters on Muslim Instagram influencers; the digital mourning after the murder of three Muslim college students in Chapel Hill, North Carolina; hijab tutorial videos on YouTube; the Ms. Marvel comic series; and the Mipsterz fashion video.